# SPORTS WRITER'S EYE

**Also by Frank Keating**

# FRANK KEATING

# SPORTS WRITER'S EYE

## AN ANTHOLOGY

Macdonald
Queen Anne Press

A *Queen Anne Press* Book

© Frank Keating 1989

First published in Great Britain in 1989 by
Queen Anne Press, a division of
Macdonald & Co (Publishers) Ltd
66-73 Shoe Lane
London EC4P 4AB

A member of Maxwell Pergamon Publishing Corporation plc

**British Library Cataloguing in Publication Data**
Keating, Frank, *1937–*
    Sportswriter's eye : an anthology.
    1. Sports
    I. Title
    796

ISBN 0–356–17843–9

Photoset in North Wales by
Derek Doyle & Associates, Mold, Clwyd
Printed and bound in Great Britain by
BPCC Hazell Books Ltd, Aylesbury, Bucks.

# CONTENTS

# INTRODUCTION

For reasons best known to themselves, I was first encouraged into sportswriting some 20 years ago by those two generous and celebrated stalwarts of *The Times*, Geoffrey Green and David Miller. They knew I was a fan all right, and reckoned I'd have much more fun alongside them in the press box than I was having, poncing around as a pretentious television producer. My only claim to fame was to have inspired a witheringly blank stare – on air – by asking the camp and crotchety old *éminence*, Somerset Maugham, whether he'd ever seen Harold Gimblett score a century for (I presumed) their native county. He did not remotely know what I was on about.

As a kid on the local rags in the 1950s, the fashionable ambition was to be a Fleet Street Foreign Correspondent. More by crook than hook, I did manage ultimately to wheedle myself into a foreign-desk job at the London end of the *Guardian*, just after it had dropped its *Manchester* bit. However, it proved not to furnish quite the 'Doctor Livingstone, I presume?' intrepid travellers' tales that this tyro glamour-guts had envisaged. Indeed, in little over a year spent putting up one-deck headlines on such half-par stories as 'Chap Missing in Chad' or 'Khyber Closed to Carts', my career itself was deservedly spiked when I missed putting the first edition to bed on the evening of 25 June 1963, on account of being unable to drag myself away from Mr D.B. Close's epic last-day innings in the second Test against the West Indies at Lord's.

1

So I joined ITV and saw the world – not to mention Somerset. Thus I contrived to be passing through Mexico in the summer of 1970 when, it just so happened, the World Cup tournament was being staged. No fool me; it was sensational stuff. Pelé was at his most brilliant and Alf Ramsey's England were at their finest; the hosts were on song and *en fête*. Geoffrey and David said why on earth didn't I send back a few coloury sporting doodles to *The Times*. I did – and, glory be, they printed them. When I got home, ITV thought it was a spiffing idea too and said why didn't I continue writing coloury doodles for newspapers – permanently. Thanks very much and cheerio.

I warmly embraced my first (and, I hope, last) love. The *Guardian* was soon to be edited by Peter Preston, whose attributes include sports-nuttery. John Samuel was sports editor, letting rip in his scattily brilliant way a Golden Age (everybody agrees) for sportswriting in the broadsheet Press.

Suddenly, I found myself carrying the typewriter and pouring the late-night drinks all round the world for such luminaries of the lore as Albert Barham, David Frost, John Arlott, Pat Ward-Thomas, David Gray, and John Rodda, who has watched more Olympic finals with a phone at his ear than Sebastian has had muesli for breakfast. I was also privileged in 1974 to be able to sit at the feet (in his favourite Baker Street Steak House) of Sir Neville Cardus, only begetter of the *Guardian*'s sporting faith. In this, the year before he died, the twinkling knight said to me 'You'll enjoy sportswriting, as long as you get on the front foot at every opportunity.'

Better advice than that was offered to me by a groaning reader after some of my early efforts. He sent me the slim volume, *How to Become a Sporting Journalist*, published in the 1930s by B.J. Evans, one of Fleet Street's best at the time. Good old BJ gets straight to the point:

Often I have arrived at a press box to be asked by a colleague if I could spare a pencil and a few sheets of paper. For my part I never arrived at this place of work without having at least three pencils sharpened and enough paper to do trebly as much work as originally planned; as I number the sheets

2

in advance I was *never* able to spare any to accommodate an improvident colleague. I once caught a rude remark about my meanness in refusing paper when I had so much to spare, but when I am on the job I have no time for other people's opinions.

Things had obviously changed when I first tremulously asked the mighty Brian Glanville if I could borrow his telephone at Stamford Bridge; *prego*, he said with a charming grin, 'be my guest'. I was lucky enough to join a laughing and encouraging confraternity: the heavyweights like Green and Miller, Ian Wooldridge, Donald Saunders and Hugh McIlvanney happily lent me pencils, and I borrowed paper from such succulent olde tyme essayists as Geoffrey Nicholson, Peter Dobereiner, Alan Gibson and Christopher Wordsworth. The pops and the posh were alike when it came to kindness, cribs, and the glug of liquid gold into the wee small hours: Moynihan, Collins and Doust, Brasher, Barclay and Woodcock, Wilson, Hart and Batt, Lander, Todd and O'Connor....

The cribs are crucial. At Seoul last year, sweating on an early morning (local time) deadline, I spied across a couple of fields the ITN ace scoopist, Jeremy Thompson, emerge from huddled conclave with Captain Mark Phillips, whose nag had just been hobblingly withdrawn from the Olympic three-day event. I galloped over, puffingly. 'What did he say? What did he say?' I pleaded. Jeremy referred to his notebook and then dictated slowly: 'He simply said, "Whoever you tell this to, make sure it's not that anti-Royal blighter, Keating, of the *Guardian*".'

A more kindly Cardinal of the Trade, E.W. Swanton, used to work in the 1930s with B.J. Evans. Once, apparently, the name of Cardus cropped up in a press box. 'Cardus!' exclaimed Evans, 'he's the effer who keeps pinching all my effing epigrams!' Swanton recalls Evans as one 'whose English in print and talk alike was almost more basic than anything I can remember'. A handful of long-running personal feuds and animosities, of course, keep the rest of us giggling into our handkerchiefs still. One of the most waspish lines I heard of was delivered when the *Daily Mail*'s old acerbic and gravelly cricket correspondent, Alex Bannister, was asked about the health of a colleague, whom the enquirer knew he cordially disliked. 'As well as can be expected, I think,' replied Alex, before adding venomously, *'between fits.'*

If rule two is to sit next to a pal with a quote or a crib, the paramount importance is to be near a telephone, preferably one that works. Nothing is more pointless (nothing is deader) than talking into a phone that does not work, especially if you've got a hard-nosed story to tell, nicely garnished with a thousand twirly-wirlies of purple prose. Once, at Jammu in the foothills of the Himalayas, I had a cracker about Geoffrey Boycott: I couldn't get it further than a Bombay operator. Another time, on the banks of the Limpopo (I kid you not), I had a real rager about the MCC cricket team being kicked out of Guyana: it got no further than the banks of the Limpopo. High up on the South African *veldt* one dead-on-deadline day I saw what all consider still to be the finest try in the history of rugby: no one in England was any the wiser. The phone didn't work.

My first ever off-the-cuff foreign boxing dispatch from the mayhem of the ringside – Muhammad Ali, no less – was worst of all. I got through to London. Hooray! While the sports desk were putting me through to the copy-typists, the local operator came onto the line to ask 'Are you through?' in pidgin English. 'Yes, I'm through,' I confirmed. Click! The line expired. For, in fact, she spoke pidgin American, and over there 'Are you through?' means 'Have you finished?'. So thanks a bundle, babe. Ali had dispatched his man long, long before my dispatch managed to get on another line to London.

Thinking up the ruddy adjectives with which to pad out your allotted space between the ads and the pictures comes way down the list. Well, first you've got to oil the Muse, haven't you? Almost to a man, I'd say, sportswriters daily and gulpingly set out to throttle at birth the wimpish, careful philosophy defined by one of the finest of their number, the American Ring Lardner: 'No one ever wrote anything as well even after one drink as he would have without it.'

Another sometime member of our clan, Norman Mailer – and he can talk! – put it more racily: 'The popular assumption that pro boxers do not have brains comes from sportswriters – but then sportswriters' brains are in their turn damaged by the obligation to be clever each and every day. The quantities of booze necessary to lubricate such racing of the mental gears ends up giving the sportswriters the equivalent of a good many punches to the head.'

You see, I have got my excuses in first – before you dip into this random hotchpotch of pieces, reprinted here exactly as they were written for the *Guardian*, dashed off to dead-heat the deadline and fill a little bit more of a daily newspaper's voracious appetites. Apart from crossing a couple of t's, the plan has been to let the stuff retain any spur-of-the-moment freshness it might have had at the time which also means that it might have retained all the original slapdash inaccuracies. So don't all write in at once.

As I say, I have had overgenerous encouragement – not to mention those cribs – from every fellow toiler among our *hic* of hacks, as well, it goes without saying, from our devoted and small band of crack troops on the sports desk of the *Guardian*, now led by that exhilarating enthusiast, Mike Averis. Thanks, too, to Lorraine Jerram for shuffling the higgledy-piggledy cuttings into such reasonable order, and to Alan Samson, who courageously conceived the idea for this series – unique in journalism, I would say – over a mellow *Wisden* dinner which greeted another cricket season a couple of years ago.

Alan enthused into the small hours about being in a dynamic age of sportswriting – and the series could run and run, as there is a new batch of quite brilliant youngsters within the Press who are refreshingly eager to make their mark once we middle-aged fogeys fall off the perch any day now. But, in fact, I told him, it was no such thing. The truth is that we guys in the last decade or three have been luxuriously lucky to have been able to turn a bloodshot eye on a quite voluptuous dynamic age of sportsmen. Well, has any other quarter of a century ever packed in the likes of Best and Pelé, Ali and Leonard – and Lester, of course? And what about Charlton, or Francome and Scudamore; Barry and Gareth,

Botham and Richards, Laver and Borg and Nicklaus? Is there even a remote possibility that we will see their like again, when spectator sport in the next few years seems to be careering headlong into cavernous, barren television barns applauded by nothing but the whirr of electronic cameras, taped and tweaked-up phoney cheers, and the cynical shuffle of soft and seedy banknotes?

We shall see. In the meantime, browse over these few doodles if you will. They tell of days when sport was sport ... and telephones didn't work. Yes: happy days.

Frank Keating, Hereford. 1989

# 1

# MUSE AND VIEWS

The emphatic gusto, good sense and vim of William Hazlitt makes him the unquestioned father of British sportswriting. Read him on pugilism, rackets, laughter, and love of life and you will be entranced. 'It is not easy to write a familiar style, which a writer of sports must do,' he said, 'for to write a genuine or truly familiar English style, is to write as any one would speak in common conversation, who had a thorough command and choice of words, or who could discourse with ease, force, and perspicuity, setting aside all pedantic and oratorical flourishes. As with writing, so with speaking.' The grand old boy, of course, died almost a century before the invention of the wireless, but his definition, as he would have surely agreed, found its personification in the broadcasting of those two resplendent sportswriters, John Arlott and Geoffrey Green, not to mention (have it your own way, for better or worse) a number of others from, as Peter Sellers used to say, 'stage, screen and radio, you know, an' that.'

But, for starters, let's bridge just the two decades we're dealing with.

# UNITED ON A DAY IN MAY
*May 1988*

29 May 1968. What a day. Youth still so clear-eyed, fizzing, full to the brim and fancy-free that we took it all in our stride at the time. Yet, inside a handful of hours, it was the time of our lives – the day of Sir Matt and *Sir Ivor*, of Best and Guest and Lester.

It was a sweltering belter of a heat wave Derby Day up on the Downs, with the classic of Classics won by, till then, the horse and jockey of the century. And in the sultry, thunderous Wembley evening, Man United won the European Cup for their manager to dedicate to his heavenly Busby Babes.

By a fluke, this small-time loiterer on the fringes of the big-time had somehow nabbed himself an intimate view of the glorious day. I was a fancy-pants, pink-shirted producer of outside broadcasts for ITV, which had the exclusive Epsom rights. It would be different in the evening at Wembley, for though we were transmitting the match the nation still tuned in, on principle as it were, to the gabby Wolstenholme waffle for soccer's state occasions.

First, early to the Downs alongside peak-capped chauffeur (ITV still had its loot-printing licence), washed and brushed-up and very much Mossed and Brossed, for one of my jobs was to liaise with the steward of the Royal Box, just above the winner's enclosure.

His name was Bernard Marmaduke Fitzalan Howard, plus a few others besides, and he was premier earl of all England and lord high marshall of ceremonial, and he had very little sniffing time, I'm telling you, for a Moss Bros oik with cumbersome television cameras keen for prying shots of Royalty at gambling. He had a rubicund, pug-doggy face, and he had crossed garters with me on other events through the year. 'Get lost, sonny, and take those wires with you,' was the tenor of his growl as he essayed a scuff at our precious cables with his bespoke little feet. But even Marmaduke left us alone to cover the race itself. It was like an oven as the sun hammered down, and the knife-sharp anticipation rose up to meet it. *Sir Ivor* was surely going to slay the bookies.

We had crossed the water a few weeks earlier to film the favourite at work on Vincent O'Brien's blissful gallops at Ballydoyle, and not one of our crew had returned home without putting his house on the dramatic, wild-eyed bay with the spectacular turn of foot. We were surer for Vincent telling us he was hoping Piggott had bagged the bridle for the up-coming biggie and more so when *Sir Ivor*'s owner, Raymond Guest, who was US Ambassador to Dublin, told us that over a year before he had plonked down £550 at 100-1 with William Hill.

The engaging Guest was furious that he would miss Epsom on the 29th because he had to attend the Wexford unveiling of Ireland's Kennedy Memorial, but when the race got under way I thought it was as well he was absent because his horse was not showing at all. The field careered like a huge colourful float down the hill to Tattenham Corner with never a mention of *Sir Ivor*. Round the bend and the long climb for home and still nowhere to be seen. Piggott was boxed in with the rear bunch that were already up in their stirrups peering into the distance to see who would win it, when, all of a sudden, whoosh! I've never seen such acceleration before or since.

In chocolate-and-powder-blue colours resembling an old-style rugby strip, Piggott launched himself out of the scrum as the horse went for the line in a way that still defies description. It was truly stunning – Piggott still reckons *Sir Ivor* his most wondrous beast – and for the first and only time I threw my top hat in the air.

I had to retrieve it soon enough, for the day was only half over. Hotfoot to Wembley. No way, though, that United could eclipse *Sir Ivor*. Wanna bet? United's progress to the final – an English club's first – had captivated all football, for it was surely Busby's last throw, exactly a decade since his finest side was wiped out in the slush of the Munich runway. But, like earlier in the afternoon, the early signals were unpromising.

9

It was bitty, neurotic stuff, with United petrified of the onus on them and Benfica narrow-eyed and oblivious to romance – though not, I hasten to add, content with anything like the tedium their team in the same fixture exactly 20 years on was to inflict on the viewing public.

The fouls went tit for tat. Eusebio did slap Stepney's crossbar with a screamer, but Best was being chopped off at the shins, Stiles was replying in kind, and Charlton was frowning and fretting, despite scoring the opening goal. The attrition wore on, the vast throng almost accepting the inevitability of Benfica's equaliser and, as soon as it came, only Stepney's galumphing last-ditch flop when Eusebio was clear put the thing into extra time. That was my cue. And the game's for immortality. And the moon's, which now raged down above the floodlit beacons, and United began to play.

By now, still in my Epsom topper and tails, I had conned my way round the touchline – no cop man enough to challenge my nobby outfit – so I was crouched immediately behind Stepney's net at the tunnel end. Extra time meant we could steal a march on the BBC and, at the final whistle, grab anyone to interview on the pitch and go live into News at Ten.

So the climactic faraway flurry of goals by the mesmeric Best, bounding Kidd and bald, brave, blubbing Bobby were only 'sensed' from my end. But I saw in close-up how the prowling Stepney, edgy till the very end, was crying too, and then, with the tumult quite overpowering, we got our hand-held shots and interviews at the final whistle as Bobby fell weeping onto old Matt's chest, the two survivors of Munich. And afterwards we searched and searched for Bobby. The celebrations were in full swing and he was nowhere to be found. We discovered him at last, being consoled by Pat Crerand, sitting in the litter and jetsam under the grandstand itself, still in tears.

We crept away, for there was another party that my gear might gatecrash to top and tail this day of days. It was already in full swing at the Great Room in the Savoy. Raymond Guest had already flown in, bringing with him Teddy Kennedy and the Irish Prime Minister, Eamon de Valera, no less. What a hooley. *Sir Ivor* wasn't there, mind, nor was William Hill – but

10

everyone else was. And as the early hours got later, the double celebration got wilder. Racing and football came together – and there drinking alone at a table was one Irishman I recognised. It was George Best, waiflike, winding down, and sadly sullen amid the crazy carnival.

He refused congratulations with a forced, dismissive smile. But he accepted a drink, and we left him to his moping. It was some 10 years later that he explained to me how that night had demonstrated to him that he was no longer part of his team's laughter or tears. 'I was there,' he said, 'but I knew I didn't belong.' All around him all evening had been men and women celebrating the achievement of their lifetime's work and determination. 'It should have been that for me, too. Instead, although I couldn't quite phrase it at the time, it was the beginning of the end for me.'

29 May 1968 was in a way, I suppose, the beginning of the end for a whole generation – and come to think of it, I bet old Bernard Marmaduke went to bed that night at Arundel quite pleased about that at least.

---

# ARLOTT AT 70
*February 1984*

His wife, Pat, brings him a cup of tea at 7 a.m. and on comes Radio 4's Today programme. By 8.15, in his bottle-green corduroy bags and anorak over the great blanket of a Swedish sweater, he is having his first solemn, plodding constitutional 'over the top' on the hillocks. Such is the minuscule one-mile-by-three rocky blob of Alderney that at most places you can see the choppy Channel fuming and frothing on the rocks at every point of the compass.

Later in the morning he will turn in the other direction from his wide, bright white house and this time the parade takes him up and down the cobbled little doll's house main street. 'Mornin' George!' 'Mornin' Margot!' 'Mornin' David!' They all reply with a hoot and a wave and a smile. First call is to the post office for the wad of letters and pile of parcels.

11

'Ahh,' comes the satisfied, familiar old growl, 'I do like my post.' It remains one of the most enduring, endearing, evocative voices known to Britain and beyond.

The telephone never stops. Indeed the volume of Alderney Telecom business that obviously increased the moment John Arlott retired to the Channel Islands gives absolute lie to the very idea of 'retirement'. It was only day-in, day-out cricket reporting for this newspaper and the BBC that ended with such wrenching finality in the early autumn of 1980. 'I can't sunbathe or sit in the garden or go on cruises. Not that I'm trying to build a career, I've come as far as I can. But I still love writing. Now I'm just coasting, not downhill, but just coasting along on a loverly level.'

There are strong hints that he is to embark, at last, on an autobiography. He has already decided on the first sentence: 'It was a fat baby of seven pounds that Nelly Arlott gave birth to at the Old Cemetery Lodge, Basingstoke, at 4 a.m. on the morning of 25 February 1914....'

Exactly 70 years on and the birthday is celebrated today with a family party for his wife, his two surviving sons and their women – and his favourite friend and cricketer, Leo Harrison, the former Hampshire wicket-keeper. And tomorrow at noon it seems that half the island will be popping in to raise the hairs from the dog with a further bracer or two. 'Mornin' George!' 'Mornin' Margot!'

This week, the old spaniel soft-boiled eyes still shining bright, the birthday boy showed me round his green-grey granitey island. We sat in a picture window watching spectacular waves snap and fret at the sea wall. It was like the royal fireworks. 'Ooh, look at that one!' 'Golly, there's a beauty for you. Wow!'

It was calmer up the cobbled street. I had, of course, to be introduced to the bearded young man who kept the DIY shop and who last season scored 216 off 51 balls on the island's little cricket pitch. 'Even Frindall says Jessop never matched that!'

After a pre-lunch bracer in the Albert – Fino sherry in tomato juice – back home for cold meats and the accompanying myriad of honest bottles – reds, whites, rosés all the way from France and Germany and California, from Spain, Lebanon, New Zealand and even England. We tasted in the slugs large and small and long. On the whole I think wine correspondent might be a better job than cricket correspondent. The newspapers have arrived from the mainland. He goes straight to *The Times* obituaries. Then to the *Guardian* sports pages. 'Good God! Lillee's put Miandad in hospital. In a benefit match, too. The bastard!'

Then an afternoon's work. He taps at his typewriter, sometimes dictates to Pat. 'I'd go mad if I didn't work.' He first discovered Alderney some 30 years ago. 'It is the most beautiful place I know. So quiet. You can only realistically arrive by air. We enjoyed many family holidays here when my late son and wife were alive.' His eldest son was killed in a motor accident. The sorrow of his loss still pains him intensely.

The isle is full of silence and the house full of treasures. In the hall is a grand and ancient old wireless set – it belonged to Haley when he was BBC's Director-General. There are water colours of Winchester and needlework of Worcester. In the kitchen is Toynbee's lively and glorious oil of 'The Nets', drawings of Hardy and Dylan Thomas and a striking portrait of Elizabeth David. In the Long Room there are the first editions – Hardy, Hazlitt, Betjeman and all – and on the walls Lowry and Rowlandson, Lancaster and Beerbohm.

John Arlott's beloved father, Jack, ended up keeping the graveyard neat at Basingstoke. He wanted the boy simply to get a job with a pension. He began in local government and then in the police force. When the young man started making his name with the BBC father and son embraced, 'and cried together at the wonder of it all'. His third cricket book, on the Australians of 1948, was dedicated 'To my father who knows nothing about cricket and cares less but who wos werry good to me.' The last sentence in that book reads: 'Is there, I wonder, anywhere in the world such a human, generous, unenvious, shop-talking, enthusiastic, mellow, craft-versed sporting community as English cricket professionals?'

He still loves his cricket though since that famous day at Lord's when the ground and players stood to him in farewell he has only seen one day's play – at Taunton when Somerset made him a life member. Hampshire have not done him similar justice. And of course he still loves cricketers. 'Of all of them over the years I think I have only known four bad ones. Yes, only four.'

Supper, beautifully cooked by Pat, is served with another swill and clink of honest bottles. You start with sherry to brace up the soup. And the stories and opinions keep coming. You ask about Yorkshire cricket. 'The only thing that can sort them out is five tons of napalm!'

You wonder if you will be steady up the stairs. You leave, early to bed, and John solemnly munching and dictating to Pat his Cheese Column to be typed on the morrow. You stagger upstairs and below the old voice is gravelly dictating: 'A deep, intense nose ... pungent taste ... but deep, creamy and satisfying....'

And in the morning he will be up far earlier than you to greet the day. 'Mornin' George! Mornin' Margot!' Happy Birthday, John.

---

# THE SQUANDERING STAR
### December 1974

Revie had just been jeered off the pitch at Wembley after the underrated Portuguese had played the dowdy English for an awful draw a week or two ago. There we all were. And high in the eaves of the grandstand, there they all were, the clap-trap chattering Olivetti chaps. England had made the media feel pretty medium that night: sad-eyed Brian James was in hunched huddle with old catenaccio himself, B. Glanville; Moynihan and Malam mumbled condolences; frizz-haired Jeff Powell, the middlebrows' middleweight, just slugged his story into the phone; our own D. Lacey took a considered swig of light ale between considered runner and even more considered rewrite; the splendidly truculent David Miller somehow blamed himself, taking it as a personal slight that they hadn't played like his prelim; Danny Blanchflower endearingly rabbited romantic reasons, on and on and on to nobody in particular; though at least Oxby and Saunders were getting on with nothing but the facts man.

Meanwhile, one man has already taken his leave, and pronto thank you very much. Grey and lean and cadaverous, but with a smile to light up all Oxford Street, he's already dictated his 1,000 words pretty much off the cuff to *The Times* and has limpingly bow-legged it off to join his friends in the downstairs restaurant. Geoffrey Green looks more than a touch like that other old relaxed scruff, Michael Foot, or did before that worthy wrapped himself up in the official steely cloak of Cabinet rank. Green shakes his head lovingly about his press-mates upstairs: 'Here we are, the fun and the laughter and the gurgle of liquid gold into the dark hours, and they're still worked up about 4-4-2 and the midfield men.'

Wise, grey Green had seen it all before; and before and before and before. Already his dictation has gone with the night wind. And to be sure he won't see his essay in *The Times* next morning. 'Haven't read the paper in years,' he says. He takes only the *Guardian*.

Geoffrey Green has only a season left before he retires. The times as well as *The Times* will much miss him. But he's leaving us a few permanent mementoes. He has just launched his book *Soccer in the Fifties* (Ian Allan, £3.95), a testament to his own handsome prime as well as, it looks like turning out, to that of the great game itself. And now the first film he has written, Morton Lewis' full length documentary on last summer's World Cup, is finished and ready for distribution.

The sporting documentary has had a run of pretty horrid form lately. Since the fine Japanese Olympic film in 1964 and the worthy, near miss *Goal* in 1966, we have had the laboriously twee urchin-runs-away-to-see Pelé Mexico 1970 effort and then, of course, the Munich Olympics' eightsome reels by the likes of Schlesinger, Zetterling and Penn which truly turned out to be a dollop of the unmitigateds. This time somebody seems to have got a grip; scarcely a quirk lurks. It seems all as straightforward and uncomplicated as a Bob Charlton whizzer. Joss Ackland, whose dad incidentally was for years on the *Daily Telegraph* sports desk, narrates, and there is a memorable score by John Shakespeare.

And then there's the script and its images: if you heard it uncredited in Iceland you'd still know it was the old entertainer's. How he loves his rainbows and windmills, his moons and stars. It starts with the final under that mesh, butterfly-winged stadium roof – 'a mosquito net where soon the gnats of fate will sting.' And sure enough Cruyff's lucid freewheeling Holland arrogantly blow it against the ploddingly earnest Jerries.... Cruyff 'lonely as a mountain wind, an original Dutch Master, he has tilted at windmills and lost … they have pricked our pretty balloon; our moon's been taken away; where did we go wrong?' The erratic Jongbloed in goal, 'all flailing arms and shut eyes, a blind windmill caught in a high gale' … and for his distressed bewildered Brazil 'once the harbingers of Spring, it is Darkness' as the Press men offer 'waterfalls of words, their typewriters as woodpeckers chipping away at the truth.'

Insurance salesmen don't usually stir in their metaphors like that. Green used to be one. When he had first left Shrewsbury he taught at a private school ('so private it cost about 6,000 quid a day'). He was Divinity master, but less than a divine instructor to such extent that at exam time he gave the boys the questions beforehand. He was summoned to the headmaster. 'You're a modern Moses,' said the Head in awe. 'The lowest mark in your class is 94 per cent.' Moses basked in glory for a night, confessed next day, and became an insurance salesman.

Head office was in Oxford Circus, his boss another Mr Green. Every morning they would say 'Morning Mr Green' to each other and our hero would be furnished with a list of clients to see; but after six months he had not sold a pennypiece of biz, not a farthing had passed hands; and the length of the list had reached epidemic, or at least loo-roll family-size, proportions. On the morning of 24 June 1938, he set off as usual with his list for the suburbs; hang on a mo, that bus goes to Lord's, the second Test starts today, and to blazes with insurance. He was one of the last in before the gates were shut. He perched high up at the Nursery end. On a green sprightly wicket the hostile Aussie McCormick at once shivered the timbers of the doughty Barnett and the two pale nippers, Hutton and Edrich: 30 for three. At high noon, in rolled the mighty Hammond, 'a full rigged galleon'. By the close of a golden day England were 409 for five, Hammond 210 not, Paynter 99, Ames 50. He never went back to the office. Ever. And Mr Green never even asked for the loo-roll list. In fact he's still got it somewhere.

So the last of the bums' trades just had to be beckoning. The knack, getting in. An attractive older lady friend of the family, it came to pass, was being earnestly courted by a sub-editor on the racing table of *The Times*. He might be persuaded to swing something. The plan was for the unemployed lank, Green, to innocently make up a four at tennis; at convenient moment girlfriend would casually drop the drift of young Geoffrey's ambition. It worked. Certain it would enhance the cut of the suit he had so long been pressing, our racing friend had an impassioned word with the boss and in no time Green was a trainee sub on *The Times*.

And it wasn't many moons before he was standing on his first touchline duckboard: 1,000 words on the Bradfield v Shrewsbury school match. Thirty-six years later, having at one time or another been the paper's cricket correspondent, sports editor and 'you name it, I's bin it baby,' he signed off from his last World Cup this July acknowledged and farewelled by the whole sad football world as the most graceful, evocative and possibly even the finest writer to have put their heady passions into words.

He might so nearly have gone in the middle of it all, been lopped off near the peak of his glory; like his beloved Busby Babes. He was all set to fly with Manchester United to a European Cup match in 1958, the same trip on which half the team, the glorious budding flower of British football, and a famous slice of the Press corps were rubbed out in an instant on the icy slush of a Munich runway. But at the last minute the manager of *The Times* cancelled his tickets – 'you understand, old boy, the budget and all that' – and sent him to Wales v Israel instead. And when he returned from Cardiff the curtains were drawn in all the little parlours and front-rooms of the land.

A whole country hunched about in black armbands. Football itself was numbed. And in a way it has never recovered its joy. 'The game's not much fun any more. It's all penguin football now, bingo between goalposts; 4–3–3 was bad enough, now it's something like 4⅛–6⅞ isn't it? Anyway, when you'd seen the Hungarians in 1953, that was probably it anyway. Flashing lights all over the place, every move like a flare going through a prism.'

But for just a little longer football will have a loving smile lurking around the corners of its mouth. For Green is still there. But when he goes it'll sure be relief to a million lily-livered constitutions – and a million or so night porters who've scurried around the hotel lounges of the world dispensing that liquid gold into the dark hours. Once in a dim Sao Paulo nighterie, a Black Power chappie swung him round and demanded which side he was on: a beatific smile, and 'I'm with the Rainbow People, baby' and the whole world was a different place as they merrily whisked him to their faraway mountain hideout to let him hear them make their music.

When Sir Alf Ramsey was fired earlier this year his agents drummed up a dreary old banquet for him in a posh London hotel: lukewarm sprouts and speech after speech of pompous elocutioned worthiness. The final speech was Green's. 'Alf baby,' he told our tight-lipped, beknighted former squad supremo, 'now that you've been put out to grass, you should look to change your lifestyle. Please join us. For when I throw down my pen and my bits of paper, some fellow old grey buzzards and I are forming a group – The Squandering Stars – and we've bagged the pitch in the underpass between Marble Arch and Park Lane. So start practising, Alf baby, 'cos it's a-going to go something like this.' And with that he whips out his mouth-organ and liltingly plays the whole of *Moon River*. The worthies didn't quite know what to do. Franny Lee, lovely chap, stood up and cheered like crazy; Sir Alf had a bash at a weedy smile and failed – and our musician, not caring a twopenny toss, beamed mightily and poured himself a large drink. Suddenly it was a memorable evening after all.

In his next life he'll settle for being the moon river

boatman. But these days he hopes that's going to be a long time a-coming. For his pride and joy, his daughter, is only five. That bewitching little sprig will probably be on his arm for his first ever film premiere. And it's not often that Rainbow People go in pairs.

---

## THE STRAIN OF BEING THE PEOPLE'S FRIEND
*May 1979*

I'll tell you one thing: Mike Yarwood can't do Eddie Waring half as well as Eddie does himself. I heard him coming a mile off as I waited for him the other day in the bar of his beloved Queen's Hotel at Leeds, greeting every Tom, Dick and gatepost in a flurry of 'Ey Oop!'s, optional aitches and jettisoned gees. Eddie Waring makes use of his vowels as expansively as Magnus Pyke makes use of his hands. A musician might call the resulting sing-song dissonance a quaver of Yorky bars. But it has the desired effect. As I say, you know Eddie's coming. Too reet an' all.

If John Arlott's is the voice of passive, pastoral summer and cool drinks in the lolling shade, then Eddie Waring's is the voice of murky, muddy winter and crumpets by the fire. This Saturday at Wembley he is, of course, hosting the nation for the big one. While a whopping majority of the land cannot name the teams involved in this year's Rugby League Cup final – let alone one of the 26 players – everyone knows the voice on the BBC, don't they? Too reet an' all.

First impressions of Eddie in the flesh are exactly what I had expected. Except he left his famous trilby with the hall porter. Everything else, by gum, was larger than life. But as we enjoyably talked through our roast beef and Yorkshire what happened? He relaxes and lets slip the mask of bluff bonhomie. It turns out he is really quite a dour one is our Eddie. Long before the pudding I sensed that it was perhaps becoming an awful strain getting out of his early bath each morning and having to don the redcoat gusto of an Uncle Ed

19

that has revived and made worth watching many a dull game from It's a Knockout to It's an Up and Under!

Like many journalists, he is very suspicious of his own trade. It takes one to smell one. When I had written this piece, he insisted, could I telephone through any direct quotes I planned to use. He said he had checked up on my 'credentials' with the BBC before agreeing to meet me. The public figure is a private man. He did not want to talk about his family at all. He was coy about his age; he said it was nobody else's business, though a friend yesterday confided that he's nearer 70 than 60, which is staggering both in terms of the all-round verve of his performances and amount of hours he crams into a day. Certainly I was not to mention the hotel he is staying at in London: everyone will bother him for tickets. The real Eddie Waring is writing a book and finding it very hard going: the television Eddie I thought I knew would surely have dictated the whole thing into a tape at one sitting.

Twice when I chided him about his privacy he did perk up for a split second and exclaim 'That's Eddie!' as though momentarily he was talking about someone else. I'm afraid I was reminded of that cracking piece about Mrs Thatcher in The *Observer* on Sunday when C.C. O'Brien said that both Dag Hammarskjold and Mrs T 'had a humourless twinkle in their eyes'. On admittedly short acquaintance I must honestly report that I had the same feeling about Eddie, the people's friend. First Dag, then Mag and now, surprisingly, the nation's favourite Wag.

It may be that he is still suspiciously on guard against the longtime criticism of his broadcasting approach to Rugby League by the game's establishment who say his commentaries turn a noble pastime into a burlesque. He knows that the BBC have been officially asked to drop him. He knows that a prim petition with an alleged 10,000 signatures was once delivered to the Head of Sport 'deploring the manner in which the BBC abuse, exploit and misrepresent the game.' Rightly the BBC answered with two words and one exclamation mark.

A couple of thousand people understand and enjoy Rugby League every weekend. Ten million people understand and enjoy Rugby League with Eddie every weekend. 'Why Mr Waring,' demanded a parochial Northerner once, 'do you always tell 'em down there that it's two points for a goal. Let 'em find out for th'selves.'

Eddie was born and schooled at Dewsbury and joined the local rag as a sports reporter. He played both codes of rugby and once had a soccer trial for Nottingham Forest. Surprisingly he cannot remember (that's Eddie!) the first time he saw a RL final at Wembley. It was a 15/6d day return in the late 1930s and all he recalled is that later that evening he fell asleep in the Palladium. By the end of the war – during which time he was manager of Dewsbury when they won the Cup – he was correspondent for the *Sunday Mirror*. He paid his own way – £11 11s 3d single fare on the aircraft carrier HMS *Indomitable* – to Australia to cover the 1946 British tour.

In 1948 he was one of three journalists asked by the BBC to comment on the final at Wembley. The seed was sown. After the 1950 tour of Australia he returned via Hollywood and he says Bob Hope and Jimmy Garner both urged him that television was the thing to get into. Next winter in England he went to a Rugby Union international at Twickenham and got a seat as near as he could to the television commentator. To get the drift, to see the drill.

By the late 1950s he was on his way – the warm, friendly voice eeing and aahing for the world's good books, for a local minority's bad books ... and for the top of the bill on the Mike Yarwood Show.

Simply, the Rugby League Cup final without him to the huge majority would be like Desert Island Discs without Plomley – no, more: without the seagulls squawking.

---

# A YORKSHIREMAN TO GO INTO THE JUNGLE WITH
## *February 1981*

The Yorkshireman was promenading along the beach in Antigua, the blissful Caribbean island that Nelson developed for his fleet and which England introduced to cricket, so that Antigua itself could ultimately produce Vivian Richards, handsomest god of them all.

The man from the West Riding presented a squat, stocky figure under the mid-day sun. The fierce hawk's eyes under the steel-grey scrubbing brush of his NCO's hairstyle were flaring at sunbathers wasting their day. He wore black plimsolls of the post-war utility variety, short yellow nylon socks, an incongruously gaudy beach shirt, and elastic-waisted shorts which looked as though they'd been cut by a blind tailor with a blunt pair of nail scissors. His pink arms and legs were spattered with angry red bites from angry black mosquitoes. He had been scratching them. Under his arm he carried a shabby old shopping bag which doubtless held a tape recorder, a travelling Scrabble set, and a pile of well-read air-mail letters. Don Mosey, of the British Broadcasting Corporation, was taking his constitutional.

From the shade of a beach-hut we watched him stencilling his Man Friday footsteps across the glistening sand. His friend and mine, Terry Brindle, of the *Yorkshire Post*, remarked: 'Y'know, it's hard to understand, isn't it, how a nation of Moseys colonised and ruled for over two centuries a nation of Viv Richardses.' The thought has struck me more than once now we are in India and I'm making my second tour with Don. He still sports his eccentric uniform, his beady eyes are ever on the lookout for a phone box that works. He still carries his always increasing bundle of air-mail letters. He's a character is Don, and proud to be. He pretends he is always a crotchety old cuss, but that's just his way. He is actually what you'd call a 'good tourist'. Certainly he is a man to go into the jungle with. He'd even smell out a phone box near the mouth of the Orinoco.

He did once. It was this time last year, the day before we were thrown out of Guyana over the Jackman rumpus. There was a match upcountry in Berbice, the ground cleared out of the jungle. Don found a hut. In it was a cobwebbed telephone. He picked it up. It worked. He got through to Broadcasting House in London. The newsroom seemed to be out to lunch except one secretary. 'Who are you?' she

22

repeated. And 'Where are you?' 'I am Don Mosey,' he seethed, 'and I'm standing on the banks of a shark-infested river in the middle of South America....'

'Oh,' said the girl, 'do you want to give any news?' 'No,' rasped our exasperated hero drawing himself up to his full pomp before slamming the phone down, 'I want to give a pint of blood.'

There have been one or two similar, if not quite so graphic, adventures on this trip, now word has seeped back that there has been some angry correspondence in the *Guardian* about his 'offensive and gratuitous remarks on India and Indians' during his broadcasts. He cannot understand it. He spent the last months of the war here, and a year after it.

'Since then, I have always nursed not only a great affection for the place, but also the determination to return one day. For 30 years since now, I'd recalled the mellow pleasure of India at sundown, the last rays of the sun on the hibiscus and bougainvillaea.... All those years I've cherished this affection for India, for its birds and butterflies and mountains. I've had this great nostalgic urge to come back, and I haven't been disappointed.'

The people, and their sense of humour and concern for their guests – 'their endearing, caring kindness' – he can get quite misty about. Nevertheless, he says, to paint a proper picture he has to mention in his broadcasts 'the dust and dirt, the communications chaos, the unfamiliar sanitary arrangements and the fine disregard for time-keeping.' For Mosey is first and foremost a journalist.

He is a Libran, born in 1924, the eldest of three boys 'of kind and loving parents who never had a penny to spare in their lives – and never expected to have.' His father worked three days a week in t'mill for 30 shillings, supplementing that with 'anything he could find' like debt-collecting, or tending the local cricket pitch at Eastburn, a village between Skipton and Keighley. Don first played league cricket at the age of 11, and was later to become the demon bowler in the Airedale and Wharfedale League. The three boys all won through to Keighley Grammar School, which was more expense.

He started 'in newspapers' at a tender age with a paper

round on his bike before school. When he was 16 his mother – 'the driving force' – presented herself at the local rag in Skipton and asked for a job for her eldest. The men had gone to war. There remained an editor and young Mosey became the editorial staff of one.

When he was of age, the boy himself went to war. He does not like to talk about it now, but he was in RAF aircrew and ended up in the Iraqi desert teaching English to Indians. He travelled a lot, and learned to play bridge – 'a great social asset'. It was also when stationed in India that he came upon another determination. 'I thought the time had come to start improving my speech. I was pure bush West Riding, "Ee, by gum" and all that stuff. Not that I had any visions of a posh accent – I was proud of being North Country – but I thought socially it could help me have a better life, just as bridge could. I thought if I could tighten up the discipline of my speech and enunciate better, it might get me somewhere in life.'

It did. But not for some time. He was an ace newspaper reporter in Nottingham, where he sent the odd bits and pieces to the BBC Midlands Radio, encouraged by the deputy news editor, Peter Hardiman-Scott. Then he was, successively, a reporter on the *Yorkshire Evening Post*, the *Daily Express* and the *Daily Mail*, in their Northern newsrooms.

One day, in Manchester, he deputised for a colleague and made a broadcast. The producer, Jack Harrison, said: 'You've done this before, haven't you?' Mosey, by then, had transferred from news to sport for the *Mail*, mostly covering cricket, and doing an increasing amount of broadcasting for Harrison.

In 1964, he resigned from the *Mail* and became a freelance. One day, Jack Harrison suggested Mosey put in for his job as an outside broadcast radio producer. 'What, a Yorkshire hobbledehoy like me?' said Mosey. He got the job and three years later he was to be senior producer for the next 14 years.

In 1973, Cliff Morgan, then head of all radio sport, asked him to join Test Match Special – and so 'The Alderman', as Brian Johnston calls him so aptly when his friend gets a touch too pompous, became part of the team that became part of the folklore of British sporting broadcasting. And that's why he's in India, filling you in every morning, usually after a maniacal game of Scrabble the night before.

Looking gruff of mien, he plods the old empire in his shorts, ever on the lookout for a phone box that works. And under his arm will be his battered old bag, and in it his bulging bundle of air-mail letters from his sons, Ian the pro golfer, and Alistair who is in Australia, but most of them from Jo, his wife. They write every single day to each other.

'She is the nicest, most placid, pleasant and easy-going wife a wandering journalist could find,' he says, 'especially for someone as mercurial and vacillating and moody as me.' And he looks defiantly ferocious again and you think how he'd have given them what for in the Raj. Unless you know that underneath, he's really an endearing, romantic, old softy.

---

# LEGEND THAT MADE A MINT OUT OF MURRAY
### October 1986

Doubtless the Australian T-shirt manufacturers will come up with a new line for this weekend. At last year's Australian Grand Prix in Adelaide they sold out of Murray Walker Fan Club shirts bearing the legend on the back: 'Unless I am very much mistaken ... Yes, I AM very much mistaken!'

Murray gives you a lot of legends to choose from. And as you read them, you have to shout to get the full effect. 'The leading car is absolutely unique, except for the one behind it, which is identical.' Or you might better consider the finality of 'Tambay's hopes, which were nil before, are absolutely zero now.' Or even print a second batch to double the profits with the even more classic and crisper 'There's Giacomelli, driving like the veteran he's not.'

If you plan to tune into BBC 2 this Sunday morning, be sure to warn pets, birds and neighbours for Murray Walker's distinctive ear-plugging shriek will be drowning even the decibelled din of the cars at Adelaide for the season's final showdown in which Britain's Nigel Mansell has only to finish third to win the 1986 drivers' championship from either Alain Prost, of France, or Nelson Piquet, of Brazil.

The famous voice was rattling the very foundations when I wincingly poked my head into the commentary hut at the Mexico Grand Prix last week. Microphone in hand, Murray cavorts around the box as charged up with revs as the cars which, by the second, crescendo past his window; distant voices are shouting back in his earphones; his spectacles glint back at the monitor set. The 200mph action is spread over three square miles. No other commentary in sport can be as difficult.

Alongside him, calmly waiting to be given, or to grab, the mike, is a calm, placid fellow in jeans whose wry expression makes him look slightly bewildered by the whole thing. James Hunt has casually strolled into the box 20 seconds before the start and will leave it 20 seconds after the finish. But in between, he puts everything into perspective. Walker and Hunt, who have the highest mutual regard for each other, are British sports broadcasting's best double act since Stewart McPherson and W. Barrington Dalby. They make the Saint and Greavsie look like quivering Hughie Green auditionees.

Walker has been steeped in the fumes of motor sport for just about every one of his 63 years. His father was a champion motorcyclist – the first man ever, in 1928, to average 80mph in winning a Grand Prix – who first commentated for BBC wireless from the Isle of Man TT in 1935. Murray jnr – who was plonked on his first bike, a 1928 Aerial Colt, when scarcely out of nappies – travelled the tracks of Britain and Europe with his dad. After Highgate, he was apprenticed at Dunlop, then commissioned at Sandhurst during the war, which he ended as a captain after the push from Normandy to the Baltic. Then a pioneering, highly successful advertising executive – he lists like sung litany all the accounts he got off the ground – 'Pal, Lassie, Chappie, Kit-E-Kat, Trill, Mars Bars, Milky Way, Galaxy, Bounty Bars and Treets.'

The first race he described for the still-infant BBC television was the 1949 British Grand Prix at Silverstone. He has not only been, I am told, the most well-liked and popular fixture round the circuit ever since, but able to enthral any occasional visitor with memories that date back past half a century.

Okay, you've seen them all, so name your top 10 of all time. 'Nuvolari, no question, the all-time great. Second must be Fangio.' A long pause till, finally, he chickens out with a great room-splitting laugh. 'Yes, I totally funk it – third place has to be a dead heat between the two Germans, Rosemeyer (killed Frankfurt 1938) and Caracciola (died 1959). Moss (alive and well and livening up London), Clark (killed Hockenheim 1968) and Stewart (still geeing up the world).'

Nuvolari was 'the best who has ever lived. His manager was a family friend. I remember like yesterday him winning at Donington in 1938 in an Auto-Union. A daredevil? Crikey, yes! And what a contrast to his supreme rival, another Italian, Varzi.

'Varzi was ice-cold, aloof, expensively dressed and a brooding womaniser. Nuvolari was a right scruffy 'Erbert, an engaging, archetypal arm-waving, laughing, hysterical Latin. Where Varzi was neat, precise and cold, Nuvolari was all arms and elbows and thrills, four-wheeled drifts round corners and smiles as he realised he'd arrived 50 miles an hour quicker than he should have, all opposite lock, and brakes and dust. Nuvolari was the guy we queued up all night for, unquestionably the greatest of them all.'

Varzi had settled in Argentina, where he helped encourage the young Fangio. 'Suddenly around 1948 this guy Fangio arrives in Europe. He's already in his late 30s but proceeds to blow everyone off the track. The furious Europeans just could not keep up with him.'

Okay, now where would his money be going if he had a bet for Adelaide? 'A calm assessment would have to put it on Prost. He's a gritty little devil, a truly great thinking driver. He is so incredibly smooth, neat and unobtrusive, he never actually looks as if he's going fast – the "crikey, he's been past and I never even saw him come or go" type of driver.

'Piquet without a doubt is one of the very finest drivers of the decade. Not in the same league as Prost, but bloody near it. He's so "basic". In the Brabham team, jokingly they say he's far nearer primeval man than anyone else on the circuit. Even in practice if, shall we say, he's taken short in the car, well he doesn't bother to come into the pits, but just lets it all go. Out of the car he has a rather bizarre sense of humour – he loves winding people up, certainly his team-mate Mansell. No one quite knows what to make of Nelson.'

So stand by your beds for 3 a.m. Sunday. Can Mansell do it? It's as exactly intriguing a scenario as the one Murray described in that classic screech a couple of seasons ago – 'and he's now totally in front of everyone in this race, except for the two in front of him.'

Now that sounds just like the perfect legend for Adelaide T-shirt printers.

---

# COMMONS TOUCH OF SPORT AND POLITICS
*December 1984*

The recent counter-attack by the hunting fraternity in the shires was as timely as it was good fun. Their gist, that if a future Labour government was going to ban fox-hunting then it should also ban fishing, must have made uneasy those Labour MPs with small majorities, and lots of canal banks in their constituencies. Fish, argue the representatives of the people, are cold-blooded and don't feel pain. Certainly they don't squeal.

It would be a quirky thing if one day Labour were to lose a few seats through the fisherman's vote. Over the years we've had elections won or lost on the serviceman's vote or the housewife's vote, but never the sportsman's vote. Forgetting the fishy business, I suppose if such a thing came to pass in the next year or so, that Labour would win by a landslide. For Neil Kinnock and Roy Hattersley – *Private Eye* mischievously calls them 'The Two Wrongies' this week – certainly represent a dream ticket in terms of sporting enthusiasms. Readers of these pages will be aware of Kinnock's articulate devotion to Rugby Union and Hattersley's to Sheffield soccer and Yorkshire cricket. Last year at Leeds I saw him accept a lift from the Queen's Hotel to Headingley with Sir Leonard Hutton. I have never seen a man – even a politician – looking so schoolboy-proud as they drove away.

Kinnock's recent *Guardian* piece on rugby seems to have been followed up in countless other interviews. I dare say the most difficult moment in his new job so far might come next Saturday when he could have to explain away yet again Wales' latest humiliation at the Arms Park. Incidentally, in an unguarded moment, he once admitted to me that long before Nye Bevan seeped into his consciousness his boyhood idols were Gilbert Parkhouse, John Charles and Cliff Morgan.

Labour have always had a pretty good record at this sort of thing. Without even taking a puff of St Bruno, Harold Wilson was always willing to rattle off the Huddersfield Town side of 1937 (Hesford, Craig, Mountford, Willingham ...). Michael Foot's first question on a tea-time Saturday was always 'How did Argyle get on?' Clem Attlee could apparently quote you verbatim whole pages of *Wisden*.

When Tony Crosland was Foreign Secretary, he once begged off an urgent London meeting with Henry Kissinger at the height of the Rhodesian crisis. The US envoy later found that Crosland's 'absolutely vital and crucial constituency engagements in Grimsby' were in fact 90 minutes at a top-of-the clash between Town and Gillingham.

The Tories don't seem able to match this sort of record. Even if their grouse moor image has taken a beating – since the year dear Willie Whitelaw enraged all Scotland, when for fun, he got his bodyguard to shoot a bird with his police pistol – the new meritocrats seem too keen to win merit marks than study the Football League tables. Indeed, soccer has been the cause of a couple of gaffes by Mrs Thatcher. Do you recall that picture of her a year or two back when she entertained the England soccer team? She is holding a ball high in the air in the middle of the group but looks nonplussed although the players are nearly falling out of the photograph in mirth. One of the team had just said to her, 'I bet that's what you'd like to be doing with every striker's balls.'

The first Cup final Mrs Thatcher saw just before her election in 1978, was that stirring day Ipswich laid Arsenal to waste. After the game she insisted in a BBC radio interview that 'Whymark was my man of the match.' The nation was convulsed. Her aides had forgotten to tell the poor woman that there had been a programme change and Whymark, injured, had withdrawn on the morning of the game.

Ted Heath, of course, had his *Morning Cloud* which was a good Central Office wheeze for a while. Then it sank and so did he. He once told me how he ran a dry boat – 'Over a two-day race I only allow my crew to eat apples or Mars bars: if I gave them fresh-made sandwiches they'd "protect" them in trouble. With apples or Mars they're happy to drop them at once overboard and start pulling ropes.'

If an interest in sport might be deemed a bonus, even almost obligatory, by the politicians' image-polishers of today, it was not always so. In a letter to his mother from Malta, in 1830, Disraeli told her how he had once been in the gallery of a racquets court where he was struck by a ball which then lay at his feet. Finally, he picked it up to hand it to a rifleman standing nearby. 'I humbly requested him to forward its passage into the court, as do you know I had never thrown a ball in my life.'

A.J. Balfour was a fine golfer. The popular weekly, *Answers*, ingenuously reported in 1904 that 'Croquet is a becoming game, but it can never take the place of golf. The Prime Minister is really a clever golfer and he possesses a remarkably fine set of silver-mounted caddies, which have been presented to him by one of his Scottish admirers.' I presume there was no Edwardian mummification of caddies, and presume they mean tees.

Ian Peebles, late and great, who once adorned these pages, told me of a discussion he had on sport with Winston Churchill. The old boy could apparently hold forth for hours on polo or pigsticking but 'when he learned I was a cricketer he dismissed his own career at the game as having ended with a broken finger when he was 10. He could not remember the rules or the names of the implements at all, but the delivery was tremendous, enhanced by those squishy sibilants.

Prompted occasionally by myself he warmed to his tale. "The ball came pascht," he said, "and hit the little things behind – what are they called? – ah yesh, schtumps." '

Once, Peebles persuaded Sir Alec Douglas Home to play in a village match in Scotland at the Peebles ground at Uddingston. Sir Alec was a very useful player but intrigued all the local lads when they noticed he had more than half-a-dozen different caps in his bag.

In his 1979 Boat Race speech at the Savoy, Harold Macmillan yearned for his old sportin' days. 'In my time one could go into sports without having first to go through a long test to discover whether you are a man or a woman. Those were the days when games were games and sport was sport. As a young man I took a great interest in cricket, knew all the batting averages, and all the great players of the day, Hobbs and Hayward, terrible degenerate days when you could still play a match between the Gentlemen and Players, reactionary, regressive, awful, I suppose. Still, a happy world....'

I remember one occasion at Lord's, possibly the only time, that three Prime Ministers were dining during a Test match – Home, Wilson and Macmillan. It was the afternoon, you remember, that there was a bomb threat. One of the great characters at Lord's, Nancy Doyle, a darlin' Irish girl who runs the dining-room, was serving the coffees when the news was delivered that there may have been an IRA bomb in the ground. 'My God,' says Nancy, bold and full of blarney, 'if they threw it in here they'd hit the flamin' jackpot, wouldn't they?'

American politicians have long realised the value of getting in on the sporting act. In 74 years since 1910, the opening day of the baseball season has been attended by 12 Presidents on 57 occasions and more often than not the senior citizen has wound himself up and winged down the opening onion. Harding, Truman and Kennedy never missed one opening day. Roosevelt attended seven and even Coolidge was dragged along to four by his Gracie, who loved the game and its guys.

Ike was right in there, and Nixon and Carter not to speak of Ford playing in the sand and snow. Remember that day Carter thought to aim for the joggers' vote, entered a marathon and was seen to be staggering around as if drunk when he hit 'the wall'? Now there's an idea for Central Office. Thatcher for the London Marathon. It looks like a must since Joyce Smith, another red-headed housewife from the north London suburbs, packed up. I really hope Saatchi and Co. think about it.

---

## 'ONCE UPON A TIME STAGE FIGHTS SORT OF HAPPENED ... NOW HOBBS GIVES HOURS TO EVERY BISH AND BASH ...'
### September 1978

Albert Finney did not look as if he was going to practise dying a dozen times that day. As he collected his mail at the stage door the other morning he had some 'Wotcha!' banter for one and all, indeed looked as mischievously cheery-trim as when Tom Jones first clapped eyes on Susannah York all those long years ago. The large white capitals ENIGMA were stamped across the back of his royal blue windcheater. Not a bad rehearsal rigout for the Thane of Cawdor. But apparently Finney had refused point blankety blank to let me see him going through his 'orrible throes at the business end of Macduff's brandished steel. 'No way! Albie'd go bananas!' was the official statement issued by a National Theatre spokesperson when I asked if I could watch rehearsals. And I had said I'd be very quiet.

They had sent me (me, a sporty type, see. Geddit?) to the National to appraise the sword fencing bits of Peter Hall's new production that opens tonight. Finney is Macbeth. Dorothy Tutin is his missus into the Mogadon – and Bill Hobbs, it goes without saying, has 'arranged' all the bouts, battles and blood. In the last 18 years Hobbs has staged more famous public fights than Mickey Duff or Harry Levene have handled hot fivers.

Bill Hobbs is 39, as fit as a footballer and as keen as Colmans. He is devilish handsome in a Stoppard-like baby-faced way. He bites his nails and hates travelling by air.

He has made fighting an art form. He was trained as an actor but even his best friends tell him he is not much cop without a sword in his hand. Lord Olivier made him Master of the Fence when the National Company was formed 15 years ago. Sir Laurence loves labels like that. 'A splendid title,' enthuses the old Baron Knight, 'redolent of times when *le mot juste* was *le mot plus splendide*, or, to be more vaudevillian, "Those days of fame/When a Pansy was a flower and a/Fanny was a name." ' (Archie Rice lives on in ermine, I'm telling you.)

Hobbs' thrilling work has punctuated European theatre productions through almost two decades now, especially when the Bard is on the boards. Germany and Denmark especially relish his stuff. But in England, unless we are tourists, it is hard to get a look-in – you, me and humdrum gateposts have to rely on his cinema jobs to jog our memory about his talent.

Remember that whirling dervish, frenzied fight by those three young gentlemen of Verona in Zeffirelli's film of *Romeo and Juliet*? Bill Hobbs was behind that. Or the whirligig, unending ketchup splattering in Dick Lester's *Musketeer* films? Or Polanski's bloody, bold and underrated *Macbeth*? Or Ridley Scott's stunning new fencing flic, *The Duellists*? All violence by courtesy William Hobbs.

Once upon a time stage fights just sort-of-happened. Men like Patrick Crean did wonders, but for the most part directors relied on the old one-two-three rudiments of Errol Flynn's simplistic combinations: top-middle-bottom, parry, parry, parry, swipe, swipe, swipe, top-middle-bottom – all repeated ad tedium with some ad lib grunting. Avaunt you cur! and the occasional jumping onto tables if the mood took you. They used to practise dying well – not killing.

As Sir Laurence puts it: 'My training in the art of fence was largely grounded on the clockwork technique of one, two, three; two, one, four; or "bish, bash, bosh; bash, bosh, bish; no, no, no, you should not do that bosh there, it is bash first, then bosh, now then, bosh, bash, bish, then backhand bosh." It could sound idiotic enough but could be quite good if you looked as if you really meant it, and used carefully practised variations of rhythm, also with a few escapes – purposely narrow escapes; then some surprises here and there, a frill or two, and your little fight could look quite respectable.'

Now the Society of Fight Arrangers, which Hobbs founded with William Marshall, has established a proficiency test which is on the syllabus of all the leading drama schools. He has written the definitive textbook, *Stage Fights* (1967) and this summer Barrie and Jenkins are publishing a completely reworked edition called *Action to the Word*. Hobbs gives hours to every bish and bash. Each one is planned to make an effect. It can take him weeks to block one sequence. 'I am simply a choreographer, making pictures out of movement,' he says. Actors tell you that he is devastating at getting his set-pieces to express the character of the combatants. Lay on, Macduff, and damned be he who first cries 'Enough!' He has worked for the full 90 minutes each day with Finney for the past six weeks. 'As a fighter, Finney moves very well and thinks very fast,' he says. Daniel Massey is Macduff.

Tonight's bloody barney will be light years away from the techniques of Sir Henry Irving and Co. Even though that worthy was myopic in the extreme, he very much fancied himself with the swishing blade. In The Academy 103 years ago this summer, the Billington of the day described Irving's fight with Macduff as 'illustrating quite perfectly, in its savage and hopeless wildness, the last temper of Macbeth.' Hobbs explains: 'Flying sparks in those days were considered an important feature of a fight. Irving was much enamoured of such effects, and would attach flints to the blade of his sword in order to achieve them. However, with the advent of electricity, Irving, in pursuit of even greater fireworks, actually had the weapons wired up to make sure they would constantly throw off sparks. Although it is not known whether he or any of his company were actually electrocuted, it wasn't long before he was using rubber insulation on the handles of the swords!'

The fight arranger does not like to talk about accidents – especially before a production of *Macbeth* which, traditionally, is the superstitious actor's most unfavourite play. Something terrible, they always reckon, happens behind the old cardboard battlements of Inverness. In 1896, for instance,

Gordon Craig cut off Macbeth's hand while laying it on too thick as Macduff; earlier the great Macready cut off two of his Macduff's digits. The worst thing that Hobbs will admit to is arranging for Oliver Reed to be stabbed in the arm in *The Three Musketeers*: 'I told this Spanish extra to stab him in the right arm, but he goes and chooses the left, doesn't he?' Communication, in films, is very difficult, he says. In the years of Sir Laurence, one of the fine, nutty fighters, who has broken many a tib and fib, a couple of ankles and a collarbone ... worst of all, he says, was probably his 'landing from a considerable height, scrotum first, upon an acrobat's knee.'

Hobbs was born in Hampstead in 1939. His father, who had worked in his brother's circus – speciality a rope-spinning act under the name of Ken Larson – was shot down in a Lancaster when aged but 24. Bill can remember him – just. He and his mother went to live in Australia, where his Auntie Lesley encouraged him to fence and act. At 14 he was a singing page in Helpmann's *As You Like It*, and at 16 he was the youngest finalist in the history of the New South Wales Foils Championships. He was in the 1956 Australian Olympic training squad but did not budge the selectors and a year later enrolled at London's Central School of Speech and Drama. However, he preferred the drama bit and by 1960, not long after his 21st, he was arranging the fights for Zeffirelli's stage *Romeo* at the Old Vic. The crits – 'revolutionary realism,' 'naturalistic fury' and all that – have been rolling in ever since.

He does not fence as a sport any more. Nor, thank heavens, jog. As a choreographer in elegant violence he thinks Muhammad Ali's early fights were magical. He says the secret of his job now is to transmit the feel of a competitive instinct to an actor who is not competitive. He has never been a team game bod, but his eldest son now takes him to Spurs. His younger one supports Man United. His wife, Janet, as it happens, is in the middle of an Open University general course and one of her setbooks is *Macbeth*. She is a distant relative of Judge Jeffries – watch tonight's decapitation scene for further hereditary symbols.

The opening production of *Romeo* at the Redgrave Theatre, Farnham, still remains, he reckons, his best stage job

('you should never fail with *Romeo*, all young, athletic people;
the whole thing so structured; no more than a Renaissance
*West Side Story*, if you like'), and if he retired after reading this
he'd like his laurels to be accompanied in *The Duellists*,
Polanski's *Mac v Mac*, and Cardinal Christopher Lee's
swordfight with Captain Michael D'York at the end of
Lester's *Musketeers*.

That last, if I remember right, had more revolting squirts
of the old tomato than the Northampton Wimpy on a busy
Saturday night. But, truth is, Bill Hobbs is wary of too much
blood. In his fascinating book he writes:

> *Blood*: This should always be minimal. To use it without
> discretion may be realistic, but it will soon lose its shock
> value. Too great a use of blood can appear gimmicky, and
> when by repetition the audience has become used to it, the
> end result will be meaningless. There are three types of
> theatrical blood: 1 Stage Blood, which is slow running; 2
> General Purpose Blood, which is normal consistency; 3
> Blood Capsules, which contain a powder pigment and are
> for use in the mouth only. *See list of suppliers* (my italics) L.
> Leichmer Ltd, 436 Essex Road, London, N.1.

I can't wait to see how his new book updates that. McFinney
might give a clue tonight.

---

# UNDER TINNISWOOD
*April 1981*

The clackety-clack of a typewriter grew louder as I made my
way down the lane. Just before hesitantly lifting the cottage
door knocker I espied, through a window, the silhouette of
the author and sage, the fierce convex of his Barrington conk
exactly in oval unison with the concave of his famous
drooping Amiss pipe. He was at work.

The lady wife greeted me with a handshake, tickling my
palm momentarily but sensuously with her spinning finger.
She ushered me into the oak-timbered committee room and

signalled me to be seated with exactly the ferocious semaphore movement of H.D. 'Harold Dickie' Bird announcing to the nation another Willis no-ball. Then, with a prim sigh, she took up the task I had interrupted and her needles glinted and flashed in the flames of the log fire as she resumed knitting yet another set of nets for Mr Alf Gover's indoor cricket school.

As I waited with trepidation to be announced into the presence, I blessed my good fortune to have been invited for an audience over luncheon in this reclusive's faraway Wiltshire village. What indeed was he like? All I knew about him – as did the world – was that he was born in the winter at Arlott St John's and he loves the summer, fine claret, Vimto, quail in season, barrage balloons, blotting paper, E.W. Swanson and his sister Gloria. For the rest, nothing. There was just time to decide to leave unasked my planned first question – 'Why does he live in a Minor County?' – before a gentle northern voice ordered me to the sanctum.

So at last I met the creator of quite the most charming, zany and downright chucklesome book about the summer game (*Tales from a Long Room*, Arrow £1.50) I have ever read. The price is a mere snip for the veriest classic of sporting daftness, a gloriously dotty and original in-joke. Peter Tinniswood has a beard of jet black, trimmed scarcely more than the Downend Doctor of legend. The famous Room, in fact, is not all that Long; only so in relation to the size of the cottage. Its windows allow, nevertheless, an unimpaired view of the backyard sunlit sward. Alongside his typewriter stands rampant a ferocious large pair of binoculars – atop a dusty pile of *Wisden Cricket Monthlies*.

He at once explained the manner of his lady wife. 'Do you not reckon,' he asked anxiously, seeking a kindred spirit, 'that she bears a remarkable resemblance to your own old hero, that great man of Gloucester, Mr T.W. Goddard, the tall fellow who tweaked the offer for years?' I nodded. He smiled slowly. We had got off on the right note. I had his confidence. The sage went on: 'It is a source of much pride and satisfaction to me, none more so than in the early days of our marriage, on that sun-dappled post-prandial session at the

Cheltenham Festival, when we were sitting with friends idly nibbling chilled Zubes and supping our mulled Chateau Dipper.

'Our peace and serenity were rudely disturbed when the Gloucestershire skipper, Mr B.O. Allen, strode up to us angrily, pointed an accusatory finger at the lady wife and said in a most hectoring manner: "Goddard, what in the name of blitheration are you doing there sitting dressed in women's togs? Get yourself off to the dressing-room this instant!" This the lady wife did. And at the end of the day she had the satisfaction of returning home having taken seven Leicestershire wickets at a cost of a mere 17 runs.'

To celebrate the memory he uncorked a full-bodied, elegant Niersteiner Guter Majid Khan. He was in a benign mood. He was this day, he said, deciding which of his two texts should be the subject of his 1981 Dimbleby Lecture. He asked me to offer my opinion between 'And behold Ron Saggers did tour England with the 1948 Australian and, lo, not a single Test did he play in,' and 'And, lo, Gordon Garlick did smite mighty sixes for Lancashire and then of a sudden he was transferred to Northamptonshire.'

He did not wait for my answer, for we were summoned to lunch by the ringing of an umpires' bell. The lady wife was a very decent 'Sam Cook' too. Here is just a selection of the veritable feast that lay before us: Duckworth a l'orange; Brain with braund and cranston sauce; Roast tim lamb with tom graveney; Dilley con carne; Van Geloven-ready chicken; Appleyard and bobbery pie. After finishing off the meal with some very savoury Jardines on toast we returned to the Long Room. Like most of the truly great in history – John the Baptist, Gandhi, Bevan, B.D. 'Bomber' Wells – Tinniswood's beginnings were extremely humble. His father was a printer on the old *Manchester Guardian* – and also a demon fast bowler for Ashton-on-Mersey. It was Dad who took his prodigy to his first Test match – All England versus All India at Old Trafford in 1946 – and he saw Voce bowl and Hammond hit a straight sixer.

The Lancashire XI became the young man's first disciples. 'They always seemed to be eating pork pies,' he recalls.

Tinniswood favoured Winston Place and chips. That sandy-haired hero 'wore his cap at a jaunty angle, and he had a jaunty walk on the balls of his feet and a jaunty smile. What a difference between him and Mr K. Cranston, the dentist with the sleeked black hair and the wife with the perfume you could smell a mile off.'

From Sale Grammar School he went to Manchester University to read economics. Then to the *Sheffield Telegraph* as a reporter and feature writer. Soon he was requested to attend an interview on his beloved *Manchester Guardian*. 'Your former Scottish editor, Hetherington, asked me who my favourite writer was on the paper. I said it was the lady who wrote the Country Diary from Keswick. His face was an absolute picture. He thought I was taking the piss.' He didn't get the job; instead it went to another Sheffield tyro, Campbell Page, who is now the *Guardian*'s Foreign Editor. 'Send him greetings,' said Tinniswood. 'Is he still flashing outside the off-stump?' I said he was.

In 1962 he cut loose on his own. Six highly praised novels, including *A Touch of Daniel* and *Mog*, have been followed by a number of plays and, of course, the Brandon family saga for television, the unforgettable *I Didn't Know You Cared*, which is now being turned into the National Theatre's first musical. Now *Tales from a Long Room*, a triumph of sustained and unrestrained pottiness. Hurrah, hurrah and hurry, hurry while stocks last. His new play, too has just opened at Scarborough. In it there are three characters called Mitten, Rowley and Carey.

Not the winter game as well? 'Certainly, sir, and if any publisher is brave enough I would like to present similar ramblings and disputations on many more of our great sports, starting perhaps with the definitive monologue on Mr Reg Harris, the bicyclist.'

At soccer the Reds of Liverpool, where he was born, remain his great passion. But his time in Manchester was also well spent – 'I'm not proud' – and with a sigh of pleasure I left him in his reverie reciting the plain-chant litany, 'Crompton, Carey, Aston, Anderson, Chilton, Cockburn, Delaney Morris, Rowley, Pearson, Mitten....'

I crept away. The lady wife saw me out; she was dressed now in her Ken Higgs autographed negligee and there was a fragrant hint of Eau de Washbrook about her presence. She forced on me a greaseproof package 'for the journey'. It contained daintily cut morsels of Pridgeon pie, Pleass pudding, some Todd-in-the-hole, and a large, juicy, steaming Rabone steak. How kind. And as I turned the corner of the village lane the good lady, having doffed her I Zingari cap, was now amiably signalling six like F. 'Cheerful Charlie' Chester on a languid afternoon at Worcester in the long ago. As I waited for the bus, I could still distinctly hear the soft rhythmic strains of his evening benediction hymn wafting from the Long Room windows and out over the meadows ... 'Sidlow, Lambert, Spicer, Taylor, Hughes, Jones, Payne, Baron, Stubbins, Fagan, Liddell....'

# 2

# THE MOST APPEALING GAME

Cricket was my first and most beguiling love – and I have no doubt that the devotion will endure however much the administrative mandarins at Lord's contrive to pop their collar-studs in collective apoplexy as they go about their convoluted, ostrich-headed moralising. Their players, almost to a man, are grown up, honest and chivalrous. But the squires farm feudal fields in St John's Wood. Ask Mike Gatting. Or Ian Botham. Or David Gower. All treated quite atrociously by their 'masters' in recent years. Talking of the galumphingly glorious hooraymanship of Botham's cricket, by the way, you'll notice in the following piece from Taunton in 1975 – just a humdrum little cricket report on a humdrum midsummer afternoon in the English shires – that I neglected to mention even once that it was the first time that I had ever clapped eyes on either Botham, then 19, or his fellow young Somerset colt, Vivian Richards. In fact Viv was out for six, which brought Close to the wicket – and when the captain departed, the gangling young scruff, Botham, made merry for a furious 45 in a quarter of an hour or so. Yet in my pleasure at watching the established legends of the game, I didn't think the fact worth mentioning in my report that evening. There's the generation gap for you!

# CLOSE THING AT TAUNTON
*July 1975*

After the first day's washout, Somerset and North-amptonshire went through some sunny enough motions on a slow but gentle turner at Taunton yesterday. There don't seem to be many realistic possibilities for the match today when, one fancies, both sides will be looking to sharpen eye and claw for the Gillette Cup tomorrow, when Somerset are at home to Derbyshire and Northamptonshire travel to Old Trafford.

Yesterday at Taunton's amiable, old-fashioned sports centre, an endearingly quaint sort of prefabricated Gothic – where even the press box still has inkwell holders – Somerset's batting fledglings put up a goodish show to help Close to 278 all out. And in the evening they took two wickets as Northamptonshire finished 224 behind. The sun shone and there was a holiday feeling, not least because Bill Alley was umpiring.

The crux of the matter was Close's combat with Bedi. One had looked forward to the possibility of such a duel as the train sped down from Paddington and, sure enough, the two enduring southpaws stepped out into the centre of the ring for a truly beguiling hour or so after lunch. Match of the Day. The bald old chewing yeoman heavy-footed his way to the wicket with unhurried certainty; Rose and Denning had batted promisingly enough, but Somerset had lost four for nearly 100; the sun and wind were now full of drying steam; the whole thing was finely poised.

Bedi came on at once – unhurried certainty, too, but of a different culture; no chewing gum for concentration and with a swot's wire glasses now, to go with a Cambridge Blue pakta. The mature student poring over his thesis. Every ball a question, experimental or imaginative or querying, every ball serenely perplexing, gently imprisoning.

For a bit the grizzly bear hung about, encouraged young Slocombe, of the shiny, prep-school face, how to play the

Indian. Answering every ball watchfully on its merits, but taking a measured chance or two in order to shake up the lulling rhythms, to grate the grooves. Slocombe was responding well, one felt, just when the placid, painstaking mesmerist's gentle curve was followed hypnotically by the kid. A dolly to one of the short-leg scavengers: 143 for five.

Close cued himself in: he had already focused his sights by twice swatting Sarfraz off his nostrils and past backward-square. Now he chassied out and twice drove Bedi straight for fours off the full red meat of his old bat. Then, flatfooted, he hoiked him over mid-on and used his toes and balance to clip him through mid-wicket. In between times he watchfully dropped a dead bat. Both men were relishing, revelling in, the differing challenge.

Towards tea-time, Willey came on. For just three relieving overs. Fourth change off-breaks. Third ball, Close, relaxing, tried to prod him past mid-wicket; it was straight and he was castled. But Bedi, out of things at third man, clapped as the rum old emperor munched his way back to the pavilion, deadpan still but somehow noticeably cursing his lunacy. The proper battle therefore remained unfinished. A draw: 190 for six and though the remaining youngsters tried manfully and with increasing swagger they could not quite reach 300 and another point. Somerset were all out for 278.

And in the evening more old friends: Virgin, poignantly leading his new soldiers back to the camp where he scored 15,000 runs, was given some cheery bird as he went out to start Northamptonshire's reply – and even more chucklingly so when he returned within an over, leg-before to Jones for a duck.

Thereafter Steele, wise and grey and unflinching, showed why he must at least be seriously recommended as England's No 3, before, off-guard, he was caught behind when the beautifully-named leftie, Breakwell, pushed through his quicker one. Breakwell continued to bowl nicely into the evening sun. There does not seem to be very much to get worked up about today. Unless the clouds of slate that were skimming across the Quantocks at dusk have some evil intentions.

# I WAS THERE WITH 'GLORSE'
*July 1977*

Gloucestershire have been up for a cup at Lord's once before, I know. But it was not the same for me, picnicking in a corner of some foreign field with a rickety wretched transistor. Today, I shall be there in person when they play Kent in the Benson and Hedges final. It was exactly 30 years ago, before the days of gold awards and silver-plated cups, that the county reached the old-time equivalent of a cup final – when the accidental arrangement of fixtures allowed the two front runners in the County championship virtually to play off for the title. When 'Glorse' lost to Middlesex at Cheltenham at the end of 1947's golden summer it was winner take all. The frenzy of anticipation for that long-ago epic has not been matched even in the West this week. I know, because, I was there. Aged nine.

Both days – it only lasted two – my uncle and I took the dawn bus over the top from Stroud to join the bleary queue of 15,000 that was to ring the College Ground. People still speak of the match today. You can meet men in pubs who recite Gloucestershire's last innings scorecard. They got 100, needing 169. Bill Edrich's 50 was top score of the match, and then Sims and Young bowled too well. Tom Goddard's 15 wickets were not enough. The very highlight was a boundary catch by an occasional First XI player called Clifford Monks who sprinted, memory says, some 50 yards to catch R.W.V. Robins. Memory also reminds me that it would have hit me on the head had he not caught it. Still the finest catch anyone could ever see. When Monks died 27 years later the *Cheltenham Echo*'s headline was 'The Man Who Made The Catch'.

With respect to Procter, Zaheer, and Sadiq (those well known natives of Dean and Dursley and Downend), what a lovely Western side that was: doughty Jack Crapp, twinkling George Emmett, the one and only Charlie Barnett, who smacked bumpers, thwack! as if he was smacking down plaice on the wet slab outside his fish shops in both 'Chelt' and 'Soiren'. Then there was farmer Neale from Grace country, and B.O. Allen. For some reason, I loved the bowlers best: George Lambert of the lovely action we all tried to copy, and his new ball mucker, great trier Scott. Goddard was my first idol. Huge tent of a shirt billowing out behind him. Huge hands, huge heart, he could wheel and deal for wickets all day long.

Goddard's appeal would reverberate round the ring from Cleeve to Birdlip. 'Eh Ta-am, whadabou' a bloke atop o' Lockhampton Hill then?' we would shout when he set his field. Once Basil Allen had to leave the field and put Goddard in charge. Over after over he bowled on, though it was not a day for spinners. Finally Goddard, completely whacked, complained to a fielding colleague, 'Why don't the bugger take me off?' He had quite forgotten he was skipper for the day.

Goddard has been dead a dozen years now. His partner in wiles and guiles 30 years ago was young Sam Cook, still with us as an umpire. Cook, an apprentice plumber, had arrived unannounced at the County Ground for the first net practice after the war. He asked which was Mr Hammond and said boldly: 'I'm Cook from Tetbury, slow left hand, sir.' The great W.R. threw him a ball, faced him for a few, then announced, 'You'll play for England one day.' And he did, almost within 12 months. He took nought for 127, conceding over seven runs an over, against South Africa in 1947's first Test, was never remotely considered again, but touchingly continued to wear his brocaded international blazer to the day he retired 18 years later.

The wicket-keeper was Andy Wilson, tiny tot with a massive appeal in every sort of way. After all his years keeping to Goddard and Cook he took bets that he would be the only batsman in the whole land to read Ramadhin's wrong'un when the West Indies came to Cheltenham in 1950. Both times Wilson shouldered arms first ball to the little long-sleeved mesmerist. Both times he was clean-bowled. That was another match that closed the gates at the College. By then new horses were leading our parade. Another T.W. too:

for in that match young Tom Graveney got top score, all blushing silkiness. And just before the start the announcer said, 'T.W. Goddard is indisposed and his place will be taken by J.B. Mortimore.' 'J.B. Ooo?' we all asked. We soon knew.

By then, too, we had 'the Bomber'. Can any county have ever loved a man as Glorse loved Bomber Wells? In his first match, against Sussex, this bumper bundle of fun arrived on the bus from Gloucester with his sandwiches and his pa-in-law's borrowed whites. First ball they put him at gulley. James Langridge cut gently, the Bomber tubbily gave chase – and they ran five. He was at once moved to short leg. At the moment Lambert was uncoiling his action the Bomber, showing he meant business, spat in his hands and smacked them loudly together. Langridge, put off, pulled away complaining. Bomber was moved to deepish mid-on and there he stayed for the rest of an enchanting career. When his turn came to bowl in that game he had the Reverend Sheppard out at once. By tea he had taken six for 47, and when John Arlott looked for him in the pavilion to do a radio interview he was told that young Wells was having a picnic with his mum on the grass by the sightscreen.

And on and on.... Now the county's thunderous trio to lead them to Lord's today are from other parts but, because of their natures and the way they play, Gloucestershire looks on them now as its very own natives. No one, not even Hammond, can have been held in more affectionate awe than 'Proc'; the same mellow drives we thought our Graveney had patented are now sketched as smooth as 'Zed'; Sadiq sparkles as Emmett once did ... and anyway still the West is served by the sturdy likes of Stovold, the bucolic charm of Shepherd; young Graveney, the nephew of Tom; young Shackleton, son of 'Shack'; Hignell, following B.O. Allen's tread from Cambridge; Childs, from Devon; and Foat, who fields as only Randall can ... or rather, come to think of it, as Clifford Monks could long, so long ago.

# QUIET POWER OF THE EVER-READY
# BRIGADE
*June 1984*

This has been the week that, annually and despairingly, I reflect how the tennis players and their umpires have come to deserve each other. There is a sullen fractiousness in the midsummer air as the magisterial district commissioners frown fiercely down from their almost comical step-ladders and speak in clipped tongue to keep the restless, war-like natives in order.

In another part of London, the throng at a far older, even more legendary, sporting arena is blessed with light and sweetness and serenity. Players in white chivalrously honour the foe; they do their darnedest to be sure, but in doing so they smile among each other and come and go with no demonstration of defiance or demur.

They are under the supervision of two quiet and calm and calming men, both in their early 50s with honest, level-gazed, watery-bright eyes and hale, nut-brown countrymen's faces. For six hours a day they stand at the Test match, unnoticed, almost anonymous, yet in a way directing, orchestrating the drama itself. The umpire is the law of cricket personified. There are 24 first class umpires – almost all former players – who officiate English county cricket. Each year an élite quintet is named for the Test panel. At Lord's today the pageant will swirl and eddy around two friends and former yeoman wicket-keepers, Barry Meyer and David Evans. And they will decide the outcome.

On Test match eve, all the young champions and their two solitary arbiters gather at the ground. Umpires aim not to get too close to the players, socially, but later in the early evening bar there is no escaping nor any doubt that the two, even briefly, are drawn in by the strands of warm comradeship which bind the freemasonry of the game.

On Wednesday evening I walked up the hotel staircase with our undynamic duo. Willis had strolled over to say hello. Now we bumped into other players. 'Oh, gosh! Got you again, have we?' says Gower to Meyer with touching friendliness. Botham greets Evans. 'Yacki da, boyo!' and puts his great paw on the umpire's shoulder in welcome. As we walk on, Evans says: 'Oh, he's a good boy, Ian,' and Meyer adds 'Yes, never any trouble with him, is there?'

Their duties start next day easily two hours before the game begins. Stadium clocks, boundary widths, sightscreens and sawdust supplies must be checked. They even re-measure a selection of balls with a gauge. The umpires' room at Lord's is thin and dingy and the window offers no view of the pitch. They have to share a lavatory with the public. But the room is very evocative. Some famous index fingers have been washed in that basin.

'Right, let's be having you, here we go,' they think in unison at 10.49 a.m. They both wear ties, carefully knotted into clean collars. In the pockets of their trim white coats they each carry a spare ball, a light meter, scissors, a knife, two handkerchiefs, a spare bail, a book of laws, and the rules of the relevant competition. In addition Evans carries six little 'beer ad' red barrels to tick off his overs. Meyer has six well-worn 10p pieces.

'But the most crucial thing I can ever take on to the field with me,' says Evans, 'is humility. No matter what preparation, you do have to take out a humility for your love of cricket. The game is fathomless in its capacity to give enjoyment. It has given me years of fascinated and profound pleasure. Much of it has been very hard work indeed – I am only an average man doing average things – but if you ask me whether every minute has been worth it, the answer is an emphatic "yes".'

The job is hard on the feet, 'but it's the truly enormous intensity of concentrating that is the tiring factor.' Like sentries they stand, never suspicious, but ever ready. Hands behind their back, or in their pockets as they notch off the minutes and deliveries with barrels and coins, plodding in from square-leg and out again, and in again ... always watching, always waiting, always prepared. When they come back to their room in the evening there is always a glass of lager waiting on the bench. Usually they are early to bed. The county motorway circuit adds to the fatigue. Once, between

48

May and September, Evans clocked up 10,000 miles. 'One day one of us is going to fall asleep at the wheel.'

Yet far younger men, the captains, stand in judgement. At the end of each match the skipper must fill in a form for Lord's and tick off one of five adjectives – 'V. good, good, satisfactory, poor, unfit.' The lovely game can be ruthless, too. Long before John McEnroe's great-grandma was born, the first-class umpires of England were subjected to annual eye tests. Every March Lord's send out a strict questionnaire for each umpire's doctor. 'Eyes and ears and everything,' says Evans, 'and of course I always ask for the tests to be most stringent, else it's not fair to the players or the game.' Their salary for four-and-a-half months' work is £6,850, with mileage money and a fair enough overnight allowance.

Evans gloved for Glamorgan from 1956-69, Meyer for Gloucestershire for two years more. They were elected to 'the list' in the early 1970s. Meyer is strong-jawed, quietly humorous, impressive; Evans a delightful, gregarious, inquiring Celtic philosopher. He recalls his first game as an umpire in 1971. 'Glos v Lancs at Bristol. I made a mistake. My older colleague didn't want to get involved from square leg. "Sorry, mate, can't help." Years later he asked me for help – of course I gave it, spontaneously and without any jealousy. Of course I did – but I thought how the wheel had turned. You mark my words, Frank, the old wheel always turns in the end.'

Relaxation for the two old friends at the end of their sun-blessed, flat-footed, concentrating days, is a half of beer to wind down as they wind up to chew the cud … remember when old Jeppo (Arthur Jepson) was ordered by Ian Chappell to stop rattling his counting coins … or how dear, lovely Eddie Phillipson would boast he would be first to his 100 lbws for a season … or when Cec Pepper turned down Mallett's appeal, saying he was aiming at three sticks in the ground, not a ruddy row of bloody railings … or how good to us when we were young were such stalwart, shining, honest men as Sid Buller, Jack Crapp or the legendary and unique John Langridge.

Eh up, boyo, time for bed … we've another long day tomorrow.

# AN INDIAN EPIC ... SCATTY, IMPROBABLE AND GLORIOUS
## August 1983

Once the heat and dust has settled, hindsight usually allows us to see clearly how great matches were won or lost, our memories of them being decorated as well with passing, pleasing, personal snippets. But where exactly was the nub of this third World Cup final? Scatty, improbable turning points festooned the whole glorious day. In the end, just the very fact of India winning was the epic thing about it.

In 1975 there was the gangling Lloyd's brutal yet almost apologetic rape of Lilian Thomson, and the memory of that superlative knock is fringed with the unknown young Richards' run-outs, Fredericks kicking his stumps, and the Australians' last-wicket run after despairing run when the ball was lost in the gloaming. Four years later, against England, that century by Richards in full flower was nevertheless eclipsed in my memory by Collis King's joyous fusillade.

On Saturday, in probably the last such final at Lord's for a long time – other countries understandably want to get in on a lucrative act – there is nothing for the memory to get its teeth into other than a glorious result and the triumph of simple faith over the hitherto invincible might.

When Marshall and Dujon seemed as if they might be turning the whole thing at the last, a friend of mine ran from his television set to the nearest church. It did the trick – on his return Dujon played on; an incredible fluke. If ever you needed proof that the Holy Ghost can bowl a cunning off-break, that was it! It reminded me a bit of Sir Neville's old ploy. Whenever the Lancashire bowlers desperately needed to get someone out he would pop into the loo – and could almost guarantee that he would miss the fall of the wicket!

The day had started badly for underdog fanciers. The Lord's gatemen were in such a mix of panic and cussedness that thousands of us were still outside when Gavaskar went. So we missed a chance to salute the wee wizard's last exit.

Srikkanth was a brief joy, as ever, twirling his moustache and his wooden scimitar, hitting Holding flat-batted to the pavilion rails then grinning sheepishly and nodding his head from side to side as is the Indian fashion. Graham Gooch, another uncomplicated opener, once affectionately told Srikkanth that his head-shaking was like one of those noddy-doggies that car drivers used to perch in their rear windows.

Scattiness continued. Of all the people to 'play for lunch' you would bet your life on Yashpal. But he blew it and at once the picnic lunches on the lawn behind the Warner were full of people certain they wouldn't be meeting again at tea-time – especially when Kapil at once fell for Gomes' three-card trick.

Greenidge shouldering arms seemed simply a necessity to get it over with quickly and give us the gift of at least seeing Richards put the Indians speedily out of their misery. The emperor seemed to have saved his most splendid robes for this last day. He dismissed the military-medium imperiously from his presence. The hauteur had him almost top-edging an amazing six to mid-wicket – but Kapil's difficult running catch did for him and, more than likely, the match.

If that was the important breakthrough the thing was settled when the gods at once tweaked Lloyd's groin muscle and suddenly his bat was no more use than as a crutch.

By then even those of little faith were beginning to see the light, and romantics' spirits were transported across the seas to the jingle-jangle jamboree of the celebrations back home. From thousands of miles away you could almost smell the joyful whiff of 5 November cordite, mixed in the sultry scents of jasmine, frangipani, cow-dung, smoke and curry. There have been few more epics deserving of a national Bank Holiday.

# HICK WORTHY TO TAKE HIS PLACE
# AMONG THE MAYTIME HEROES
*May 1988*

Should young Graeme Hick complete his 1,000 first class runs in May when he 'resumes' his innings against the hapless Somerset bowlers in the match starting at Worcester today – in Worcestershire's last championship match at Taunton Hick took his bat in at 405 not out – it will be the most startling arrival to the merry month's mythical four figures of all time. Cricket's traditional calendar has been so frigged around that it seemed unlikely that anyone would manage the feat again. The last was Glenn Turner, on 31 May 1973, when playing the full first class month with the New Zealand tourists.

Hick needs 185 more runs to obliterate Don Bradman's earliest achievement of the mark, 27 May 1938. If he manages it in the first innings he will have needed only the same number of knocks, seven, as Bradman needed that year. If he does it by next Monday, his 22nd birthday, he will be the same age as Bradman when he first logged 1,000 in May, in 1930. Even Bowral's boy did not manage an undefeated quadruple century in his two cavalier opening charges. Nor do the men who have fielded to Hick this spring stand around gammily with their hands in their pockets as some photos show the 1930 pro-am county players to have done.

Besides Bradman (twice) the other six to have run amok in May are Dr Grace (1895, 10 innings, aged 47), Tom Hayward (1900, 13, 29), Wally Hammond (1927, 13, 23), Charlie Hallows (1928, 11, 33), Bill Edrich (1938, 15, 22) and Turner (1973, 18, 26). Except for Hammond (28 May) and Grace (30 May) the rest posted the figure on 31 May. None of them had to intersperse his first class innings with one-day knocks which do not count in the historians' dotty calculations but are nonetheless crucial and played in front of far larger crowds.

The exclusivity of the list is proved most easily by its omissions. The game's run-stealers, like Hobbs, Hendren,

Woolley, Mead, Sutcliffe and Graveney, as well as such purple patchers as the Richardses, Gavaskar, Hutton and Compton never got near the target. But the litany of legendary names, let alone records, means little to the upright, blushingly boyish Hick. Growing up on his father's tobacco farm in Zimbabwe was no place to hear of many more heroes than his own namesake, Pollock, whom he was taken to see by his sports-loving father when he was five. Indeed the most famous English cricketer he had come across in person was Robin Jackman, livewire local coach, who presented young Graeme with a bat in 1972 after he had scored his first century for Mangula junior school at the age of six.

He hung a ball from an acacia and, with his new bat, thumped it hour upon hour, straight and true – which might account for the way he is now so powerfully, innately sure through the V between cursing bowler and colliding mid-off and mid-on.

If anything the young Hick considered hockey his favourite sport and that good game could well inspire now his glorious, wrist-rolling drives, played late off the front foot, that curl, screaming past cover's left hand or mid-wicket's right. He was also more than nifty at golf – hence, doubtless, those sure-swung, leisurely sand-wedge sixes that pepper the traffic behind the Worcester pavilion. But cricket could not be denied and by 1983, just 17, he is in that famous mass-photograph at Lord's, in the far left-hand corner – the youngest ever to play in a World Cup tournament. He had few opportunities for Zimbabwe then.

Next season, though, sponsored by his home union in Harare for a season with Worcestershire 2nds, he made the First XI in the last match of the season against Surrey at The Oval and *Wisden* reported that 'the unknown showed real promise' at No 9, adding 133 for the eighth wicket with his captain, Phil Neale. Hick made an undefeated 82 and thought 'great, but it was never in my mind to make pro cricket a career'.

But the buzz of playing a big innings was something he found he relished like a glutton. It reached outrageous and sublime proportions a fortnight ago at Taunton when he was left 19 runs short of the highest score ever made in English cricket when his captain, Neale, declared. On the same ground 93 years ago Archie MacLaren marmalised 424 off Somerset before he was caught. 'MacLaren? Sorry, I've never heard of him,' said Hick when he walked off undefeated on 6 May. The evening before he had come in on 179, red-cheeked but still unsated, and later in the bar, showered and half-a-shandied, he stood modestly in the background as his estimable mentor, Neale, explained how earlier, when the team had lost quick wickets, he had demanded of the young batsman that he 'set himself a target'; and Hick had replied: 'Skip, I have done just that.'

In the evening old hands ruminated on that precocious answer. Was he going for his highest score for Worcestershire, 212? Or his best for Zimbabwe in England, 230? Or his highest in Africa, 309 (v the Gents of Ireland in 1986)? Then, above the bar at Taunton there is a memento recalling Vivian Richards' 322 on the same ground. Was Hick going for that? No one even thought to mention MacLaren.

Hick, without a jot of conceit or complacency, is not unduly impressed by heroic tales. W.G. and the later Gloucestershire giant, Hammond, he is told, both received lump sums of money when they made their 1,000 in May. In 1895 public subscription raised £9,073 8s 3d for Grace. And in 1928 the *Bristol Times'* shilling subscription made £319 for Hammond, plus a gold chain and watch. 'Money doesn't come into it, does it?' says Hick. 'Scoring runs is satisfying enough. Just playing the game. If my stamina holds out, I'd like to retire with a few thousand in the bank, sure. But, if you're having fun, how can you look to a fortune?'

Hallows, Lancashire's left-hander, intrigued him. In his last innings of May 1928 he needed 232. He got them, exactly, and next morning in these columns Cardus snorted: 'The Sussex bowlers did their best to make Hallows' task easy. Was it cricket? Nobody would wish to be a spoil-sport in this hour of Hallows' splendour ... still, the game is the game; besides, Hallows is quite capable of dealing with *good* bowling.' Hick will have no 'gimmes'. When Bradman posted his 1,000 on 31 May 1930 he admitted in his diary that even he had been

54

offered some dollies: 'Southampton. Light bad, rain about ... I wanted seven more when rain started. Newman sportingly tossed up two slows. Immediately left the field and play ceased for the day. Dramatic. To the Empire Theatre in the evening.'

Eight years later, after Bradman had repeated the feat on 27 May, again at Southampton, the Australians travelled to Lord's to play Middlesex. On the 31st young Edrich needed nine for his 1,000 but there seemed no hope for Bradman himself was batting and only half an hour remained. Then Bradman uncharacteristically declared, saying 'Let's see if Bill can get his 10 tonight.' Edrich opened with Compton and, as he took guard, Bradman warned him, 'You're going to have to fight for them, lad,' and he directed Waite and McCabe to bowl flat out. But Edrich nurdled his tremulous 10.

Worcester is perfect for this week's latest wonder. Hallows saw out his days as the county's much loved coach; Bradman set himself up in early May with those two dashing double centuries in both 1930 and 1938; and Turner took out a mortgage on those two Severnside creases. But not, probably, as high a one as the amazing Hick.

And more records? 'Oh yes, I hope so. I just like batting, I suppose. If my stamina keeps up I'd have a go at them all.'

---

## GLEAM IN A VENGEFUL EYE
*June 1988*

The new Test series offers a genuinely intriguing sub-plot which many lip-smacking students of human psychology will be relishing far more than the actual five-act drama on which the curtain rises at Trent Bridge today. How, quite simply, will Vivian Richards cope – not only with the doubters' renewed challenge to his own smoulderingly brazen batting pre-eminence, but with the gathering criticisms of his ability as captain to meld and weld his transitional young team into a willing and winning combination? Is the awesome, brooding commander leading too awestruck a brood? The very possibility of such a stress fracture in West Indies' morale must at least offer England a glimmer at last after two successive 'blackwash' defeats against the hitherto unassailable team from the Caribbean.

England have not won a Test, against anyone, in the last 13 attempts – but neither have West Indies won a Test series of their last four, during which time, under Richards' leadership, they have also rather gormlessly surrendered supremacy in one-day competition, underlined by England's 3-0 win in this summer's single-innings pipe-openers.

For a lionised decade under Richards' predecessor, the seemingly placid, avuncular diplomat, Clive Lloyd, successive West Indies sides cruelly rode roughshod and rollicking over the rest of the cricketing nations in an unprecedented rampage based on an unending seam of ruthlessly talented, cold-eyed fast bowlers. Suddenly this summer, will that sometime embarrassment of riches be turned into the embarrassment of Richards? Great kings do not necessarily make great captains. Richards' peerless, almost frightening batting has been based on a kestrel's eye, and fierce pride fused with a withering scorn for mortal men attempting to bowl line and length. Eyesight, pride and scorn are not essential ingredients for leadership.

Was it really a dozen summers ago that I framed with devoted awe a picture for my bedroom wall. It is still up there – a riveting colour shot of Viv at the wicket, laying the Britishers to waste, a picture personifying the utter hooraymanship of those heat-wave glories of 1976 when the dazzling new star came among us. In eight months round the world that year Viv announced himself to posterity with a joyous and breathtaking power that brought him a record 1,710 Test runs at an average of 90 and, as John Arlott suggested on these pages, 'exerted a headlong mastery even more considerable than Don Bradman at the same age.'

The point with the picture on my wall is that in it Viv is smiling broadly and with boyish, bubbly content. There was a joy about him as he relished the uncomplicated proof of his talent, and as such he was utterly relishable to the whole game. Viv Richards does not seem to smile any more. This summer, in his team's preamble round the shires, the queues have been as long as ever, enthusiastic to glimpse his every entrance. What they have witnessed, from behind the ropes anyway, has been a lofty, stone-faced, shrugging champion.

Sage and sympathetic counsel seems difficult for the Master Blaster – and when his turn comes to bat, a savage venom fills his eye and makes him blind even to the very consideration of playing himself in. It had become a commonplace, almost a cliché, to talk of Richards over the years as an emperor, but by his whole swagger and audacious bravery the imperious mantle does sit on him well – but now, like the Roman fool, is he too readily falling on his own sword?

The churlish, sudden sacking by Somerset 20 months ago still rankles. 'I gave my heart and spirit to the place, only to be chopped down like an unwanted tree,' he says. Nor remotely healed, I fancy, are the wounds inflicted by the West Indies Board which for so long pusillanimously hesitated over the captaincy when Lloyd was considering retirement. Starting today, Richards will, as ever, be playing his game for the ordinary West Indian supporter in England – 'you know, those fellows who don't have too great a life, working on your buses and tube trains and that' – but also, this time, that vengeful eye will be cast across the seas to those Caribbean administrators he suspects of stifling mean-spiritedness, not to say treachery. I sense he feels let down by more than Somerset. When Viv mistrusts, he harbours the grudge, and he still feels on trial as a skipper as he seeks to mould, with steely, cruel wrist, his new side into his own image rather than Lloyd's.

In spite of his languid, even laid-back reputation, Viv is a complex and wary man. He does not trust easily. Nor is he totally bound up in cricket. The *Guardian* writer, David Foot, a biographer of Richards, sat alone in the dressing-room at Taunton with Viv just after he had brought his bat in for a record 322 for Somerset three years ago. 'We talked for half an hour about loyalty and religion, with never a mention of cricket.'

In the early middle 1970s, when we would make the

pilgrimage to Somerset Second XI matches to see the smiling prodigy with the walking-stick swish of stroke-play, Foot was commissioned to send back reports of his progress to the Caribbean Broadcasting Service. 'He was boyish, shy and most engaging. He is still shy, actually, but over the years I have seen a change in him, not personally but in his relationships generally. Not surprising, I suppose. But Viv has increasingly struck me as having an air of preoccupation about him – his eyes can glaze over and his mind will be darting off somewhere else.'

Foot thinks his friend will end up in West Indian politics. That indeed might be a reason for his comparative lack of acceptance as captain by the conservative West Indies Board, for as another of his biographers, the broadcaster Trevor McDonald, has pointed out, the board worries about 'his unbending affection for his Rastafarian friends. He sports the movement's colours as a sweat band on his wrist and is deeply fond of the music of the movement – his favourite is Bob Marley's *Redemption Song* – and he considers most authority out to demean him, to belittle what he has achieved, to make him less of a man, somehow to rob him of his pride and dignity.'

The brooding venom is being stored for more than the English bowlers this summer. His disdainful dismissiveness is retained, too, for sportswriters' guff which 'suckles fools and chronicles small beer' (*Othello*, Act two, Scene one, most apt) and Viv has muttered answers to routine questions on over rates and bowling changes. And if you ask who he aims to demolish first from the English attack, the glare turns up a withering beam or two, as if to say 'you name them, they'll go'.

It will be daunting and dramatically revealing to see how his team respond to such ruthless leadership. Personally, I would bet on a century at Trent Bridge, then a crowning, crowing 100th 100 at the shrine at Lord's in a fortnight. Emperors usually have the last word.

# THE GUILTY MEN OF LORD'S
*June 1988*

There is a dramatic unity about Lord's latest cock-up. For exactly two years ago this very day, 10 June 1986, Mike Gatting was called into the gents loo behind the home dressing-room at Lord's and offered the captaincy of the England cricket team in succession to David Gower. He accepted and at once the bitterly disappointed but ever chivalrous Gower presented Gatting with his T-shirt, which read 'I'm in Charge'. Yesterday's tragic second anniversary sequel which resulted in Gatting's unceremonious sacking strikes me as a scandal – the Test and County Cricket Board over-reacting to some Fleet Street trivia.

If Gatting two years ago had realised what traumas he was being lumbered with, he would not have touched Gower's T-shirt with a jumbo sized Duncan Fearnley. The job, however, was accepted proudly. Since when it has turned the young man from a universally admired, combative, uncomplicated, intelligent, heck-of-a-good-egg sportsman into a suspicious, defensive, stubborn victim of his ditheringly feeble, not to say hypocritical masters. All down the century, Lord's administration of cricket has pottered about between fifth form housemastership and the nanny-knows-best hand slap if the workers get out of line. This latest outrage of theirs because four players had a party with four girls on their day off takes the cream cracker. They still plough feudal fields in St John's Wood.

This time Lord's have contrived a botch too far. Who the hell are they to tell a grown man who he should or should not have an off-duty party with? The matter is surely the business only of the persons involved and – possibly – their father-confessor and spouse. Truth is that the mandarins of Lord's are about the only folk in the land who do not treat the gutter Press as a joke. 'By Jove, chaps, the *Sun* have done us again. Hell's bells, set up another full scale inquiry – and round up the usual suspects.' Why does this presumably grown-up body of men dance with such despairing, gormless regularity to every tuneless sleaze of the tabloid Press?

Lord's fall every single time for Fleet Street's brazen three-card trick – one titbit of scandal, the horrified setting up of a full inquiry, so the story runs and runs till Fleet Street (or rather Wapping) gets bored. The incredible thing is that on the issue of discipline on the field of play itself, Lord's recent record is pathetic, pusillanimous and prevaricating. When the opening batsman, Chris Broad, flouted the game's very fundamental rule in the winter by refusing to leave the field when given out by the umpire, he got off scot free. When, a month or so later, his stumps were stirred, he bashed them down in a fit of pique – and this time he received a paltry fine from the same men who have now instigated their righteous full inquiry into players' private lives.

More, when Gatting himself had his unseemly barney with the Pakistani umpire, Rana, in Faisalabad in December, the upshot was that Lord's presented each player with a *bonus* of £1,000 for, one can only presume, sticking so loyally behind their beleaguered captain. Nor have we heard one peep from Lord's of apology to Pakistan for their indescribably insensitive and patronising decision which fuelled the whole umpiring row in the first place – the refusal to comply with Pakistan's totally legal complaints about the British umpire, David Constant, on their tour of England last summer. No full inquiry there.

Best story that explains Lord's double standards is of the MCC committee meeting a few years back. In 'any other business' there were two items: a) that a senior member had been summoned in the courts by his ex-spouse for 'incessant wife-beating, permanent drunkenness and depravity', and b) that another member had been reported for breaking a hallowed club rule by 'eating an apple in the Long Room during the hours of play'. The chairman dismissed the first complaint – 'a feller can do as he wants in the privacy of his own home, what?' – but the pippin muncher was severely warned as to his future conduct. Apocryphal no doubt, but the yarn does illustrate how Lord's have been always in permanent dithering flux over morals relating to life, cricket, and 'the club'.

Even before this latest non-event of Sunday's fountain-frolic in the shires, Gatting was looking down the barrel of Lord's olde tyme musket because his ghosted book on the calamitous winter tour is out imminently, and his masters demanded his chapter on the umpiring fracas be excised. Instead, the ghostwriter simply put the captain's words in the third person singular. The censors called in their solicitor to see if Gatting thus remained in breach of his tour contract.

Of course, in the old days following a tour was a leisurely job for a cricket writing gent. They concentrated on the pace of the pitch and the quality of the cover drive. They did not rock the boat, and left all social stones unturned, for as often as not they were themselves getting even drunker than the players and, indeed, only passing on the groupies to the pros when they had sampled the goods first. Now the poor self-respecting cricket writer trying to concentrate on googlies and over-rates often finds himself sitting in the press box next to two, or even three, fellow hacks from his paper who know not of the difference between silly mid-on and a bag of Typhoo tea, but are in attendance only for the post-match titivating trifles that sell the *Sun* newspapers and get Lord's to set up inquiries.

A couple of springs ago I was privileged to be invited to a lunch to celebrate the late, great Bill Edrich's 70th birthday in London. It was a week or so after the *News of the World*'s 'revelations' about Ian Botham's 'night of bliss' with a model in Barbados. It was the talking point of the lunch, which was attended by many of Edrich's cricketing contemporaries. Ban Botham for life, chap's a disgrace to the game, fellow's an absolute bounder, was the tenor of all their rheumy-eyed and bitter old venom – but as the port went round so did the tales of far pavilions in their own youth: remember, ol' boy, how you got totally pissed the night of the Sydney Test, and what you didn't do to that Sheila and her mate before you passed out ... and what about that night in Jamaica with those three darkie bints and the rum punches ... and, by heck ol' boy, those tarts in Capetown are something else altogether, and so on and so forth. Yet Botham was a disgrace to the game, even though he was suing the newspapers for libel and is, and has been seen to be, a happily married family man. The old men were simply falling for the Lord's syndrome: it's okay as long as it doesn't get in the papers.

All these same old pros will be wading into Gatting and his pals this weekend, demanding life bans and what have you. How times change: when the two gnarled old pros, Trueman and Lock, were hauled over the carpet for being, allegedly, rude to two white women in a lift in Barbados in the 1950s, the manager, Palmer, and the captain, Hutton, called in the episcopal journalist, E.W. Swanton, to adjudicate at the 'tribunal'. Fleet Street was a safe house in those days.

On the next tour by MCC to the West Indies, in 1960, the manager, R.W.V. Robins, had a public slanging match with Peter May, the captain, over the continuing presence of May's wife on the trip. That didn't get reported either. Amateurs could be accompanied by women, professionals never. The autocratic May, chairman of the selectors, of course, sat as yesterday's lord chief executioner on Gatting's career.

It has even taken well over half a century for the fact to emerge that the most esteemed amateur of them all liked his 'frolics' too. They didn't set up an inquiry into Sir Pelham Warner, did they? In Gerald Pawle's 1986 biography of the doughty old England player, R.E.S. Wyatt, he recalls the trip by MCC to Australia in 1932 aboard the *Orantes*: 'The team took full part in deck games. Wyatt had the job of chasing up competitors behind-hand in playing their matches. Discovering Duckworth, the Lancashire wicket-keeper, was the chief offender and was two rounds behind in the Mixed Deck Quoits, he told him to contact his partner, "if you know who she is".

' "Aye", said George inelegantly, "I know her by sight, she's Plum's tart", referring to the very dignified lady who had befriended the chairman of the selection committee.'

Plum's tart! If the *Sun* had been on board, Lord's would have had to set up a full investigation.

# TRAITS OF THE GREATS LINGER

*September 1983*

There was not a helmet in sight: as the only concession to the current funk of youth, the youngest man on the field, Richard Hutton, wore a thigh pad. Everything else was nostalgia; even the weather was a bit Oval, 1948. The bowling was, frankly, geriatric; the batting sketchy, to say the least. The memories were rich: one or two shots wound back the clock if your eyes happened to be half-closed – a push to mid-wicket by Sobers, a beef past point by d'Oliveira, a cover-drive by Harvey, and a sliced carve by Close – but most of the time the mortality of man was being undermined.

Olde Englande beat the Olde World by 137 runs at The Oval on Saturday in a match sponsored by Courage Brewery. On a pleasant enough, blustery autumn day of scudding grey clouds and sunny patches, only about 2,000 souls speckled the wide terraces which was a meagre turnout since cricket people, above all gamesmen, set great store by antiquity. Perhaps a more compact, parkland setting in the provinces would better house such a carnival than the empty acres of dear old Kennington. Still, £3,000 was raised for the Ken Barrington cricket centre.

Jameson, d'Oliveira, Denness, Close and Edrich each got a few as England's ancients made 224 for five in 40 overs. Trueman, Snow, Titmus and d'Oliveira dismissed the even more ancient visitors for 87.

I met a friend who brought me a present – the late Denzil Batchelor's carefree character sketches in his 1952 *Book Of Cricket*, illustrated with evocative sepia period pictures of cricket's heads of state of the time.

And out there yesterday under the gasholders were two from that sepia cavalcade – Ray Lindwall, 'the holocaust who consumed, oh, how many magnificos as victims?', and Neil Harvey, who at 19 in his first Test against England, the book described, 'dashed away, driving and heaving to make Bedser look plodding and Pollard wildly despairing.'

There they were, the stocky bowler with creamy-white hair and still with a frisbee of an outswinger from an arm now a long, long way from the perpendicular. But still the outline of the action. Harvey, in dark spectacles – 'I can see the scoreboard now' – was as tidy, trim and hostile as ever in the covers and, at the crease, all nimble charm and footwork.

Age cannot wither the outlines, the gait, the little manifestations of swagger and character. Trueman has a more beautiful, fluent and venomous action than even Lindwall. You can sense it still: it will not go away even when wrapped in a comedian's beer gut and a seasick matelot's rolling waddle. Fred was puffing like a grampus; of a sudden, the turkeycock's chest and strut broke through when he speared out Sir Gary's off-stump.

All our yesterdays. There was Gibbs, still as slim as a girl, arms still high, tweak still sharp, and bouncing in on feet at 10-to-two; Kanhai was greyer than ever and Close more bald. There was Engineer behind the wicket, still contriving to shout, smile, and stump someone at one and the same number; Murray, still finding it impossible to squat without first the necessary ritual of tapping the tips of his gloved fingers together and readjusting his always-blue cap peak. There was the Noob, the one-eyed prince still daydreaming in the covers; Simpers as keen as mustard; Griffith still bounding in.

D'Oliveira still walks through the wicket gate as he ever did; stately, solemnly, staunchly. It was 15 years ago last month that he walked on to this same metropolitan paddock and in one day changed the face of contemporary cricket history.

The night before his innings against Australia in 1968 he had telephoned his wife, Naomi, in Worcester and said: 'Pull up a chair at 11.30 tomorrow, love, turn on the telly and enjoy it, because I'm going to be there all day.' He was equal to his boast and his destiny: he scored an heroic 158 and a Dr Vorster of Pretoria reckoned it was all a put-up political job.

As the sun dropped over the river for the last time in another cricket season, I spied Sir Leonard Hutton, almost anonymous, watching from a quiet corner of the Long Room. His eyes were glistening in a faraway reverie: 45 years ago last

64

month, on this same grass, he logged a run for every day of 1938; 30 years ago last month he brought home the Ashes and received the mythical gift on that balcony up there; out there on that field he reached his 100th 100 with one of cricket's – and Hutton's – lovelier strokes, the silken cover-drive. He caught my eye, and he knew that I knew the sort of thing he was ruminating on, and he smiled an old man's smile.

# 3

# ALL BANDS TO THE POMP

The Olympic Games bring out the worst in me. Giganticism gone potty. For the last two I have flatly refused to scribble so much as an exclamation mark on either the opening or closing ceremonies. If you want it covered, I tell them, go get the opera critic. In fact, let him stay for the whole flaming fortnight. And yet, and yet ... every mammoth, indigestible fortnight every four years still manages to throw up sublime sporting moments which catch the breath and warm the cockles: Coe's fifth gear overdrive off the bend; the remarkable Thompson's attitude to both winning and, just as memorable, losing; British lack of inhibition in, of all things, hockey; and African ditto in any race they have entered. The best foot race I ever saw was when Ed Moses led his two pals into the promised land at Rome in 1987. The most coruscating was Ben Johnson's in Seoul – till, three days later, the lights went out. Unless the athletics world watches it, the lights might not come on again. Or how about races between *chemists*? I wasn't always so cynical, mind.

# AN INFANT IN THE GAMES
## TELEVISION PLAYED
### September 1988

The Beeb is up against it this time. ITV is on the rampage with its Olympic coverage. ITV's network sports committee has a new, abrasive head, Greg Dyke, who says that cricket is crap – 'Nobody watches it' – and bowls is boring. He also has plans for soccer's goalless draws.

Dyke fancies that the Dallas Dudes versus the Cincinnati Slobs is the very stuff of British traditional sport – let alone, say no more, Mr Tyson versus Master Bruno. Our traditions are in danger of being showbizzed beyond redemption. I know, because I was a pioneer. I helped produce the very first ITV Olympics – blimey, almost a quarter of a century ago. They called me Editor of Outside Broadcasts, and although I was youthfully ravenous to get outside and edit outside broadcasts, I knew nothing about satellites. The first had winged into space only months before. We had to make do.

Us v the BBC. We were given a matchbox-tiny dungeon near the Middlesex Hospital. There were about 20 of us, mostly light-entertainment bods whistling Russ Conway and very browned off. Generally, sportswise, we had even less clue than budget. The much lamented, cheerleading Graham Turner and his quaking OB editor kept insisting that we would manage. In fact, we began breakfast television. Though no one had made the remotest plans for relaying the results across the world – for the first time, don't forget – I suppose it was my job. But I'd only left the *Guardian*'s subs' desk the week before.

The Games began. 'Give me some results of the heats of the 100 yards,' shouted Turner. I put my raincoat on and hared 100 metres to the Cleveland Street corner up the road and jogged desperately on the spot waiting for the first edition of the *Evening Standard* to reach the 'StarNews'n'Standard' shrieker. Then I hared back, shamelessly ripping out the stop-press tabulated, early-morning results, and plonked them breathlessly in front of our long-suffering genius presenter, Kent Walton. How he put up with it I will never know, but Kent has ever remained, for me, the most troubadorious old trouper of all time. After that he stuck to wrestling commentaries – Dyke is going to kill those too.

We worked manically round the clock. And slept on the floor. We would watch the suave BBC transmissions and swoon at their competence and calm. Peter Dimmock was arrogantly twirling his moustache, Coleman was beginning his years of pioneering brilliance. We hadn't a hope.

In the early hours of 14 October 1964 (funnily enough, the very morning baby Steve Cram in Gateshead woke up early to see what present his ma and pa had given him for his fourth birthday), I was shaken awake by my favourite PA, Suzanne, and told, 'She's done it. She's gone and bloody well done it.' I sat up, took a puff of the pipe, and said, 'Hooray, but what do we do now?' For Mary Rand had not only won the long jump, but had broken the world record. We were on the air in just an hour or two. We had no sound commentary, just a few fuzzy monochrome pictures. What the ruddy hell do we do? Coleman and Co. would have it taped.

We hired a car and sent it into the Home Counties to fetch Mary's infant daughter, Alison, who was being baby-sat for the month by the former Olympic athlete, Diane Leather. Reluctantly, Diane agreed to come to the studio. To this day I send her kisses.

What an Olympics that was. We did the same sort of stuntish thing when Lynn leapt, when Mrs Ken Matthews tumbled on to greet her walking chap, and when Ann Packer fell into Robbie's arms at the end of the mesmerising, first ever women's 800 metres final. But we ITV-ites were first with Alison Rand. Oh no, you cannot take that away from me.

Diane and the mewling Alison came out of the panting minicab. The show was almost over. The BBC had done a sterling job from Tokyo. But an engineering genius had somehow kept us in landline contact. We put a mike to the mite. 'Hello, Alison,' squeaked a breathless Mary. 'Hello, mummy,' mumbled the woebegone tot in Diane's arms. The hundred or so ITV viewers, including my mum and dad, had only time for a sigh before the pips went and Alison bawled.

Mary and Tokyo were cut off – and we still had at least two minutes to the end of the programme. The beaming, brilliant Kent was doing his best above the bawls to pour balm and for the umpteenth time brag about another British gold medal. But even he was stretching things.

I carefully placed the braying brat on the concrete floor. In the excitement of the morning I had forgotten to purloin the *Evening Standard* stop-press results. On my knees in the tiny studio space, amid near-panic, I scribbled out a note to Kent on a piece of paper and thrust it under his nose as he played for time. It was a good wheeze – especially as I was throttle-stifling young Alison Rand at the time, rolling her over on the floor to keep her quiet. My note to Kent said: 'Ten minutes to titles. Close the show by pacing out – VERY SLOWLY – Mary's new world record of 22 feet and two-and-a-quarter inches across the studio floor, to give the folks some idea of what she has achieved.'

Good old Kent, ever the pro, got up from his desk. As if we'd rehearsed it for a week, the grand old trouper slid into the routine, smiling and fluently waffling about the great feat (while the tyro producer and the babe writhed at his feet) that had been logged in all-time history that very morning.

I grabbed dear, darling little Alison and rolled over on the concrete floor like I was a scrum-half waiting for my forwards to come and save me with the ball embraced lovingly. Kent stepped adroitly over me as he continued his crablike shuffle sideways, his beetle-browed gaze never shifting from the tracking camera as he expansively marvelled at the Somerset girl's feat and counted out the yardage. Mary's world-record long jump had been just over 22 feet and two inches. At about 19 feet and 11 inches, Kent and our tracking cameraman simultaneously hit the wall. Clang.

Literally. Clang. The shuddering populist reverberations of Kent and Keating are suddenly being heard a quarter-century later. ITV takes on the BBC this fortnight with a vengeance.

# EE-AYE-ADDIO, THE CHATTY GUY WON
### *August 1980*

*Moscow*: A friend summed it up immediately afterwards. 'I have never seen an English press box look so happy since Leeds United lost the cup.' Poor Ovett. He shook hands graciously at the end and put on a brave face at the medal ceremony. But I noticed that as soon as he stepped down from the podium he took off the little bronze biscuit and stuffed it in his pocket. At the packed conference for the world's Press, Ovett's chair was empty. Last week he had boasted: 'I am 90 per cent sure of winning the 1,500 metres.'

Later last night he admitted: 'I couldn't raise myself after the 800, I suppose. But I don't hold any grudges for Seb.'

Said Sebastian, 'Of course I feel sympathy for Steve. A genuine trouble with competitive athletics is that someone's a loser. This week we have both won and we have both lost. Before the race, in the tunnel, I wished Steve well and he wished me well and I said I hoped we'd both run the race to the very best of our capabilities.'

How did he climb the mountain after such a fall last week? A long, long pause. 'The 800 metres was a terrible, terrible disappointment, a disaster ... do you know I would still have preferred to have won last week than tonight. The 800 was the race I'd come for, the race I'd dreamed about for years. Not that I'm complaining about tonight – and all week I insisted to myself that I could never again run as badly as I did Saturday. I studied the video and the only good to come out of it was that we noticed I finished that race very fast. Too late, of course, but very fast.' He sat holding a bunch of flowers that a Russian girl had given him. Our gentle, gifted boy who prefers watching his beloved Chelsea FC to athletics, had a dazed and faraway look of ecstatic self-satisfaction. A job well done.

Why had he stared at the wide Russian sky during the medal ceremony? 'Did I? Did I really? I wasn't aware of that. I suppose I was thinking "well, someone up there loves me after all!" ' Did he miss the national anthem? 'A decision was made that British winners would have the Olympic hymn played. I am fully aware of the reasons behind that decision and I certainly respect the decision. But I heard the crowd singing *God Save the Queen* as loudly as they could, so I didn't miss out at all, did I?'

Once he took the lead we held our breath for Ovett's famous kick. It never came. Coe had taken him too early and wrung the zip from him. 'What was it, 200 metres out? No, about 180. I felt settled and comfy; I felt I was beating out a real rhythm; I thought "Now", knowing Steve's ability to go when others aren't ready and once I took that initiative I had to keep it.'

He ran the last 800 in one minute 47.5 – only 1.6 seconds slower than on Saturday – the last 200 in 25.2 seconds. And the last 100 in 12.1. That's why Coe beat Ovett.

Coe's father and coach Peter said: 'You can do all the training, all the routines and all the schedules, but it is those famous words in the last analysis – it's all about character. Running at this level is more than just putting one foot in front of another. You've seen an athlete come back from the grave. He's got all the guts in the world.'

---

# TEARS FOR THE FORGOTTEN HUNGER STRIKERS
*August 1980*

*Moscow*: Just after I left my hotel for the Lenin Stadium yesterday evening a small sad group of Jewish people approached and asked if I would go with them to report their demonstration. Would I talk to some friends who had been on hunger strike for the duration of the Games in protest against Soviet anti-Semitism. 'Sorry,' I said, 'terribly sorry,' but the closing ceremony of the 22nd Olympiad is very, very important. Sorry. But have a good demo.

The dancing was fantastic, and the gymnastics elastic, though the smiles very plastic. Those children on the far bank were at it again with their coloured cards, creating superlatives, multi-coloured mobiles and mosaics. There were banners everywhere, fluttering yellows and blues and greens, but mostly reds. There were fireworks and cannons that made us innocent mortals cower.

There were doves and girls and soldiers and more girls and more soldiers, then even more girls with heaps of hoops. There was Shostakovich and Rachmaninov and Artemyev and Pakhmutova. There were national dancers and national costumes and national songs and national nations. On massive screens there were replayed highlights of the sports, and, as the programme put it, 'shots of friendly encounters in the Soviet capital.'

Allowed for some reason into this rigid jamboree were a token six athletes from each participating delegation. A right rag, tag and bobtail mob they were. They quite ruined the spectacle. Well, for one thing, they had not been practising for the march all those years, had they? They didn't take up much time – so the bands were allowed to play on. Nothing was spontaneous. Everything ordered, rehearsed and very, very spectacular.

The retiring president of the International Olympic Committee, Lord Killanin, came to the podium. A gold for Ireland at last? No, the old boy made his farewell speech, repeating his constant appeal for the separation of sport and politics. Then the Olympic Flag was Basil Fawltied off by eight junior ministers at the Department of Silly Walks – for a moment I thought they were walking threateningly over to toss M'Lord in the blanket like at a prep school birthday party. But they wandered away, heaven knows where, and our eyes were drawn to the flame high, high up against the evil, thundery night sky. The flame started to flicker and then the darned thing went out completely.

Darkness for a moment. Then, let there be light, and half the Russian army marched on, blowing bugles and crashing cymbals and putting not a foot out of place. The whole shebang was led by a pompous drum major. Then everyone followed him out, a ridiculously precise great crocodile of flags and hoops and cymbals and symbols and, I suppose, people.

Oh yes, then the mosaic children conjured up a last picture of Misha, the Russian bear. And, do you know, they made it cry real tears. Hundreds of feet high and it cried real tears – and that determined me to leave the Lenin Stadium at once and try to find my sad little knot of very, very brave Jewish hunger strikers.

---

# PAPERING OVER CRUELTY TO AN INNOCENT
*August 1984*

Even the choirs at the canonisation of St Sebastian could not drown the debate. Even Carl Lewis leading what amounted to an old-time Bible meeting – 'I did it all through the power of God, hallelujah' – could not deflect totally from Budd and Decker and the drama of the night before.

All day Mary Decker was poking her drawn and tear-smudged face out from the protective bear-hug of her discus-throwing fiance to insist that it was all the fault of the transplanted South African waif. All day Zola was kept in camera, reportedly weeping now and then, as the top brass of the *Daily Mail* decided on how brassily they could play it. And all day, television and radio here overwhelmed us with live reports from Pretoria and Bloemfontein wailing the Afrikaans equivalent of 'we was robbed'.

It seems to have been South Africa's lowest night since Mafeking. To my mind, Miss Budd was totally innocent, though almost total inexperience of racing against humans as opposed to just running against Rolex and roebucks might have contributed to the accident. But it was Miss Decker's head-girl vanity that got her into the mess and the agonised come-uppance. No barefoot pipsqueak was going to lead the grand dame of front running.

But how gloriously and fortunately it got the *Daily Mail* out of a hole. And South Africa too. ZOLA's FLOP … THE BUBBLE BURSTS was a headline that would have been embarrassing. Now, thanks to Decker's dramatic arrogance, the headlines can read: ZOLA – AGONY OF THE LATEST CONTROVERSY or whatever last milking of the mileage is printed this morning. The harsh fact that the young phenomenon was sadly and cruelly entered out of her class in the race can now be conveniently forgotten. Indeed had it been a 3,100 metres race she would have been last and, in the circumstances, ignominiously last.

Everyone from the *Mail* seems to have been over for the swan and to cheer their cygnet home. Viscount Rothermere, chairman of the group, has once or twice been spied dazedly and bouffant-grey wandering around our hotel during the fortnight. Nobody it seems had told him Zola might not win. Sure, he had heard of Decker, but not Puica, Williams, Cunha and Co., let alone a totally vindicated Wendy Sly.

The morning after the night before, the editor, David English, called a council of war in his Beverly Hills HQ. How many pages would they need to raise a hullabaloo over the Decker latest drama and so cover up somehow the failure of the prodigy to get anywhere near even a bronze medal? The results of such hard-bitten executive deliberations are on our news-stands this morning. Great story, eh?

Thanks to Decker's dive – and together with the pre-exclusive syndication deals – the Zola story remains a viable investment. But for how long? What happens now to the little girl with the shiny new British passport? Her coach was insisting last week that he, anyway, had to return to his teaching job in Bloemfontein. Certainly, Zola can still pull in some money for herself and her investors on the European autumn circuit – but now only as the one-time phenomenon who was seventh in an Olympic final. Will she lose her precocious ability once her body grows up?

How long will she stay in her adopted land? The South African people obviously and genuinely would love to welcome her back. But, how does the South African government stand? It is as intriguing as it might be harrowing as we wait to read the next exclusive instalment.

# YOU'RE RUNNING ON AIR ... THEN IN MUD
*August 1986*

Landy v Bannister, Elliott v Hewson, Bayi v Walker: old hands at the Commonwealth Games are ever ready to nominate their favourite foot races, memories of which still stir the blood. Perhaps it is simply a generation thing. Or was it the fact that slow-mo replays had just been invented or that everyone suddenly had a colour television set to see the blue on the red and the stars from their spikes?

Or perhaps just that the romantic unities so sumptuously came together 16 years ago this very week – and in Edinburgh again – when the epic 5,000 metres ended with two blue-shirted Scots youngsters careering to the tape, legs stride for stride in an egg-whisk whirr over the brand new rose-red tartan track. The two Ians, Stewart and McCafferty, with Meadowbank's crowds almost as delirious as Coleman's crescendo at the mike.

Ian Stewart was obviously chuffed that someone had thought of talking him through that sweetest of Scottish afternoons in 1970. The one-time boy wonder has little, indeed nothing, to do with athletics these days unless it concerns business at his swish sports shop in central Birmingham. He has not been so much as telephoned for an opinion, he says, in the past five or six years.

He has lost all touch with the sport, and far prefers motorbikes. He is up at today's Parade of Champions – riding from Birmingham on his high-handlebarred full dresser Gold Wing, power chrome and glitter and noise, CB radio and stereo aerials flying, and capable of vrooming at 140mph away from the Queen's highway.

Stewart still relishes speed, just as he did in the last week of July in 1970. 'It was quite a field, wasn't it? Ron Clarke, Kip Keino, Dick Taylor, McCafferty and a pile of other fellows who could really run a bit. I was only 20 and the European champion. I really felt unbeatable. Lasse Viren once told me that winners are always the men who think they will win.

75

'Everything the winter before had gone perfectly. I was carrying 120 miles a week, great cross-countries and no injuries. In the spring at Stockholm I'd beaten Clarke: simply demolished him. And as far as I was concerned that put him out of the Edinburgh race. So it was Kip and me and Ian – even though we heard that Clarke and Dick Taylor were planning to team up against me and try to break me early with some venomous kicks. Warming up, Geoff Ware, his coach, asked me how fast I could run if they put me under terrible pressure. I said I must win in 13.05. Geoff reckoned 13.20 would do it – still the fastest in the world at that time.

'I said I was going to totally ignore anyone else, but hit Keino so hard with 500 to go that he just wouldn't realise what the hell was happening to him. Everyone else those days was so mesmerised by Keino they were scared to death, they just let him toy with them.'

The start: reds and whites and greens and yellows – and, of course, two blues. 'The gun, Dick [Taylor, still a firm friend] looked really magnificent. He picked it up at a creaming pace. I was determined to sit calm if his pace was fast enough. But it was ruddy fast, and it's a hell of a long way. Dick was looking to demolish everyone: 75 seconds for the first lap, 73 for the second. He was through 3,000 in 8.05 or 8.07. He had burned off everyone except Clarke, Keino, McCaff and me.

'Nine laps gone, and we knew – and Dick knew – that he wasn't going to get away. We had him. Two-and-a-half laps left: at the top of the 100 metres bend, Dick suddenly cracked, down to a crawl. Should I take it up? Should I surprise them all and go like mad? I had that split second to consider the dare, when McCaff suddenly jumped ahead like a shot-at rabbit. Nerve! Brilliant, but would it work? Certainly he killed off Dick at once, and then his 60-second lap left Clarke bewildered and well behind with nothing left.

'Now only Keino and me could possibly catch him. The bell. I went, Keino followed. I beat him to McCaff, and we passed McCaff at the top of that last long, long back straight. I was surely going to do it. No! Suddenly I could hear Keino still behind me. On cinders, sure, you can hear the crunch of someone behind: on tartan it's an ominous pad-pad-pad.

'I was holding him off. I was flying. I surged again. Curved into the home straight and let fly once more. Would I have anything left? All of a sudden there was a great noise in my ears, not pleasant, like bees buzzing in a hundred hives. Oh, why can't they stop? Just stop for a moment so I can hear if the footsteps are still behind me. How close is this ruddy African? What has he got left? I've done everything right – everything except drop him. Have I blown it? Or has he? He can still attack. I can only run.

'And somebody is coming. Try and surge again. You can't! He's up to my hip. He's alongside me now. Christ! It's McCafferty! Fifty metres left, then 40, then 30.... You have to have a last burst. There must be something left. Arms high! More breath. Please! You're running on air. Then in ruddy great army boots in mud. All those winter days across country. Help me now.

'Go for it! Suddenly I'm there. I am. Not him. I've won and the noise now is not that of any angry bees, but a great choral whoosh of cheers and glee. The home crowd, the blue vests, the flags of Saint Andrew and the pipers all sort of merge into one sensation, one feeling. And you gasp as you totter and you think of nothing and everything and turn round on your haunches at last and see it really is McCafferty next to you and that only him and me had made it and Keino was far behind, and Taylor and Clarke and all the rest were still running.

'McCaff, wonderfully, had done everything right – but I'd done everything righter! Thirteen minutes, 18 seconds: Geoff had been two seconds out!'

---

## WHITBREAD'S BITTER YEARS
### *August 1986*

The Fats and Tess show runs and runs – but no episode in the already epic serial can have matched yesterday evening's drama in Edinburgh. How does the billing go? 'Just two ordinary girls who grew up to be extraordinary, drawn together by their singular infatuation. No love is lost in this saga of Passion! Intensity! Intrigue! Vengeance! Suspense! And there can only be one winner.'

Not, as you might think, a fly-on-the-wall report from Holyrood, where Mrs Thatcher dined with the Queen last night, but the latest spellbinder from Javelin Junction.

Fatima Whitbread, dark and intense, and Tessa Sanderson, black and beautiful, had their last run-in at the Coliseum in Los Angeles two summers ago. Tessa won that, but Fatima has extracted vengeance, month after month, with the cruel unending relentlessness of Scottish rainwater torture. With throw after throw in city after city she made poor Tess pay for her nerve that steamy night under the Californian stars and also for her exuberant rubbing-it-in when she lapped the field in honour wrapped in a Union Jack blanket.

Much as these comparatively minor victories gave pleasure, to turn the knife at a major championship was the satisfaction she craved. It was a two-year wait. In between times the rivalry had been batted back and forth with locker-room comments in sullen whispers as well as screaming headlines in the public prints.

Tess, her once massive confidence in shreds now, bellyached about Fatima's sponsorship by industry and about Fatima's step-mother, who was at the time a British team official, having her priorities twisted into favouritism. Fatima's answer to such seeming jealousies was to throw longer and faster whenever poor Tess was present.

The girls, who used to be buddies, sending each other good-luck notes signed 'Fats' and 'Tess', now only referred to the other, if at all, as 'Her'. In public anyway.

There was no way, you felt, that Edinburgh's rain would dampen Fatima's revenge. All seemed predictable. Fatima sat in the little mobile trackside hut. For four throws she did all that was needed. Tess sat away from the hut, alone under a blue-striped golfing umbrella, changing in and out of her tracksuit to throw in moody concentration, almost resignation.

Sanderson paced out her run for her penultimate throw. Her strength and speed had been okay all summer, she was as fit as a flea, and only her technique continued to worry her. All week in the Village she had worked at it. Oh, if only the timing could come right now. She took up her spear, wiped off the rain, settled herself, a long pause – and then a skip and run-up with a lithe and rhythmic bounce. A last whipcord flick of wrist and shoulder accompanied with an orgasmic half-shriek, half-grunt. Straight as an arrow, not too low, but not too high; flat and not dying; on it went. Ecstasy on the runway.

Fatima had one attempt left. She tried to calm herself. Panic obviously set in. She paced about as if suddenly caged and trapped. Tessa jogged and jigged loosely and she could not help having seen her from the corner of an eye. Panic and one last throw. As it had been ordained, it was limp and damp and depressing.

And so Tessa doubled the dances and the jigs and jogs and giggles and laughter. The crowd all round the crescent of the Kop responded. Fatima collapsed in a heap, a distraught heap, quite inconsolable. She untied her laces and then tied them up again. She buried her face in her hands and then rolled her eyes despairingly to the heavens that had so wretchedly failed her and blessed her rival. The poor woman sat there in brooding anguish for fully half an hour as her mother and friends and officials tried to rouse her. And all the time, perhaps milking her triumph just too unkindly much, just 20 yards away, Tessa signed and sang, cavorted and caroused with the cheering crowds on the trackside. She did chivalrously (or gloatingly?) go over to shake Fatima's hand. But she was waved away.

Finally, the once and newest champion was shepherded off – and only then was the loser helped up and limping away. Off the podium, on which she looked a painful picture of distress, Fatima ripped the medal from her neck and then, bravely at least, attempted to speak. It came out, poor girl, in a monosyllabic whisper: 'Twelve long years and it all ends like this, 12 years of hard work. Still no medal. I'm sorry I seem unsporting. I'm so upset. She doesn't know how it feels. I've performed so brilliantly for two years, the one time I needed a lucky break it didn't come. Twelve years is a lifetime. It's shell shock. I still can't believe it.'

She made a point of congratulating the Aussie blonde who had won the bronze. 'I regarded her as a bigger threat than the winner. Unfortunately, the gods weren't shining on the right person. I've waited two long years since LA. Two years for the gold medal in a championship. And now I'm humiliated. The next Olympics? Sure. Two more years. I'm a very determined girl.'

The Fats and Tess Show. They never close. Passion! Intensity! Suspense! And Revenge!

---

# THREE TIME WINNERS
*September 1987*

Nobody could remember a triple-header like it. McDonald Bailey, Remiqino, and McKenley at Helsinki in 1952, said one old timer, mopping his brow with all of us. But that race was four times as short and before such electronic sophistication. Other Limeys were tossing about names like *Dawn Run, The Minstrel*, and *Hot Groove*.

After the stupendous charge – six eyeballs rolling grotesquely, three faces gruesomely contorted – the throng, also drained, fell momentarily silent and 80,000 turned as one to the large screen above the stadium for the television replay. There was a huge and collective intake of breath and a sort of gigantic question-mark seemed to hang on the heavy, sticky air before the cheers rose up. It was a dead-heat surely?

If high technology had a hell of a job sorting it out, oddly enough the three runners seemed to know the score at once. Said Moses: 'At the tape I knew they were still behind. Fortunately in this game 2,000th of a second is as good as two metres or 20. Everything went to plan, after the 10th hurdle I knew they'd be coming all right, and they did too, didn't they? You sense when you've got it, you sort of just "feel it".'

Harris too: 'No, I didn't think it was me. I ran a personal best so I'm not sad, in fact I'm thrilled. I didn't take the last hurdle well, but no excuses.' Nor did Schmid have any complaints: 'My best run ever, the best by anyone ever from Europe.' He held out a finger and thumb showing the gap of a millimetre. 'I'm just this distance behind Moses now. It was so close, in my heart and spirit I know I'm level, with him. Edwin just made one mistake today – he didn't slow down quite quick enough.'

The old emperor, beard still glistening with sweat but face now serene, and you might say appropriately biblical, was not going out on this high. He's 32 but wants to keep the old legs moving. 'Give up? This race was the fastest ever in history, it was an orgasm of p.b.'s – and I won. With a bit of rest I could still go for another world record this year. Retire? What else do I have to do but keep running? I have definite plans to do a job at the Olympics, then maybe the World Cup in 1989 and, sure man, I'll be hanging around somewhere in Barcelona in 1992, I guess. But though I say it myself, I've created a monster, a rod for my own back, for this little event of ours is so rapidly improving day by day and month by month that it makes every race tougher and tougher, pain humped on pain.'

But the pain was over now and everyone was beaming contentedly just to have taken part in what they knew history would log as their event's most epic occasion.

The experience was worth a few seasons of pottering about Crystal Palace for Akabusi. Brand-new to the event he was seventh, the six in front of him all being Olympic finalists. He held his own till the three-man gale blew him away. 'I panicked when they went past. Once they had there was nothing else to concentrate on, so I just put my head down and ran after them like an animal.'

Ah, the bulldog spirit of olde Englande.

---

## NEW ERA BEGINS WITH A CHILLY DAWN
*October 1988*

I do not know how many Olympic competitors say their prayers night and morning as a matter of course, but I bet a heck of a lot more than usual woke up to Seoul's chilly grey dawn yesterday and, with a shiver, offered thanks: 'There but for the grace of God go I.'

Ben Johnson is taking the rap for a pretty large army. Even the most conservative pre-Games estimates admitted a substantial group of athletes were taking performance-enhancing drugs. The president of the International Olympic Committee medical commission guessed six per cent – that is over 500 of those who woke up in the Olympic Village here yesterday.

Last month, when presenting the official report of the committee of inquiry into drug abuse in British athletics – commissioned by the British Amateur Athletic Board and the Amateur Athletic Association – even the chairman, Peter Coni QC, had to concede, when asked about the prevalence of drug-taking among today's athletes, that 'it would be a brave man who said that one in 10 was not a possibility'. So in a British team here of 96 athletes, officialdom reckons 10 of them may be doped up – and Coni's brief, of course, took in none of the other Olympic sports where this pathetic pill-popping is even more prevalent.

It is a special thrill to witness a world-record run – and particularly so in the breathtaking short sprint because, stripped of tactics or intellect, you have before you the very basic proof that no one in the history of mankind has run faster. Well, all right, if you must, since the stopwatch was invented last century. Even if your great-grandchildren prefer piano playing to sports, they will be mighty impressed that grandpop actually witnessed a bloke being the very fastest man in the history of the universe.

In Johnson's case, twice in 13 months, for on Saturday in Seoul the Jamaican-born Canadian became the only man in history to break his own world record at the 100 metre dash. So, perhaps, we should have been suspicious – as indeed we were. But excitement of the moment readily files conjecture to the back of your mind and submerges cynical suspicion.

But what do we tell our grandchildren now? Wide-eyed innocents on your knee should not have to ask why Stanozolol makes a man run faster. Johnson now forfeits his new record – but his old one of 9.83, set in Rome last year, will stand, for he was not officially nabbed for any illegality then. So for how many years will the new kids to the sport be chasing a tainted record? Will they grow up to know only that to break sport's classic barrier you have to be abusing yourself?

Unless the authorities really have broken through with a new and highly sensitive testing kit – and unless Johnson, as he claims, was nobbled – then the now former champion or his advisers must have been astonishingly lax at not coming off the drug in time or not using a masking agent to hide its use in the bloodstream.

Johnson's performances in the last couple of years have, after all, been such to make him the rumour-mongers' prime suspect – especially those who knew him as a skinny medium-pacer of a few years back. Even the NBC commentator for the programme beamed to the US forces out here was a touch near the knuckle during Saturday's race – 'Wow. He had another gear there that we didn't even see in Rome when he broke the record. The man's incredible.' And later, on NBC again, Johnson's fierce rival, the American Carl Lewis, who was second on Saturday, brazenly told his interviewer 'He just wasn't the same person he was yesterday (in the qualifying heats). I don't know how he did it. He must have been hypnotised or something, but he did something to stimulate himself in the final.'

Lewis was also quivering with innuendo in Rome, after which he called a Press conference to complain about drugs wrecking his sport. He did not exactly name his great rival, but he was miffed to say the least, telling how Johnson had been an insignificant rival all through the early 1980s (both men are 27), running about 10.1 or 10.2 for the distance until 1985. Then Lewis had 1986 off for a knee operation, and when he returned 'I saw old Ben suddenly running better than anyone else; he didn't look the same and he certainly didn't run the same.'

Poor old fast-footed, slow-witted Ben, carrying the can for his greedy little cadre of 'advisers' – as well as for those cheats, who must be numbered in tens of thousands, who call themselves athletes from all over the world, east and west. But a sad and sorry day for the Olympic Games and for sport?

Not a bit of it. Just like the nippy, milky-white dawn that lay over our Village compound, brightened up with a fierce sun as the story, too, got hotter, so with a bit of luck and even more vigilance might 27 September 1988, turn out to be a glistening day, full of light and hope, for honest sport.

# 4

# NEW BALLS, PLEASE!

A snag with the lovely game of tennis is Wimbledon itself. Especially for the Brits. Even before the midsummer fortnight in London's SW19 became the utterly depressing commercial fandango of the 1980s, most of Britain, I fancy, thought the world's best tennis players practised in private for 11 months of the year solely for their four-week public appearances in Europe in June: slow courts and fast women in Rome, heavy balls and long matches in Paris, as a preface to the world championships at Wimbledon. There, the machine-gunner's fast grass and the pompous officials with the military mien sort out the brats from the boys. Nonsense, the same circus has been hitting the globe, town after town, week after week for 12 months. Modern tennis pros are tired-out troubadours. In 1990, the inmates take over their own asylum – the clowns and gymnasts running their own circus – and we shall see what we shall see. I was in on the very beginning of the revolution, in Dallas in 1972, when the break-away World Championship Tennis group established itself by the immense good fortune of staging what is generally considered the finest championship final in the history of the game. And to be sure, Laver v Rosewall, 1972, made even Borg v Connors, Wimbledon 1980, resemble kids' stuff.

# WHEN 19 YEARS ROLLED AWAY
*May 1972*

*Dallas*: Nineteen fifty-three – Churchill in power, the Queen crowned, Sir Gordon's Derby, Sir Stan's Cup final, Sir Len's Ashes ... and Ken Rosewall, at 18, won the Australian and French Open tennis titles. Nineteen years on and Rosewall, incredibly, is still at it. Last night at the Moody Coliseum here, he retained his World Championship of Tennis title and won $50,000 when he beat his great rival Rod Laver by 4-6 6-0 6-3 6-7 7-6 in a magnificent final. There were tears at the end. Rosewall himself broke down at the presentation ceremony. And even after a night's sleep those with long memories in the game were still insisting that last night's excitement at the very end transcended anything in their recollection.

They had been playing for three hours when, all square, they went into the final set. Rosewall, already visibly distressed, called on the old legs for a last despairing spurt. They responded, carried him to a 3-0 lead then, seemingly, surrendered. The little man was left to fight with only his instinct. Laver pulled back to 4-4, but somehow Rosewall, on principle as it were, clung on to 5-5 6-6 and a tie-break, best of 12. Laver went 4-2 up; then 5-4 and serving. Suddenly, miraculously, 19 years, just for a moment, rolled away, and with two backhand strokes of rare daring and beauty Rosewall took the lead 6-5 before Laver returned weakly into the net and Rosewall, unbelievably, had won.

The drama of the final play-off muted even the backstage whisperings here about contracts and options. Earlier all the gossip was about whether John Newcombe might yet be defending his Wimbledon championship. He has been quoted as saying that he desperately wants to, and is convinced that he has an option on his WCT contract that legally entitles him to turn up at Wimbledon in June. But WCT says the contract does not expire until the end of the year; indeed are insisting that Newcombe appears in their

86

tournament in St Louis which has been arranged to clash with the first week of Wimbledon.

Meanwhile, back at the Coliseum, the day of this folksy friendly but impressively run promotion opened with a short ceremony, made longer by television advertisement pauses, which included a cornet solo from a nervous local band leader and a booming introduction of the gladiators – Rosewall in a strip of Blackpool tangerine and Laver in the powder blue of Coventry City.

At the end Rosewall was presented with the cheque which brings his earnings for the year to $104,000 (Laver incidentally took $20,000 to end his season with $122,000), the massive gold World Champion trophy, and a diamond ring. Mike Davies, the WCT executive director, made a short speech. 'It was the finest exhibition, the most exciting game I have ever seen.' And so said all of us. And later a cleaner found an envelope which had been left behind on the presentation dais. He handed it in. In it was a cheque, made out to Ken Rosewall – for $50,000.

---

# A DISH TO SET BEFORE THE QUEEN
### *July 1977*

Virginia Wade is the Wimbledon champion at last – and it didn't matter one jot that it was one of the worst finals in memory. The day will be long recalled for the ecstatic scenes at the very end when the Queen gave her the trophy and even starchy All-England men and matrons relaxed upper lips and thunderously let go with 'For she's a jolly good fellow.' Whether the anthem was addressed to the Queen or Miss Wade they cared not a fig. And nor did England. But by Jove, Miss Wade made the nation sweat as ever. She has been trying to win the thing for 16 years now and it was not until well into the afternoon that nails stopped being bitten. She beat the mountainous Dutch girl, Betty Stove 4-6 6-3 6-1.

Miss Wade's first year at Wimbledon was 1962 and coincided with the Queen's first visit. Afterwards Virginia said it had been so joyously noisy that she had not heard all the Queen had said to her at the end. 'It didn't matter, it was just great to see her lips moving.' Rampant patriotism apart, it must be said that it was an awfully dank, dull match full of terrible unforced bloomers by both girls. The Queen's long-known aversion to lawn tennis cannot have been changed. Indeed she had pulled on her white gloves, was straightening her skirt, glancing at the clock and looking to get away to the tea-time racing results mid-way through the third set.

From the start both players were as nervous as field mice at harvesting, the Dutch girl seemingly the less so – for she won the first set – at the end of which you could probably hear the silence a mile away. It looked as if we were in for the biggest anti-climax since the *Titanic* similarly came across something large and unexpected all those years ago. It was 3-3 in the second set before the despairing, muttered prayers of 14,000 people got through to their girl in the cathedral. It worked! Virginia reeled off seven games on the trot to take the second set and squat, unassailable, on a 4-0 lead in the last.

She was greatly helped, it must be said, for poor Miss Stove continued to serve a basket full of double faults along with no end of all-round unforced errors.

The power of prayer! Miss Wade's father, a retired arch-deacon, also did his stuff. 'Yes,' he admitted before the match, 'I did pray for Virginia this morning.' Though he added after some meditative thought, 'But then I always pray for everyone each morning.'

---

# COOL BLACK CAT
### *June 1975*

Arthur Ashe is back in his beloved London. As ever, it is good to have him back. And, as ever, he is thinking of buying a flat and basing himself here for a year or two. It would have to be near the Westbury Hotel though, so he could send out for their Eggs Benedict for breakfast.

How he can rabbit on about why he likes us. All about our traditions being more traditional, our royalty being more royal, and how, at most parties in the world, a beautiful woman comes up to him and asks why that cute Nastase wears powder blue shorts and carries on in that awful way, but in London all she wants to know is why Nasty isn't so effective with his cross-court underspin backhand when he's returning second serve against Antipodean left-handers.

Arthur Ashe's father was a park policeman in Richmond, Virginia. His beat took in 10 public playgrounds. The family lived next door to one. All public facilities were segregated then. Within a 400 yards radius of the Ashe kitchen were basketball courts, baseball diamonds, football fields; a swimming pool, and a tennis court. The gawky black lank with wire specs loved it; he even loved school, and can still remember the name of every teacher he ever had. When his mother died, Dad brought up the family with an affectionate sternness: he insisted the kids take a nap in the middle of every summer's day, he made them eat whole-meal bread and brush their teeth in baking soda to stop them getting any cavities (and they never did).

A hundred miles away from Richmond, at ominous Lynchburg, lived a well-off black doctor, Walter Johnson, who loved lawn tennis and who had a dream: he wanted to see a Negro win the National title at Forest Hills. One day in 1953, by accident, he came across 10-year-old Arthur Ashe playing in his Dad's public park. Arthur started going over to Lynchburg to practise tennis in his summers with a few other black nippers. Two years later Dr Johnson was driving through Charlottesville one July when he passed a white youngsters' tennis tournament at some very swish courts. It was the all-America National Inter-Scholastics. 'How does one enter?' he asked with daring. All schools were segregated then. The kindly tournament director agreed that if Johnson held his own all-comers' black tournament he would guarantee the four semi-finalists a place in next year's draw.

Johnson beavered away teaching his volleys (he didn't rate ground strokes), held his 'qualifying' tournament – and all four were beaten 6-0 6-0 in the next year's first round. But *amor vincit omnia* and six years later, in 1961, Arthur Ashe did win that same National Inter-Scholastics tournament. And in 1963 he won the National High School title. And in 1968 he won Forest Hills itself. His Dad, in tears, posed for pictures with him after he was presented with the cup. Dr Johnson cried a lot, too.

Arthur Ashe has been one of the world's 10 best tennis players for a decade. Last year he made 129 aeroplane trips, slept in 71 different beds, travelled 165,000 miles. His first service whistles down at 135mph. He owns property and a Rembrandt. He is certainly an ambassador and would not mind being an Ambassador. And now he is an author. His new book, tidied up and semi-coloned by the very accomplished Frank Deford, is called *Portrait in Motion* (Stanley Paul, £3.95) and is outstandingly done; unquestionably the best thing sporting Stan ('In the fifth Test we batted first and I was lucky enough to get 364 which at that time was, as it happens, a world record') has given us in ages. It is written in diary form. A year in the life of. From Wimbledon 1973 to Wimbledon last year.

All of human life: from the politics of the Wimbledon Strike of 1973, when Ashe's baby squawked unwelcome into our world as the ATP ('I lay in bed a long time thinking. It was the first time any athletes had voted, on principle, to withdraw from their championship of the world. I could hardly believe what we had done'); through the bread and circus of big-time tennis ('you eat, drink, practise with him, chase women with him, play doubles with him, and two weeks or months later you draw him again in Barcelona or Manila or Chicago, and all of a sudden you look across the net and it occurs to you that this is the same sonuvabitch who once beat you in Vancouver and you give him no quarter and ignore him when you next pass each other between games, and then you shake his hand when you beat him or he beats you, and you have a beer together and share a cab back to the hotel.').

There's romance, too, and the sad, sad break-up with the lovely, lovely Kathy Benn, of Toronto ('When I helped her on that train it was one of the hardest things I ever had to do in my life. I just stood there and watched the train go down the track. Also this afternoon we got beat in the doubles.').

And humour: 'Everyone likes Nikki Pilic. One of the first times I met him in the locker-room he put his hand on my head and held it there for a while. I didn't know what the hell was going on. Finally he said: "Iss not like the steel wool. You know what I mean? Iss not the steel wool at all. Iss soft." '

Or two chapters of high diplomatic drama in South Africa, which Alan Paton would have been proud to write; or Behind the Scenes at Wimbledon – 'one fellow named Peter who has been here for years or generations, and all he does is escort players to the Centre Court. The only fresh face I've seen this year around the locker-room belongs to an elderly newcomer who serves Robinson's Barley Water – orange, lemon or lime. There is still no guy to serve ice with the Barley Water because there is no ice to bother with.'

To loll this midsummer week away at Nottingham, eavesdropping on, and chatting with, Arthur Ashe was to be pleased to do what one was doing and to be pleased to be alive. Even the elderly Midlands tea-ladies duffled up their perms and fluttered about with an extra rub for his white tablecloth. Eavesdropping was best as the soft-drawled cool cat purred on; the claws came out but they were loving scratches. 'We need a cadre of touring professional umpires and linesmen (I bet he gets them); we don't need head-to-head betting – we're a clean-cut bunch of fellows y'know, let's keep it that way; women are important for this game, but "The Old Woman" [Billie Jean] has got it all wrong.'

He is best of all on his fellow pros. **Cox** Cleverest of all. **Taylor** If you aren't as handsome as Roger, you figure you get all the bad breaks with women. If you are as handsome, you take the women for granted and bitch about line calls. **Paserell** If he could have been a bit quicker he could have been the best in the world. **Lutz and Smith** Big party man, Bob. He and Stan have played doubles since they were kids. But always the odd couple. Even as juniors Stan would stay back in the dorm and jump rope, and Lutz would round up a few guys and drink beer. **Connors** He'll do it, just like Smith and Emmo have. He's meaner, too. He'll make the necessary sacrifices to win. He'll chase everything down. But a guy like

Vijay Armitraj, it comes so easy, you question whether he'll work hard enough. **Okker** He's going to retire as a Dutch esquire because of his one great shot, a crazy top spin forehand he hits off the wrong foot. Anyway he doesn't worry. If we were all like Tom, psychiatrists would be out of business. **Hewitt** We seldom bother. We've not exchanged four sentences since four years ago when we had a spirited discussion on apartheid. **Nastase** When he makes fun of an opponent he is only being childish. He is so vain he doesn't realise what he is doing. But he is so good I can actually get inspired watching him play. A man who can lose from 5-2 40-love. Impossible to fathom him.

And on and on. Arthur Ashe, good fellow, good tennis player, good writer, reckons he might have five years left in the game – 'but by then I guess the whole tour will be made up for guys like Brian Gottfried, practising 12 hours a day and sleeping the other 12.'

---

# TO THE WINNER: £5
*September 1979*

On the desk in the neat and cosy study, there is an elaborate writing set, inkwells and calendar holders in that ghastly dated onyx stuff that used to be so fashionable. Engraved on it is a brass reminder that it was presented to the owner after Britain's last successful defence of the Davis Cup in 1936.

Above the fireplace is a charming Riviera seascape. Bunny Austin bought it with his tennis winnings. 'In those days a tournament victory meant a £5 voucher to spend at Mappin & Webb, the jewellers,' he said. 'I always asked if I could have a voucher instead for Tooths picture gallery. They usually let me. I was runner-up at Wimbledon twice. Runners-up got a voucher for £2 10s.' Buster, Mark, Dave and John would have a fit, and as for their agents....

Britain's last single victory in a Davis Cup challenge round was in the opening rubber against America 41 years ago when Austin defeated Frank Parker in straight sets. Between 1929 and 1937 Austin played 24 Davis Cup ties, winning 36 of his 48 rubbers, all singles. He won eight rubbers out of 12 and five out of eight 'live' rubbers in his six challenge rounds. Only his great pal and partner Fred Perry keeps him off the top of the all-time record lists. Between 1929 and 1939 Austin only once failed to reach at least the quarter-finals at Wimbledon. Yet he remains the object of an annually prolonged snub by the membership committee of the All-England Club.

In that 1937 final challenge at Wimbledon, which America eventually won 4-1, the British team stayed overnight at the RAC Club in Epsom and were driven up each afternoon. He thinks Queen Mary was probably there. Certainly tea was served to the players on court in individual teapots at four o'clock. In the last 'dead' rubber, Austin and Donald Budge fooled around a bit. 'In the last set I remember we swapped rackets.'

My word, how the baby Busters have come a long way! Exactly 50 years ago when Austin was 23 and Palm Springs was not even a dot in the desert, Davis Cup players seemed to spend most of their pre-match preparation on railway trains. Under the clock at Victoria Station was the place to get sportsmen's autographs in those days.

In 1929 there was a total of six days in the train on either side of beating Poland 5-0 in the first round at Warsaw. The next round was also a whitewash against South Africa at Bournemouth (he vroomed down to that in his Jowett 9) after which it was a mad dash back to Victoria and the boat train for the third round against ... well, that year the tie between Hungary and Holland was held up by rain so the British squad entrained to Basle where they awaited a cable to see who they played next. It was Hungary, so they went on to Budapest. Had the Dutch won they would have simply returned to Amsterdam. Occasionally, they even flew, the dare-devils. These pioneering sports jet-setters once flew to a match in Holland. 'I remember we had to get up at some ridiculous hour in the morning ... rain and wind caused the aeroplane to roll, which meant continually altering one's position to remain upright in the wicker chairs. An unpleasant climax was reached when the lady seated in front of me was overcome by the unfavourable conditions.'

The British team could probably club together to buy a jet if they win this weekend. Still, Austin is fond of his onyx inkwells. He lives in a tiny oasis of genteel calm just a couple of Tilden serves away from the fume-laden frenzy of that same Victoria Station. The walls of his charming house are dotted with sepia memories in passe-partout frames – upright men in short striped blazers and long white flannels, (Austin, sensationally, was the first leading player to wear shorts: in 1932 he had his tailor run up a prototype 'modelled on what was then worn on the rugby field') smiles and handshakes at the net, Borotra and Vines and Perry and Budge vying for wall space with other friends from the 1930s – Lawrence Olivier looking like Ronald Colman, Alfred Hitchcock looking like a young Lord Goodman, Shaw looking Shavian, Edith Evans looking beautiful.

On a sideboard there is a framed photograph of Arthur Ashe. He has a great regard for that fine American player. Borg impresses him, too: 'Such composure. When he almost went out to Ayala in Wimbledon's first round last year his expression was exactly the same as when he was winning the final.' Now he thinks there are 'about 30 players as good as we were' though he reckons that Vines, Perry, Crawford, von Cramm and Budge would have been great in any age. 'They were all very, very powerful.'

Austin himself was more the Rosewall type. He looks like a pale and elderly little Muscles even still. 'I didn't have a big serve or volley. I was a ground-stroke player. I was reckoned to return well – except when Vines beat me in the Wimbledon final of 1932. He won that match with an ace. I still don't know which side the ball passed me; all I can remember is the thud of the backstopping behind me. I didn't play well that day but, by jove, Ellie did. He served 30 aces in 12 games. Six years later, in my other Wimbledon final, I did much better but Donald Budge was so good that day he was unplayable. He devoured all my best shots. He was truly magnificent.'

His father, a stockbroker, used to play tennis at the local South Norwood club to keep his eye in for cricket. At Repton, though Bunny helped build a tennis court and won the national schoolboys' championship three times, he was a celebrated cricketer. He opened with B.H. Valentine, who later captained Kent. 'We would invariably reckon to put up the hundred.' He always suffered from ill health. His housemaster at Repton wrote: 'Always a small and delicate child, he had to be dieted carefully and sent to bed occasionally for a few days' rest.' Yet it was still in year one at Cambridge (honours in history) that he got to his first Wimbledon quarter-final.

In 1928, travelling by Cunard to Forest Hills, he met Phyllis Konstam, the beautiful young actress who was crossing to play on Broadway opposite Olivier. When they married in 1931 it was the society wedding of the year. It was a highly dramatic, extremely theatrical, greatly loving relationship. In 1933 Austin met the Oxford Group and discovered Moral Re-Armament. It has been his guiding beacon ever since. Phyllis was violently antagonistic towards the movement for six years. When she finally saw the light, like most converts, it burned very bright indeed until her death in 1976.

By the war he was in America working for the cause. He served in the US Army but a malfunctioning liver and a strained heart disqualified him, much as he tried, from both the officer training corps and overseas service. Innuendoes from that time, apparently, rankle still with some of the All-England buffers, but mostly they rear up about Austin's devotion to Moral Re-Armament. On his return to England he was told that his membership had lapsed 'because he did not pay his subscriptions during the war.'

'Well,' he says now, without any malice but with a shake of his head, 'I don't suppose many soldiers did: I can't imagine a man fighting at El Alamein saying "Hang on a minute, Gerry. I just want to post off my All-England sub." '

In 1962 he officially applied for re-election. His friend, Herman David, the chairman, agreed to support him, but warned 'It will be very hard to fight through. There are some who do not want MRA in the All-England.' Acceptance has to be unanimous. He is still on the waiting list. 'I have to face the fact that MRA is a militant force. It challenges the way of life of some people. Of course I'm sad when Wimbledon comes round each year for I'd like to be included among my old friends so I can go and meet them and greet them on level terms. But they all get me tickets and Fred (Perry) and others always take me into the members' tea-tent as a visitor.'

He realises that 'if they don't want to re-elect me it is their affair. But only to a point. The reason for rejecting an application is important. If it is on account of a man's religious convictions it is dangerous. The very essence of sport and the hope it offers to the world comes from the fact that it is above discrimination. Will we begin to apply this discrimination to Jews, Catholics or those of different coloured skins? Where does it end?'

But the snub does not bother him overmuch, says Bunny Austin with a glance at the onyx writing set on which the brass engraving is so very highly polished.

---

# WATCHING BRIEF
*June 1982*

Wimbledon's numbers two and three courts are divided only by a steeply raked grandstand pyramid. When there is a lull on one court spectators at the top of either stand can lean over the dividing wall and take in play on the other. Yesterday, simultaneously, Martina Navratilova was on Court Two, Christine Lloyd was on Court Three – and across the concourse, in the cockpit itself, was the astonishing Billie Jean King. Of a sudden the Centre Court exploded.

Immediately, Mrs Lloyd netted an easy cross-court volley in her match against Barbara Potter. At almost the same moment, would you believe, Miss Navratilova fluffed a backhand return against Joanne Russell. They were two of their rare mistakes in the hour. The news had engulfed them too and they knew that their women's game had been ignited once more by its very founder, the bow-legged brave in the glinting granny glasses. Aside from that passing swirl which prefaces great dramas in store, both the first and second seeds yesterday moved comfortably – perhaps a little too comfortably in these new circumstances – into their semi-finals.

'Hey, c'mon!' said Mrs Lloyd crossly to herself when she let slip her only game in the second set. The few points she lost on account of Miss Potter's youthful power she would say 'Yep!' and nod in appreciation across the net to her opponent. She left the court smiling and sweetly signing a string of autographs – and off she went to a remarkable 11th successive Wimbledon singles semi-final. Over the crowded pyramid, however, it was very much a team effort. Sterner stuff, which makes you feel that really there can only be one result in Saturday's final.

Accidentally (promise!) I sat next to Miss Navratilova's 'seconds'. I could not resist furtive glances as Renee Richards made copious, amazing notes on a loose piece of paper torn from a school exercise book. Every shot she logged and every point. Minute and zany hieroglyphics the like of which would have made Sir Mortimer Wheeler twiddle his moustache with one hand and get out his magnifying glass with the other. Stuff like an Arabic Bill Frindall scoring a century by Botham in Dubai. The grey-haired – with a tiny trim of ginger – Renee herself made the code up. Next to her is the clean-limbed, bouncy redhead who translates it into words for the handsome, passionate, superb sportsgirl out there.

Renee is the brain coach; Nancy Lieberman, former basketball player, is the buddy who is the brawn coach, the cheerleader. Renee writes on; 'Right on!' says the pretty redhead, scarcely audible, but her eyes show that the player picks up the signals. 'Way to go!' or 'pick yourself up, girl'. One time, as another clinically outrageous pass stirs the tramline chalk, Nancy shouts 'Oh, shot!' at exactly the same time as the passed and despairing Miss Russell says 'Oh shit!'.

And, at the end, across the court from the umpire's chair, Martina secretly and fleetingly throws her team of two the most beautiful of Slavic smiles – and bobs a tiny, scarcely noticeable curtsey.

# LOVE-ALL AS PM BLESSES TENNIS THRILLER

*May 1985*

Chrissie, the long-time queen of tennis, wore a bright green blouse, and thought to curtsey as the Prime Minister approached her. Mrs Thatcher was in a bright, almost peacock blue. They talked about frocks, and whether they watch themselves on video after their respective performances. Neither of them enjoy the experience, they agreed.

We are in the high season of tennis parties – and, as these things go, this one, on the roof garden of a swank London disco, was certainly different. Mrs Thatcher was there because her journalist daughter, Carol, was launching her biography on the tennis players Chris and John Lloyd – a torrid tale of passion, love, and love-15 across the continents, or, as the blurb puts it, 'a unique glimpse into the glory and the thrills, the pressures, and the pain of life and marriage at the top of the tennis circuit.'

Daddy came too. Denis beamed, got his first round, a large Plymouth and tonic, and settled down to discuss the sad state of English rugger. The rule about releasing the ball when tackled makes the one-time referee very gruff indeed.

The Prime Minister called for sparkling Malvern water, and posed for pictures, with the writer, the written-about and the respective parents-in-law of tennis' newly-happy couple. Was she here because at times like this every girl needs her mother? 'No, I'm here to pay tribute to a wonderful book.' Mrs Thatcher was introduced to Ted Tinling, dress designer to the game, a totally bald lamp-post of a man who sports a diamond earring. 'I dream about you,' said Ted. 'How nice,' said Mrs Thatcher. 'Could I thank you for saving England,' said Ted. 'How kind,' said the Premier.

From the back of the throng, just out of earshot, a mischievous hanger-on asked if Mrs T could help, as he was having trouble organising his postal vote in Brecon and Radnor.

But it was an English day. John Lloyd, not to be outdone in

a silk brown suit and pop star's hair-do, was saying he had managed his best ever preparation for Wimbledon, and he felt more confident about the tournament than he had ever done before. We had heard that in umpteen mid-Junes, but it was the sort of stuff to put a sparkle into the lady's Malvern water – though luckily Mrs Thatcher had not been around earlier to hear John admitting that the patched-up marriage had foundered on his passion for video nasties.

He had sought escape from his failed tennis career. 'I was vegetating. I spent too much time watching television. I was watching till two o'clock in the morning, and often I would make sure I was back during the day to see a programme I'd already seen 20 times before. If I was going for a run and a programme came on, I would stop my run. It was a way of escaping from things. I didn't have a goal.'

The Lloyds are deservedly a popular couple on the tennis circuit. They said yesterday that a book on their troubles was the last thing on their minds. Carol Thatcher had first approached them two years ago, and then pestered them into happy agreement after last year's Wimbledon.

Miss Thatcher, a square-chinned girl with riveting blue eyes and a winning smile, tracked them down through the year, travelling 52,000 miles. As the Fleet Street cameras clicked away at her mother yesterday, daughter cheerfully asked her to move a little backstage. 'Carol, I am not moving from here,' said the definitive, unwavering mum. But in the end, she did.

---

# ACE FOR FREEBIES, SECOND SERVICE FOR THE FAITHFUL
## *June 1986*

Wimbledon's poignant moments repeat themselves each year – and I don't necessarily mean John Lloyd's moist-eyed impersonation of Kim Hughes as he handed in his badges after yet another first round calamity, or even Annabel

Croft's ditto departure. The poor lamb said afterwards she'd had a rotten headache all through the match, but her new agent from Mark McCormack's IMG was undaunted. 'It should be easy to find lots of sponsors for her because she is so attractive,' he said.

Wimbledon is a sponsors' beanfeast now. If Wimbledon didn't exist, no sponsor could have dared invent it, but seeing it's there, they are working on it. Oh boy, do they keep in the poignancy! Though it easily could be arranged to sell a number of season tickets on a first-come, first-served basis to the general public for the fortnight they do not do so because nothing is more poignant each day than to have the privileged corporate guests helicoptered and limousined past the bleary, blanketed, tennis-loving hoi polloi who have camped outside the gates all night. This is one hippie army the establishment does not move on, for this lot proves the very point of their privilege.

That 12 o'clock rush by the dawn queue for any left-over standing room on the Centre Court used to be a touching thrill to be in on. Now it seems as seedy and forlorn as it was always unfair. For just across the way, out of sight, the smoked salmon and champagne is being guzzled by captains of industry, who can't tell a backhand pass from a tennis elbow, and their clients, who can tell even less. The grandest parade at Wimbledon these days takes place long after play has begun, when the captains and their clients, cigars chomping at one hand, and a parasoled poll at the other, hold sway. Every day this week they have stepped blinking and briefly into the real world of unshaded sunlight, sweaty armpits and concourse crush to make their way as quickly as possible to the reserved exclusive reservation of the Centre Court seating.

Wimbledon – quite simply the finest laager in the world. Wimbledon is now a corporate outing. A freebie for BP, ICI, BAT and all that lot, and the talk is not of sport, but of deals and dollars. Wimbledon is big business – and business is business in Mrs Thatcher's brave new world of macho money men and their haughtily mournful mascaraed molls.

Of course Wimbledon and its oligarchic All-England Club

(membership less than 400, with three free tickets each day) was ripe for the plucking from the moment some years back when old Bagenal Harvey, the same London agent who persuaded Denis Compton to smarm his hair in Brylcreem, suggested that Wimbledon charge a little more for Robinson's Barley Water to put their product under the umpire's chair. Now it is Coca-Cola, of course. You might not have actually seen any player this week with tell-tale brown stains smudging his lips after quaffing the revolting American fizz, but as long as the paper cup has Coke printed on it, that's good enough for the marketing men. Business is business, and business is booming.

They make strange bedfellows, but opposites attract. Big business does the deals while the All-England keeps up appearances. At Wimbledon sweets are called bon-bons. Alongside the Centre Court there are a series of temporary crush bars where you can wash down a £1.50 hot dog on a paper plate with a £22 bottle of non-vintage champagne. Or perhaps sir would like 10 soggy strawberries in a paper bowl at 10p per strawberry. You stand with your paper plate on this acre of concrete surrounded by signs which read 'No glasses may be removed from the Lawn – By Order of the Committee.' Lawn? What lawn? The committee bangs on: 'Spectators are requested NOT to take crockery or cutlery away from the catering area.' Crockery? Cutlery? What age are they living in?

The clock of St Mary's church strikes four – and the Royal Box rises at once and goes in for tea. If a match stood at two sets all, 5-4 and 40-30, they'd still go in on the stroke of four. And that's where the real crockery clinks. Sarah Ferguson was there on Tuesday. She seemed to enjoy it. Martina was playing, but about 50 cameramen kept their lenses trained on Sarah throughout. The bon-bons passed round the Royal Box like at a pantomime matinee. Sarah had more than most. In front of the seat for the royal personage there is a miniature television set. In black and white, of course. On Tuesday it went on the blink for a bit, but nobody bothered to tune it. Not a thing to do with white gloves.

A couple of years ago, John McEnroe's father asked if he

101

could meet, at his convenience, the Wimbledon boss, Air Chief Marshal Sir Brian Burnett, to clear up a couple of matters relating to his son, the champion. 'Impossible,' came back the withering message via a minion, 'Sir Brian is far too busy entertaining Royalty.' What a heck of a two-week job for the old boy. Mind you, this week has been a bad one for the club. Stares are blank and upper lips twitch when you ask a member about the essays their former supremo, Major David Mills, has been contributing to the *Sunday People*. In his three-page spread last week the Major, 16 years the club's secretary, unaccountably and luridly filled in the space under such headlines as 'Sex Scandal of the Women Stars,' 'Wimbledon's Sodom and Gomorrah,' 'Perils of the Women's Locker Room' and 'The Day I Nearly Spanked the Brat.'

This was the man who for so long called Royalty in for tea at 4 p.m. precisely. If he had stayed longer perhaps he would have flogged the Royal tea-time to the highest bidder. Which is that company that uses chimps in their ads? Somebody did once say that if two such simians made it to the final the crowds would still throng in and clap. 'Quiet, please!' Come to think of it, that command is one of the sharpest reminders of old imperial England that remains at Wimbledon. Quiet, please. You natives must stop being so restless.

Except tea-time, everything else has long been up for grabs at Wimbers. The small print in each day's official programme reads like an old theatre cast-list below which the producers thank such as 'Puma, who provide the footwear for ball-boys ... Radiol Chemicals for massage creams and other products in the dressing-rooms ... Sunsilk for hairdressing services for lady competitors ... and Slazenger sport toiletries for anti-perspirants.'

Soon after tea, the Royals have gone and so too, after a final few for the road, those in the chauffeured helicopters clutter up into the evening sky carrying the sozzled wheeler-dealers of industry and their still deadpan dolls. Then the Sunsilked players come out to talk – Tim Mayotte, all-American Gatsby-type with eyes closer together than Borg's; Ivan Lendl, pouting distractedly as if programmed by some Ruritanian Karloff; the still bewildered Boris Becker who is learning fast, however; Mikael Pernfors, new man with old-time shorts and early Steve McQueen hairdo.

John Lloyd offers yet another sad farewell; Jimmy Connors, as game as ever, says he'll be back, you betcha. He had better be. Yet did old Wimbledon end the very day Connors first came?

Dusk and dust. Someone is sweeping the paper 'crockery' from the concrete lawns. And outside in the street the cheery, bleary little handful of sport-lovers puff up their sleeping bags in readiness for another long night with the pavement as their pillow. All very poignant, ain't it? Must keep that bit in.

---

# THE FUNDAMENTAL THINGS STILL APPLY ...
## *November 1987*

*Paris*: It was an odd place to come across him. Or rather the whole tribe of them. Well, you fancy, a group of New York Irish millionaires would be out on the town, living it up on Hallowe'en, and not sunk in sofas, sipping sodas in the tinkling hush and lush-carpeted corner of the piano bar of one of the ritziest, chandelier-dripping hotels in Paris, just down from Place Vendome and with Tuileries as a backyard. And Tatum came too, looking very, very pretty. And Mom and Pop were along for the ride as well, and his doubles partner, Peter Fleming, and a handful of other minders and help-mates that celebrated international sportsmen need to have around them these days.

In his famous Paris entourage once, Sugar Ray Robinson included a barber. That is the last fellow John McEnroe needs. It is 15 months since I last saw him, finally and almost tragically taunted out of Europe by the Wimbledon Press corps, and while he looks as if he's lost quite a bit of weight in that time, even from his boyish frame, he sure has lost some more hair. The hairline is receding fast to the baseline. By the time he's 30 we might even be calling him bald. John McEnroe 30? Impossible! But that's what he will be in just

103

three more Februaries. The Kid. The Brat. The Prat. The Squirt. The Genius. McEnroe is back on the road after a sabbatical which took in marriage and fatherhood and, alas, not all that much relief from the hassle of being a public property.

It is not an easy road. Last night McEnroe's interest in the Paris Open was terminated in the quarter-final by a qualifier, Sergio Casal of Spain. A 6-3 7-6 defeat – 11-9 in the tie-break – left him wondering whether his target of reaching the Masters tournament this December was still feasible. Earlier in the week the hotel waiters, well-trained, crept about the thick pile carpet with eyes respectfully lowered; the pianist, too regularly I thought, kept getting round to *As Time Goes By* – and then as midnight approached John and Peter had to go out on court at the cavernous Halle Marcel Cerdan at the new sports centre in Bercy.

It was well into the witching hours by the time they had won the three-setter enlivened by a spat with a lineswoman whose signals exasperated him – 'Get your stupid hands away,' he sneered. She witheringly looked him straight in the eye, as only a Frenchwoman can, and that seemed to calm him. Yesterday he earned a $3,000 fine after an altercation over a line call with the British umpire Chris Shales, whom he described as the worst he'd ever seen. The game surely needs his electrically instinctive touch and feel and daring to illustrate to the grim-faced muscleman Lendl and the heavy, bounding Becker that subtlety and stealth can still dilute the big bang. But yesterday's lapse brought his total of fines since he started his comeback to $8,850, which will mean an automatic three-week suspension.

His appearance in the B and H tournament at Wembley has been thrown into doubt. 'It seems probable I won't be playing in London,' he said. 'I cannot have much chance for the Masters, but I'm going to give it the best shot I can. I've left it late – unfortunately I've had a few personal commitments that have prohibited me playing in a few key tournaments. I've had to make my schedule so much in advance – sort of up to nine months you could say.'

His son, Kevin, was born in May. He married the actress

104

Miss O'Neal in August. They had bought Johnny Carson's Malibu beach house in January so he could, he says, have a chance to wind down. Wind down? How could it be possible for this young man to escape the arc lights? The Press, for instance, would report the tiniest marriage aspect, turning an ordinary row into a spectacular gossip column headline. And if anything, his young wife had lived even longer in the hissing pressure cooker. Frenzy, phoneyness and fame. What a price they pay.

The young man still looks distracted with those red-rimmed eyes. He still scratches his head sometimes to ponder a question like Stan Laurel did; he still can convey that uncertain wonder as to why everything should be happening to him; like, as someone said memorably at the 1985 Wimbledon, one of those little boys in the Maurice Sendak stories who go to bed feeling normal and then wake up in the night to find themselves hurtling through the starry sky. And a new adventure, over which he has no power, has begun.

And it all seems to begin and end at the Press conference. As he said after his comeback singles: 'I don't think there is any other athlete in any other sport who goes through what I go through. Everything I stand for is different from what they in the media say. It's incredible that it has come to this. It is mind-boggling to me that I have this image.'

Since Muhammad Ali's prime, has any sportsman been so recognisable round the world than this pouting man-child? Perhaps it is because, like Ali, he inspires the underdog in all of us by going out there to meet the great power-house hulks who rely on shoulders and strength and elbow grease rather than strategy, and the frail man toys with them and laughs at them before dismantling them.

All this week in Paris, he has come on court acknowledging the applause with an emperor's salute, wearing a shirt and socks of regal purple and even if, as he says, 'the timing is a bit off' he still uses the racket not as a bludgeon, but as diversely and freely and pliably as if it were a baseball glove wrapped round his hand. When he first returned after the six-month break, he put himself through what he now admits was a ludicrously tough regime. 'The diet was too strict, you know, and then all that yoga. Mind you, I guess I could still recommend you to try yoga for enjoyment. I might even do it again some time, I wasn't doing it specifically for tennis. Anyway, for the time being, I'm going back to the things I feel comfortable with, the things I've always been used to, so in three or six more months down the long old road I'll see where I stand in the rankings and then we can judge if I've planned it right.'

And somewhere along the road, Lendl and Becker and the new gang are waiting to ambush him. Becker these last few weeks has put Lendl in his place. 'Boris must be playing well, must be high on confidence right now. But no, man, I'm not conceding any place. If I can improve as much as I think I can I see a real good chance of getting myself to the very top again. I think I've got the game to do it, the game and the mentality – it's just a question of putting it all together. That's what the challenge of being number one is all about. I've done it before – though sure I realise that a new generation has come up and I've got to deal with them. Do you remember when my best matches in history were with Borg and Connors – but now it's Becker, Edberg, Pat Cash, if he makes his way back, and Wilander. Do you realise Leconte is four or five years younger than me?

'Course I don't feel number one any more. You have to have results to be number one. Right now though, I don't feel I'm necessarily number 10. But I've gotta just pick up my game and deal with Lendl and Becker in the not too distant future. Sure, I feel confident about that. Now, please can I go to bed? I'm getting up early these days. No, man, not to practise. I get up to play with my son.' And on into the early hours in the posh Paris pub, the pianist was still making too regular a trip to *As Time Goes By*.

# 5

# GRAND TOURS

Even your sports editor would see you off from an English winter to the sun by inadvertently letting slip, 'Have a good holiday!'. He should have known better, for the truth is that cricket tours (whatever the myriad bonuses) were long and often tedious slogs that have broken, over the years, a heck of a lot of pencils, tethers, spirits, not to mention marriages. But I wouldn't have missed any of mine for the world. Even when you got back from a cricket tour in the spring, got rid of a pile of laundry, and then hotfoot it out for the summer with the British Lions rugby boys. I was lucky, too, with my tours – my Press pals in the caravan were all fellow cricket lovers, beguiled by the game. These days, alas, Fleet Street's crazy circulation wars have them sending out blokes with eyes sharper even than their suits, and with a snide relish for gossip-columning, if not downright crime writing. No way these days, for instance, that the eminent knight, Sir Geoffrey Boycott, would have allowed a gentleman's-gentleman from the Press to dress him for an evening engagement.

# GEOFF PLAYS THE PRINCE
*January 1980*

*Australia:* Our last few hours in Sydney went from the sublime
to the ridiculous. A lunch in the blissful shade of Watson's
Bay at Doyle's celebrated seafood restaurant meandered on
past tea-time. It was followed by a few gentle digesting swipes
as a cooling breeze tinkled the gum trees around the Royal
Sydney Golf Club. Then, believe it or not, we went to a seedy,
raucous little dive just off the city's red light area to see
England's premier batter be a disc jockey for half an hour and
a hundred quid.

'And now, the moment you've all been waiting for,' said a
spotty, pale, night owl with sweat stains in his armpits and
pretensions to punk. 'Here he is, the new sound of Sydney
from out of the West. Guys and gals the Zoo Disco is proud to
give you – Geoffrey Boycott!'

Our rum hero pranced on to the stage and gave his
emperor's two-armed salute like when he hit the famous
on-drive off Chappell at Headingley three years ago. Only
this time the applause was, to put it kindly, not quite so
ecstatic. There were one or two amiable jeer-cheers from the
back bar of this darkened dump, but most of the sad,
over-made-up little girls with slits up the side of their frocks
looked gawpingly unimpressed, took a slug of Bacardi and
coke, scratched themselves and itched for the next record. In
a corner of the cellar, unbeknown to our star of the show as
the strobe lights surrounded him, sat Bairstow, Emburey,
Dilley, and Colonel Ken Barrington, absolutely creasing
themselves with mirth.

Geoffrey wore tight black slacks and a frightful gaudy shirt
of purply flowers. Not a hair of his hairpiece, preening and
pommaded, was out of place. The lights kept changing – red,
green, amber, you name it. His bright, blue-tinted contact
lenses turned positively and glaringly Martian green when
the lights were on amber. The first record he put on was *Baby
Love* and he jived in time to it, sticking out his bottom and

clicking his thumbs and middle fingers in the prescribed fashion. It seemed he did not actually have to say anything for his £100. He and the Punk just put one deafening record after another on to the turntable. Geoffrey's lopsided grin got wider and wonkier. He genuinely seemed to be enjoying himself. 'Come down and 'ave a dance,' asked a little black girl in a little black dress with golden glitter glued on her eyelids. 'I can't, luv,' said the greatest living Yorkshireman, 'I'm putting on the records you see.'

He especially enjoyed giving away the spot prizes just before the evening's grand finale when he and the Punk played cricket with a child's plastic bat and ball. Afterwards he was elated as he signed one or two beer mats before collecting his little brown envelope. 'I were all right, weren't I?' 'Yes Geoffrey, you were absolutely terrific; they really loved you,' I assured him. 'Yes, they did seem to, didn't they.'

One day I wouldn't put it past England's very own, sweatbanded Hamlet to ask if he can play the lead in *Hamlet*. Now that would really pack 'em in. Meanwhile the din went on and Geoffrey went up into the night and back to his hotel bed, reet chuffed with himself. Disc jockey-ing was almost as much fun as batting.

---

# SONNY BOY
### *February 1981*

Into Indian territory ... down the long road due south from Port-of-Spain, in and out of potholes and past the mangrove swamps where the scarlet ibis roost, over the Caroni river, on the banks of which some embers still swirl sad smoke into the eyes of some remaining mourners from a Hindu cremation yesterday.

A diversion to spick and hilly and sunbright San Fernando to see the actual and famed Last Train, an ancient dinky shunter which is newly painted in blue and black and silver and mounted in concrete in the city centre opposite Woolworths and the Convent of the Holy Faith. For some reason they pulled up all the railway lines in Trinidad when independence came in 1962 and this truly was the very last train, the 7.10 out of Port-of-Spain, to San Fernando. 'If you miss this one, you'll never get another one … tiddly-om-pom to San Fernando….' We hum the catchy tune and drive on, deeper into Indian territory. We stop for a minute or two beside a lifesize statue of Mahatma Gandhi girding his loincloth about him, and as you squint up in reverence, the weathered bronze against the shining sky and the jug-handle ears attached to the tiny head seem more out of proportion than you had imagined.

Then off again – to nod a tiny tribute to another diminutive Indian with jug-handle ears. A different sort of mystic. There is a steamy, damp, paddyfield sort of heat to the day now. We are in the country of V.S. Naipaul – mystic masseurs and miles and miles of sugar-cane which stops abruptly to make room for the village of Esperance. Some of the men have long caught the dawn bus to town, or are those distant specks hacking and bending at toil in the fields. Mangy terriers sleep in the shade. Serene old women squat on doorsteps watching beautiful children sleepily play.

Two plots up from the Yellow Bird Café – 'Licensed to sell spiritous liquors' and 'No obscene language here' – is a quaint and aged wooden house perched wonkily on spindly stilts. On the verandah, from a creaking rocking chair, an old lady in plum-red hand-stitched dress watches her clothes dry; they are spread around her on every available bush and rock and hedge. She is not expecting you, but when you announce yourself she beams a mouthful of gold teeth and greets you by putting both her hands on your shoulders, as is the custom.

Please to step inside, says Mrs Sumintra Rocke. At once I am transported back three-quarters of my life to that high summer morning in Gloucestershire full 30 years ago when poor old Dad had to work and couldn't come, and Uncle John and me and our Mum's sandwiches in greaseproof paper, caught the first bus of the day from outside Woolworths in Stroud. Our Jack Crapp's heroes batted first. Just for an hour or three. Jack himself couldn't have got very many that day. If any. Only our blushing lank, young Graveney, had the remotest clue about playing the spin bowling of a tiny man with a pencil moustache and a plum-red cap, with a pattering neat little run-up and the sleeves of his cream shirt buttoned tight at the wrists.

Sonny Ramadhin, that same mystic mesmerist who bowled off-breaks and leg-breaks and straight ones – but no bat knew which until it bounced – arrived at this very same house in Esperance to live with this same auntie when he was orphaned at the age of two. He was born on May Day in 1930, and now, just like one of his celebrated predecessors, Lord Learie, he has become an adopted son of Lancashire in England, where he is much loved and owns a pub in Saddleworth which is far more swish than the Yellow Bird Café in Esperance.

The old lady's husband, Soodhat, had a hobby. He enjoyed making picture frames in black or silver passe-partout. This little house is a shrine to his hobby and his nephew. A large framed picture of the Sacred Heart has pride of place – many Trinidad Indians are Christians – but then every available inch of wall space in the three little rooms of the wooden house is covered with faded sepia snapshots of one of the most legendary wizards of tweak the noblest old game has ever known. And everyone is glazed and framed lovingly in black or silver passe-partout.

Before he came to England in 1950, Sonny Ramadhin had only played in two first class cricket games, and those were the two trial matches for the tour. (He took 11 wickets.) That had been the first time he had travelled up the long road to Port-of-Spain, and the first time, too, he had made the acquaintance of his friend, Alfred, a myopic teenaged Jamaican in wire-rimmed specs who was even more shy than Sonny, but bowled left-hand round the wicket with just as much of an assassin's knife turn. Oh, those two little pals o' mine, Ramadhin and Valentine.

Aunt Sumintra proudly showed me the picture of the 'spin twins' in that team for their first trial match. After that there seemed to be a picture of every team they played for: Sonny, in the early days, always standing in the far left of the back row, and only later when he was a touch more portly and the centre three places of the front seated row were taken at last, not by haughty white men and managers, but by the handsome black Worrell and the two other Ws, he would be seated next to them in stately seniority.

There is a photograph of him bowling against Yorkshire at Bradford, the second match of that 1950 tour. That was the day when, having taken a couple of wickets as soon as he came on, he approached the player who had taken the bewildered boy under his wing, Gerry Gomez, and enquired: 'Mister Gerry, will you tell me when this great batsman, Mister L. Hutton, is coming in?' Replied Gomez: 'My dear Ram, you've just got him out, caught in the leg trap in your first over!'

There is a faded portrait on the wall of Frank Worrell. It is inscribed 'Happy thoughts of years of pleasure – Frank.' There is one, too, of Weekes – 'To Ram, my truly good friend, from Everton.' There is a studio study of Ramadhin himself, taken on the day he left on the boat for fame and faraway England. He was wearing a trilby-type titfer on the crown of his head and looked for all the world as solemnly sinister as a Hollywood extra playing a Chinatown hood. There is a picture of a starchy white-tie-and-tails banquet at London's Café Royal in the summer of 1950. Surrounded by knights with garters and peers without peer, Sonny Ramadhin is the only diner in the photograph wearing an ordinary necktie. He probably bought it at Woolworths in San Fernando in the days when the railway trains ran.

---

## SLEEP LIKE A LARK ...
### *March 1981*

*Bridgetown*: He had been so hale and full of beans. So dynamite chuffed at the end of the West Indians' innings in the morning. His nose crowded out the already jammed pavilion long room bar. His smile illuminated it. If, batting first, a side did not make at least 300 in this place they could consider themselves well and truly stuffed – and he was

112

beaming because his boys had just bowled out the unbeatables for 265. Across the change-of-innings pavilion barge and bustle, I caught his eye. You could only grin back as he gave a thumbs up. The last time I saw him was a little later on the players' balcony during England's afternoon collapse – choked he was, but always first up with a great big consoling arm round the incoming batsman and some perky get-stuck-in encouragement for the outgoing.

Then, late in the evening, somebody whispered me off the dance floor and told me the numbing news. It just could not be true. Why, he was so very happy that his wife had come out for a holiday only last week. No, you could not take it in – nor could the players after the team manager Smith had summoned them before breakfast to his room at the end of the pier that juts from the hotel into the Caribbean. The young men tiptoed back across the boards almost in single file, the tan drained from their faces and looking shellshocked as if they'd heard their very best friend had died in the night. For many of them he had. Only since knowing him these past two months did I realise how heartfelt, even desperate, had been the demand from the players and the Press that he be added to this touring party as assistant manager. When it was named in the autumn he was missing from the list for the first time in England's last five tours. Lord's were cutting costs – but the genuine outcry was relentless enough to make them admit their mistake and change their minds.

He was the players' man, both spiritual and temporal. Each morning he gave them all their individual alarm calls. In the nets he bowled at them and followed through to cajole or advise with tiny hints on technique; always a smile; always relishing the day like mustard. Perhaps he knew there wasn't all that much time. On match days he was ever lifting spirits and humping kits. In the evenings his boys would gather themselves and a few beers around him and listen to the tales of long ago when cricket tours might have been to other planets for all these new jet-aged players knew.

Ken Barrington had done it all. The first of his 20 foreign centuries for England had been here at Bridgetown. For a dozen years till a first warning heart attack in 1968 when the doctors ordered him to take off his pads, he had squared his shoulders, jutted his jaw and come back for more; he was England's rock-solid, often unconsidered trellis around which the public's favourite fancy Dans and flash Harrys entwined their colourful summer blooms. He was invariably up the other end, grim and determined as he conscientiously swept the stage for the entrance of the Mays and Cowdreys and Dexters and Graveneys, the last great quartet of the golden line of legend. They would not have done even half as much without Barrington.

I will never forget that midsummer Monday in 1963 during that second Test match of unremitting tension at Lord's when in the last innings, England, needing 233 to win, lost Stewart, Edrich and Dexter to the blazing fires of Griffith and Hall with only 31 scored. Barrington and Cowdrey dug in and ducked and battled it out on into the afternoon. They were on the point of swinging the match with an epic stand when a withering delivery from Hall broke Cowdrey's forearm. Crack! At once Barrington, in answering fury and in spontaneous hate, struck Hall for venomous one-bounce fours over mid-on. The rage was on him in manic defence of his wounded officer – but then just as suddenly he took a deep breath, calmed his soul to concentrate, and turned to stand again to see out the day in England's cause. They always called him the Colonel, as befitted a soldier's son. But he was more of a kindly sergeant major without any bark or bite, mind you, just a large beak and larger beam.

He first signed for Surrey as a leg-break bowler, but they soon realised that he had too much grit and guts to stay long messing about with the twiddly stuff. In the end, it was a grim business he had worried and worked himself into. But after his ticker first complained at the unrelenting life at the top, he emerged to everybody's astonishment and joy from behind the ropes with one of the loveliest, hail-fellow natures that could be imagined. He bought up a successful Surrey motor business then asked if he could be of any more help to cricket.

Now he was in his element, talking about the old days. When one of his youngsters complained a fortnight ago about some aspects of the hotel service in Guyana he said: 'I dunno. When I first came here in the 1950s with Peter May we stayed down the road at that wooden place and the cockroaches were so big that you'd tread on them as hard as you could and you'd lift your foot and they'd wave up at you, say "good morning", and potter off into the woodwork without a care in the world.'

When his boys moaned about tedious waiting in VIP airport lounges he'd grin: 'Blimey, we had 27 hours in a Pakistan train once with only a bucket as a latrine.' Or: 'You should have come out here with us, mates, in our banana boat. First six days through the Bay and all that time you wouldn't see another player except the dying geezer in the next bunk. We were all simply seasick.' Or a complaint that a Trinidad steak was a bit small: 'Crikey. I had five months in India and Pakistan once when my total diet, honest to God, was eggs and chips. Closey, my room-mate, was so ill for days that all he could do was crawl from his bed to the loo on all fours every five minutes. He'd had a curry. I stuck to egg and chips. You can't muck around with eggs and you can't muck around with chips, can you?'

We would log his malapropisms; some pinched-lip types thought we were sending him up. He loved it, and laughed back at himself. 'Well, Frank, you all know what I bloody mean, don't you?' Sometimes they were quite ingeniously perfect. A batsman got out because he was 'caught in two man's land'. When that minor riot occurred last month in Port-of-Spain, it might have been worse than one he had encountered in Bangalore. Because there, to mingle with the crowd, the police had sent in '200 plain clothes protectives'.

Between their sobs yesterday his boys could only have faith that now he will 'sleep like a lark' in eternal peace.

---

## BOTHAM'S BIT OF HUMPETY
*January 1982*

*Indore*: A stupendous, power-crazed innings by Botham electrified Indore yesterday. Indeed his 122 lit up the whole legend. It took 55 balls and 55 minutes. It included 16 fours, seven sixes, three twos, 10 singles and only 19 dot balls off which he failed to score – and 11 of those in the first three overs when he was playing himself in.

The central zone fielders were reduced to a shambles. He went from 50 to his century in 19 balls and, before he was caught, at deep mid-wicket, the previous four deliveries had gone 6–6–4–4. Gatting turned the knife with a sparkling century of his own. Botham arrived at the wicket at 87 for three to join Gatting, who had not scored and had managed three when Botham reached his century. England had made heavy weather of things and in fact there was a whiff of fury in the air. Cook had been given out to a questionable catch and Fletcher, having angrily joined in the resulting kerfuffle, was immediately caught at mid-wicket, obviously still seething at the decision against Cook.

The Somerset celebrant of swipe strode in looking none too pleased. He'd had supper the night before with Cook, one of his particular buddies and who, as everyone knew, was playing for his place here. For once, I noticed, Botham didn't cheerily swing his arms as he bristled in, his now curly long, gingery locks twining round the edges of his floppy white sunhat. He doesn't trust Indian barbers and isn't going to cut it till home. He played himself in with narrow-eyed and untypically heavy menace. The night before, in a throw-away forecast, he had promised 'a bit of humpety in the morning.' Cook's dismissal determined him on it.

This was an hour great-grandchildren will gape over – Botham at Indore. It has the same ring already as Jessop at Hastings and Harrogate, Fender at Northampton or Gimblett at Frome. You name it, Botham hit it. Even, like W.G. used to do, his blocks were going for four. Twice he tried two of his patented reverse sweeps. Four, both times – for the last man a captain wants for Botham is a third man. In all the glorious, galumphing mayhem, as always with Botham, there were one or two quite mesmerisingly wondrous strokes; this time, the ball after celebrating his 50 (34 minutes, 28 balls), with a forearm heave over mid-wicket, he stepped inside a delivery curving in on leg stump and bludgeoned it in a soaring arc high over the long-off boundary.

You feel even Hammond wouldn't have attempted that shot in a first class match. Then, after scoring his first two to take him to 61, he predetermined a sweep but, as he genuflected, the ball dropped shorter than he expected and still on one knee, he adjusted to send the battered red apple soaring high over the mid-wicket line. The century came with a genuine sweep for four (50 minutes, 48 balls, 14 fours, five sixes). When, five minutes later, he walked in to tumult from the disappointingly small crowd of 10,000, he received cheery garlands of oranges. Grinning again, he met those too full on the meat of the bat: Gatting had given all possible strikes to his marauding friend. Of the 55 balls Botham had needed, the stand of 137 only needed 75.

Once Botham had departed, Gatting himself cut loose. By now, of course, the bowlers were shellshocked and what's another mortar or two then? Gatting's sprightly manner took full toll and there was no end to the merrymaking until the shadows lengthened and the umpires called a halt, with England 367 for five, Gatting on 108.

The innings has probably saved Gatting's Test place. It was wretched luck on Cook, who batted doughtily and well in only his second knock in the middle for a month. He mistimed a hook and shortish mid-wicket, diving, scooped it up and claimed the catch at the second grab. Fletcher was so upset at the decision that he lost concentration and left at once, livid. That would have been the story of the day, I'm afraid, except that Botham was next man in.

---

## GOOD MEETS WICKET
*January 1982*

It was rest-day morning and the remainder of Fletcher's England was still dreaming dreams of run-rates and declarations, when a couple of us crept out of the Grand Hotel at dawn. We went to the slums to see Mother Theresa at work. In her line of business you've got to get up early.

The Convent of the Sisters of Charity is down an alleyway

off Calcutta's north circular road. Outside are a group of urchins with empty tummies and, when you put an arm around them for a cuddle, wide, white smiles. You knock on the door of No 54A. Inside, seemingly some hundred nuns are bustling, washing, working to prepare their day. In the small room that is open to this courtyard there is a smiling portrait of the good Pope from Poland as he bends to listen to a little old lady in white. There is also a simple crucifix and one or two amateurish pious posters framed with loving care and passe-partout. You don't hear her coming, but suddenly she is there.

'Cricket?' she says. 'Is it played this way?' And she flaps a wrist in over-arm mime: 'or is it this way?' And her arms essay a baseball swipe. You are not in awe any more , and you are laughing with her and want to call her 'Luv'. Without the slightest corniness, Mother Theresa, of Calcutta and the world, tells Bob Taylor, of Derbyshire and England, that she and he are both equally serving Christ. 'You must play this game of yours simply to the best of your ability, for if you are doing your best you are pleasing mankind and thus you too are doing God's work. And never forget to smile to show you are happy doing your work for God.'

Tomorrow, she said, was going to be the happiest of days for her. 'It will be exactly 52 years that I arrived in India.' Since then business has boomed. Today, for instance, she would be serving meals for 7,000 people. Her nuns are not allowed to beg. 'We have never once asked for gifts or money, but just relied on them to be given us with love for then they come from God.' Only once did such faith flutter for a moment, only once in 52 years. 'One morning, just like this, my sister came to me and said "Mother, we have no food today, no food at all". I knew we could only wait. And then a lorry arrived. And then another. They were from heaven. They were both full of bread. Just for that day, for some reason, the government had suddenly shut down all the schools. They brought us their bread. There was so much bread, oh dear, all Calcutta ate bread for two days.'

Asked by the world record wicket-keeper, 'Mother, why do you smile so?' the Nobel Peace Prizewinner replied: 'Because

118

a smiling face is an integral part of Christian love. You should know that, you are a sporting man whose job is to give people pleasure. Remember how St Francis and his friars laughed so? In every clown there is a saint and in every saint there is a clown.' And up the road, in her hospice for the dying we saw she had taught old mortal men in ultimate agony to smile serenely. And in her orphanage too there seemed just as many smiles as empty stomachs. So we went back, refreshed, to the Grand Hotel for a slap-up Western-style breakfast.

---

# CURRY AND FAVOURITES
### March 1982

*India*: Everyone jumps to it when she gives an order, so, following her phone call out of the blue, I was smartish into best bib and tucker. I had been summoned to supper and she was sending a car in half an hour.

Mrs Marshneill Gavaskar, just turning 30, is a jolly attractive and carefree young spirit. She isn't in a sari, but wears a blouse and jeans and a smile. I was expecting something quite different and she laughs a lot when you tell her how reputation and rumour have preceded her. And that she is the certain power behind the throne, that not only are the old establishment codgers of the Indian Cricket Board in dithering fear of her, but that she as good as picks the Indian team, and even dips in her oar about which umpires will stand in the Tests.

Marshneill? What sort of name is that? Her husband calls her Pammie. He sits opposite her and smiles like a mischievous and knowing schoolboy who is also in love for the very first time. Sure, they've heard the rumours. They hear them every day, and of course they're not true. Not that it wouldn't be a bad thing if they were, thinking of the backslapping bureaucrats and the politicos' jobs-for-the-boys that pervades Indian sports' hierarchies.

The smoke without fire, you fancy, is that Sunil Gavaskar himself, after a decade of running battles with the Board, is now securely in the driving seat and the old boys are desperately hanging on to the tail of his lorry. As well as being as bright and determined as his wife's eyes, he is unquestionably the most prolific batsman in Indian Test history. With already more than 6,700 runs in the bank he should, if alas Geoffrey Boycott's international career is really over, comfortably pass the Yorkshireman's world record aggregate some time next year. Gavaskar is 31 and has played in 75 Tests. Boycott is 10 years older and has played in 108.

Gavaskar's brother-in-law, Gundappa Viswanath, comes to tell us supper is nearly ready. He looks even smaller than his friend and captain, whom the books log at five feet four inches. Vishy is also beaming. When is he ever not? He can't half bat too; having made 5,751 Test runs. He pours another drink and beams. The girls, the Lady Macbeth of Indian cricket and her husband's younger sister, wonder if their curry is too hot for a cold-blooded Britisher. Weedily, I don't dare ask who lived in this gracious house of her businessman father's when the incredible British Raj lived over the shop. So we talk about cricket.

Vishy is a few months older than Sunny. Both were born two years after Salman Rushdie's 1947 'Midnight's Children,' but both, like the Booker prizewinner, were brought up 'listening to Polly Umrigar scoring centuries on All-India Radio', unlike the final guest Pammie Gavaskar had asked to dinner. The sun had dropped fast and the night started humming. It was lighting-up time for the stars that Kipling knew in the wide, black skies of Northern India. Not many leagues over yonder flowed the Ganges in her wintry trickle. Out of the shadows, clutching a glass and with a glint in his one good eye, emerges another cricketer of legend 10 years older than his friends, preceded by his patrician's nose and Wykehamist tones. It is Mansur Ali Khan, the Nawab of Pataudi, 'The Tiger,' the son of a prince, who was coached by Frank Woolley.

He played for Sussex at 16, lost an eye in a car crash at 20, yet only a year later became the youngest Test captain in history and scored 3,000 international runs, including six centuries and a double-hundred against England. In a country of eagle eyes this one-eyed man was king for 14 years. Only three Indians have ever scored a double-century against England – the very three men who were here asking me if I really liked mango chutney.

We eat a feast and the two super sisters-in-law are smiling pleased. Our host helps to clear up. For once Vishy's face clouds over when I tell how a fellow hack from England had cried 'Eureka' the other day when he discovered that Gavaskar had only been given out lbw four times in 66 Test innings in India – a staggeringly low ratio and proof surely that the little man had home umpires in his pocket. 'Ah,' said Vishy, pained for the slur on his brother-in-law, 'see how his feet – or rather his bat – is always in the right position, for if you look up the figures for his innings abroad, I think you will find he has only been given out six times for lbw in another 59 innings.' Touché with knobs on.

Tiger readily admits Indian umpiring is awful and leaves it at that. But though he accepts 'cricket is a hard game for hard men with a hard ball,' he is saddened that the old chivalries are being disregarded now, especially by the English. There is a thought that it's never been the same since Tony Greig's era. Vishy told how, when he was captain of India in the 1979 Jubilee Test in Bombay, Bob Taylor was given caught out when he never touched the ball. He was halfway back to the pavilion when Vishy caught him up and brought him back. Taylor then put on 171 for the sixth wicket with Botham. 'Do you know,' said Vishy, his eyes sad again, 'I'm still being pilloried and sneered at for that, and in India, too.'

Mrs Vishy, Kavita, had now come back to the room, and her brother, Sunil, told her to tell me a true story. In the first two matches of this series Vishy had been in miserable form. His brother-in-law (or possibly his sister-in-law) was on the point of suggesting he be dropped from the team after 77 Tests. He was given one last chance for the Delhi Test at Christmas. On the day before the match the young couple went up to the great temple on Tirupathi Hill to pray for success to their god, Venkateshwara. They vowed to offer the god as many grammes of silver as Vishy would score runs in the Test. Vishy hit a dazzling 107 and that night telephoned his mother-in-law (and captain's mother) asking her to organise her Bombay silversmith to make a silver bat weighing exactly 107 grammes, which he would present to the temple – and to send the bill to him.

The bill came on the eve of the next Test in Madras, Vishy's home town. It was for 222 rupees. I would, said Vishy in a throwaway line to Kavita, make another bat for our god weighing 222 grammes if I could get that score in Madras, for that is one run more than the highest score ever made by an Indian against England – his brother-in-law made 221 at The Oval in 1979. He never thought another thing about it until he was bowled by Willis three days later for 222.

The two players had to go back to a lonely bed to the same hotel which half the English team were sharing with their wives. The Indian Board makes no allowance that their captain's wife comes from Kanpur. I suppose old disciplines live longer here, though not always. Both the wizard midgets twinkled as they kissed their wives goodnight and left by taxi.

Tiger Pataudi poured me one last nightcap under the stars. 'Tell me,' I asked, 'after the accident and the loss of your eye, when did you first realise you had a chance?' 'When I saw the state of the English bowling,' was the reply. Mrs Pammie Gavaskar laughed fit to bust at that. She twigged the same philosophy 22 years on.

# 6

# RUGGER TYPES

I remember one sweltering beach day on those cricket tours to the Tropics when Chris Old, Ian Botham and I tweaked an old radio knob hither and yon, trying to tune into a rugby international back in the blizzards of home (that Chris' brother, Alan, was playing for England at Twickenham made us doubly desperate). And it's a fact that after a few winters in the sun, I did miss the home fires burning, and as a bits-and-pieces sports freak, I knew I missed particularly the unique and homely flavours of those chapped-lip, foot-stamping, frosty-fresh international rugby weekends when even those who didn't have a clue about the difference between a corner-flag and a traffic-bollard, or a left-wing and a right-hook, got worked up about 'the match'. They are celebrations of big-time sport and small-time nationhood when, in turn, each of five ancient cities present in their daft and differing ways a weekend carnival of comradeship, crunch and colour – when the whites play the blues play the reds play the greens. Not to mention, with slightly different rules, the 1985 Rugby League Cup final at Wembley, which remains the most voluptuous exhibition of rugby I've ever seen, or am likely to.

# NO SING-SONG IN THE HOT SPRINGS
*June 1983*

*Rotorua*: The Lions were not in a sing-song mood as we switch-backed south by coach, up and down the gravelly, asphalt slalom that leads to Rotorua, skirting misted mountains and scattering a few of the million white dots of mutton that speckle every hillside. The team were still licking wounds after Auckland's well merited victory on Wednesday. Still, it's early days yet and morale and endeavour were certainly intact when the coach, Jim Telfer, put them through the hoop on arrival in this decidedly one-off, one-horse town. It seems even more of a wooden, bungaloid, frontier post than Wanganui last week. We rode in, still scaring sheep and chickens, with all the commotion and grandeur of a motorised Wells Fargo stage.

There was a decided pong about the place. Like the All Blacks had decided to greet us with stink bombs. It's because Rotorua is ringed by sulphurous geysers and hot springs. It stands on the rim of a steaming lake with the same name as the town. Anywhere you look on terra firma can suddenly, from the minutest orifice in the ground, steam up before your very eyes. Even in the main street. Thousands of individual little kettles boiling away – and they still can't make a decent cup of tea, bless 'em.

On the titchy main street corner is the rugby museum. You have to pay a dollar to duck behind a curtain and enter the carpeted, soft-musaked, sanctum. It's mostly old programmes and club-housey, glass-cased, venerable jerseys. Nothing as riveting as Bob Scott's toupé, or Mr Kelleher's whistle (or even his right arm) with which he sent off Colin Meads at Murrayfield. But there were photographs of Barry John opening a hotel here in 1971; and there's Terry Cobner's Pontypool shirt looking so tattered that he might have taken on the 5th cavalry in it (which in a way he did). And there, too, is enshrined the Stradey programme and a scarlet shirt, badged with 'Cymru am Byth,' from the day they showed the mighty Blacks what for.

Ah, how Carwyn James would have revelled in his fortnight's build-up to a Lions' first Test against New Zealand. Perhaps the present, but differently Celtic, management team of McBride and Teller are hatching something. You never know, but I suspect they are playing it straight down the middle, not using any intellectual devices to keep the All Blacks' selectors guessing. For all their bravado-tinged-by-insecurity those worthies – a brand new panel this year – have just funked naming their first Test side for a further week. It was due out this weekend. Are they panicking? Or are they conning Willie John? It's all part of the fun.

Anyway, I'll be interested to see next week if it's really true that the New Zealand Radio play solemn music from a neighbouring antechamber throughout the day the three selectors are in conclave choosing their XV. Every five minutes, apparently, they go over to the reporter who intones, in hushed voice: 'Still no news, I'm afraid, but we'll interrupt the music the very moment we have any' all flaming day sometimes. Once when they were in such a flap about Carwyn's 1971 team, the chairman of selectors finally emerged, reading the team, and someone ran out of the crowd and clocked him on the jaw. Carwyn obviously revelled in such intrigues and passions. I can see him now, taking a long drag at his Senior Service, twinkling eyes through the smokescreen, and readjusting his twitch of a smile to deadpan. The New Zealanders loved him grudgingly, but couldn't make him out – though not a day has gone past here without at least one person remembering him with sadness and warmth.

---

# KISSING GOODBYE TO A QUANDARY
*June 1980*

I felt drained of emotion at the end of 80 minutes of truly epic rugby when the Springbok players of South Africa welcomed themselves back into some sort of civilised sporting

125

society by beating the Lions in a coruscating, unforgettable first Test at Cape Town on Saturday.

Fifty or so of us British sportsmen and hangers-on were welcomed, dined, and wined in the very lap of God's own country, but found ourselves increasingly unable to ignore the sounds and the fury going on around. Some of the players have realised already that those muffled shrieks signify something. And all the rest have seven weeks left to tour.

After the humdinging match there was a humdinger of a private party in a marquee near the ground. The South Africans were understandably exalted that their team had played so well. Dr Danie Craven – bridge building a speciality – is the long time theologian-in-chief to both world rugby and apartheid sport. He has seen a new light in the last few years, he says. He offered a heartfelt harangue from the pulpit. Imagine Jimmy Cagney playing a scrum-half. But the Doc has even more fire in his eyes. 'Tonight,' he said, 'I'm elated. We should all be elated. Today has been one of the greatest days in South African sporting history.... You know what the world asked us to do and we have done it. Only things that are seen and done in any country of the world are being seen and done in our country today. Study history and science and you will agree.... A British Press man this week called us "Yobboes". To that we take the strongest objection. We are not. We are proud to be what we are.... You Lions, please excuse us for being so delighted tonight and know that by coming you have contributed to South Africa and to the game of rugby more than you will ever realise.'

Back at the hotel a friend of mine, a Lions player of long standing, said to me: 'Didn't you want to puke at Craven? I had to go out of the marquee till he finished.' I bought him a drink and passed over a local newspaper story, tucked away on page six. It read: 'A South African Railways police constable yesterday told blacks, who had first class tickets, to leave a whites only coach – although there were no whites in the coach. There were only two non-white coaches on the crowded train. About 80 to 100 people got into the coach and the train left. When the train got to Germiston police forced the occupants of the coach to leave.' Then all the Lions became jovial rugger-buggers again and we hangers-on hung on and all of us got drunk at various times and places. The only consolation as the night wore on was to know we had taken part in or witnessed such a fair and fast and vibrant match. The Springboks have certainly set off with a thrilling, cocksure certainty. The injured Lions limp on to face the fires again in a fortnight's time. Till then, Billy Beaumont's bedtime book must be Henry V.

So, drained and relieved, I pack for home as a black waitress brings up a final drink. She is sad that the Lions lost. But she is worried more about getting to work tomorrow. The schoolchildren and their militant leaders plan to stone more buses as they leave from the townships. 'They are very bad people, sir' she says, but then falls about in a convulsion of giggles to join me in my own joke: 'People in grass houses shouldn't throw stones!' Even later the grey fingers of dawn got a grip on the grandeur of Table Mountain where we've gone for a last looksee. Somebody reminds me of the Catholic priest we met from the Ciskei tribal homelands who remarked of his country: 'Those who know don't talk, those who talk don't know.' Fair point. Is there a brighter prospect up here? Two weeks ago in Natal we persuaded Alan Paton, revered old author, to attend his first rugby match for 27 years. That, he admitted, was certainly some sort of progress. Like he signed off in *Cry the Beloved Country*: 'It is the dawn that has come, as it has come for a thousand centuries, never failing. But when that dawn will come of our emancipation from the fear of bondage and the bondage of fear, why, that is a secret.'

So this sportswriter comes home to Wiltshire with relief. And the good, brave, now only half blind Lions travel up west to Windhoek. They are still extremely worried about their injury problems, bless them.

# GREAT SCOTT – THE ALL BLACKS
# ARE BACK
*December 1986*

Thirty seasons ago, the All Blacks came to Twickenham – and so did I, for the first time. A spluttering old village charabanc carried up our school party. We smoked Woodbines in the back seat and boldy bellowed out the chorus of *If I Was The Marrying Kind, Which Thank The Lord I'm Not Sir*. We parked on the verge on the Chertsey road and suddenly we were midgets again. We crocodiled to the ground, one priest and 20 little boys, muffled and mittened against the cold, ears frozen numb, eyes and heart furnace-hot with anticipation. I looked up the contemporary reports this week and learned that 17 tons of straw were raked off the pitch before the game started. The backdrop to the whole bewitching afternoon was sprinkled with snowflakes and wispy swirls of chaff. Not counting us, there were 71,980 in the old cabbage-green amphitheatre.

England had Regan and Rimmer, Butterfield and Davies, Stirling and Sanders and that unquenchable back row quartet of John, MacGregor, Kendall and Carpenter. But the greatest to us was Woodward, the prime and beefy blond butcher, the High Wycombe Wasp on the wing. He did not so much run as rumble, a roll of thunder over the frost-hard turf. I wonder how many times England's wingers will get the ball at speed today? My memory insists that Woodward never stopped rumbling and rolling along that day: time after time he would charge the line.

We were standing on the half-way line, right under the press box in which I shall be swanking it today. The mighty throng craned forward to block my view of the game's only try, scored by Dalzell after a forward rush to the Clock corner, but I did see Scott's torpedo-true conversion from the very touchline bisect the old perpendiculars. Great Scott! Bald and brave and beleaguered at full-back, he would catch everything in the swirling gales and then feint and dodge and grin genially before setting up the counter-attack. In *The Times* the next morning O.L. Owen described the New Zealanders as 'a great pack – and Scott.' In the following Friday's *Spectator*, J.P.W. Mallalieu said the All Blacks won because they 'had one thing which neither England nor perhaps any other football side in history has ever had – a full-back like Scott. I can only say of him that he was always there and that danger vanished at the sight of him.'

Scott is in his early 60s now. I had promised myself to visit him when I was in New Zealand this summer. He owns men's outfitters shops now. I never managed it, but on other occasions this June, up in the grandstand or over at the bar during an after-match function, someone would point out the rheumy-eyed, stooping but still square-shouldered old warrior in crumpled, tent-wide and beloved black blazer, and I would think: 'I saw him in his prime, laying waste the whites that very first day I saw an international match.' And the memory spool flickers back to Twickers. Even by New Zealand standards that must have been a truly wonderful pack. The two massive Whites, Snowy and Tiny; Bill Clark and Bob Stuart at seven and eight, and the hooker Ron Hemi, who had a sensational game, taking 10 or 11 tight-heads against England's Eric Evans. Yet Hemi acknowledges still that Evans was the best hooker he faced on the tour – 'he didn't have a shove with that England pack, but when he played for the Barbarians he was real class.'

One of Hemi's props was the fearsome Kev Skinner, a teak-hard former New Zealand heavyweight boxing champion, who recalls that his opposite number that day was England's captain, Squadron-leader R.V. Stirling. 'When their scrum wasn't going too well, Stirling shouted, "By jove, you chaps in the second row, can't you drop your shoulders a little under my rump, there's good fellows!" When our scrum wasn't going too well later on, I hollered at Tiny White, "For Gawd's sake, get your effin' shoulder under my effin' arse!" Stirling looked horrified.'

Three years after that match, Skinner told me, he was coaching Pohuturawa workers who were building a big dam. He was helped by Sid Tangira, a war-like Maori who kept needling the players during coaching sessions. 'One day he kept calling this Maori winger a yellow belly. Finally, this guy was put in the clear and sprinted down the sideline – a sure try. Suddenly he sighted Sid. He stopped, put the ball down, came across and king-hit Sid; went back, picked up the ball and all but scored a try!'

On another occasion during that project, Tangira called a public meeting to discover which of the workers had got one of the village girls pregnant. 'Sid spoke in Maori for about 20 minutes, then asked the guilty man to stand. All 50 of 'em stood up!' Grand days.

---

## GLORIOUS GLOSTERS
### *September 1976*

It is hard to think of the biggest of big matches being held at Kingsholm on a Wednesday, in the evening ... with the sun still there at kick off, and floodlights on at the end. As Gloucestershire celebrate their Rugby Union centenary, my memories will sharpen of Kingsholm as I knew it on 'County Day'. That was always a Saturday. If not muddy slime, then always footstamping cold. And always steam from the scrum as it seized and shoved and stirred to our raucous bias. The Saturday morning buzz and burr before a county match at Kingsholm represents just about my first warming memory in sport, my small mitt enveloped in my father's hand as he did his rounds at the old cattle market, which is no longer there; it is the bus station now. On those mornings the auctioneers' staccato would rattle about their lips with even greater frenzy so that everyone and everything could be loaded up and fed and watered and hosepiped clean in ample time for the kick off.

On those afternoons the *Gloucester Citizen* employed extra boys to race the reports like crazed short-trousered Obolensky's from the press box, a run down Dean's Walk and hare up Hare Lane with a breathless skid into the sports editor's tray in St John's Lane. The world was waiting. And the world then meant the *Citizen*'s sister 'Pinks' at Cheltenham and Bristol. Is the *Citizen* still the only Pink in Britain invariably to lead its front page with rugby? By the tag end of the 1950s I was working on that same southerly sister, the *Bristol Evening World*. It was like yesterday sweating on the runner of 1959 final as the paragraph came into the office from the Memorial Ground. We were leading the match until near the end and I had even written the headline 'Gl'shire Do It!' – then the last flashes came through telling of Warwickshire's final try and the last nail being riveted in by George Cole, of the boot.

That was the start of Warwickshire's seven titles in eight years. Nobody has bettered that mighty span. But Glorse have come close in these 1970s. Since 1970 they have been finalists an astonishing eight times, winning four and losing four (and at least twice those defeats have come, to the whole country's exasperation, only when they allowed their well-muffled pomp to turn into bullying arrogance. Why do they do it? Since their first championship title in 1910 Gloucester have won the thing 13 times and been runners-up in 10. They have contested every third county final that has been played in 68 years. They may play their cricket like a Graveney, but they have ever played their rugby like a Bradman – relentless accumulation first and the fancy stuff as decoration.

I was privileged to be in on John Blake's running team at Bristol in the 1950s and 1960s. What a man! What a dancer! He revolutionised the game long before new rules could. He had to run – because he could not kick. Week after week he inspired his mates to run through every tackler as though all 15 of them were demented electronic pinballs. Blake's Bristol scored glorious try upon try. And an England selector once came down to pick him for Twickenham but sadly pronounced – 'Brilliant he is, but how can a man play for England if he cannot kick.' For all that, Gloucestershire rugby more than most owes its present strength and historical eminence to the small clubs it so voraciously feeds from.

Time without number have I scanned the names of the latest county selection we print and been despairingly bored by the parenthesis 'Gloucester' or 'Bristol'. We exiles want to know where a new lad named learned his game – in Lydney or Cheltenham, in Stroud or Clifton or Cirencester, or Cainscross or the Gordon League, or Painswick, or Pates or St Pauls … simply, if you want to play for the county you have got to join Bristol or Gloucester. To play for England is simply an extra bonus. The schools, of course, were the founding fathers. The first time a rugby ball rolled in Gloucestershire was at Cheltenham College in 1843. Clifton College got going in 1862. Cirencester schoolmasters first started a town side between themselves in 1866 and a year later had encouraged the local agricultural establishment to have a go.

I once played at Painswick – for Cainscross United as a fancypants scrum-half who had been dropped on the previous three Saturdays by Gloucester United, Stroud Nomads and the Cainscross firsts. Bomber Wells, that marvellous cricketing character, was the ref. I needed him against those trampling from up the hillside on the Recreation Ground. He was a fine ref. After half-an-hour the Bomber blew shrill his whistle and brought the game to a stop. He ordered my battered body to the wing – or else, he said when I got my breath back, he would send me off. 'Hey, you can't do that!' said my captain. 'I can,' said Bomber. 'It's to save him from further punishment!' I staggered to the touchline as if it were heaven.

Not long after that I switched from boot to bike. Soon I was reporting for the *Stroud News*. We had a front row forward called Roy Fowke, whom the whole county by then loved as Our Fowker. He should have played for England – certainly after he moved to Gloucester. He was a bargee on the Sharpness Canal. Up in London to play the split-shirt Harlequin nobs, Gloucester gave them a good thumping as usual, after which Fowker twigged it was the form to get pally with the opposition in the clubhouse. His giant fist curled round a pint mug, he then engaged in conversation with the pukka Harlequins and England stand-off – I forget his name. Or was he a winger? Anyway, he was certainly a blazered barrister, a bit of a Whatho Wodney in Cavtwills and Quins Quavat. Fowker's chat-up went thus:

*Fowker*: What be y'doin' furra livin' then?
*Quin*: Actually, I'm working at the Bar.

*Fowker*: Which one?

*Quin*: Lincoln's Inn, actually old boy.

*Fowker*: What be 'ee there then? Potman, is it?

Ah, Roy Fowke, of blessed memory. They don't make them like that any more. Oh yes, they do – in Gloucestershire they do. And today it's congratulations all round.

---

# D'ARTAGNAN VS THE MAYOR IN A BANQUETING DUEL

*January 1983*

*Paris*: The reverberations of Garuet's sending-off continued in Paris yesterday. At Saturday night's post-match banquet in the posh Grand Hotel there was a sotto, but nevertheless highly dramatic and emotional public clash between the two unquestioned leaders and totems of French rugby, Albert Ferrasse, the autocratic president of the FFR, and the captain Jean-Pierre Rives. The tubby, shrewd and dominant Napoleon versus the dashing D'Artagnan with the flaxen corn-stoop hair and deep philosophy of comradeship. Ferrasse was incensed that Garuet had fouled the fair name of France. Rives was incensed that one of his warriors was being castigated. The timeless confrontation between them and us. Garuet, raged Ferrasse, 'was an imbecile' and would be severely punished. Replied Rives: 'We dedicate our great victory to our brother Garuet.'

After such matches as these there is an hour or two allowed for media mayhem down in the locker-rooms' dungeons. Then both teams had about an hour in their hotel to change into black tie and dinner jacket. Garuet himself came to dinner cosseted and whisperingly encouraged by the warmth of a team's freemasonry. After the roast lamb and the claret came the champagne and the pudding. The menu called it 'la bonne surprise' and it was. Ferrasse rose. He has all the provincial pomp of the Mayor of Clochemerle. He said: 'Garuet behaved like an imbecile. His action was a terrible blow to France and French rugby. Bravo to Monsieur Norling for his exhibition of refereeing. Garuet will now have to be left aside. In my 16 years as president of this federation a national player has never been so disgraced. It is unfortunate to see any foul play in international rugby. He knows he is very guilty and he will be punished severely.'

The disgraced Garuet, the squat, sad-faced barrel of a boy, rose quietly from his place at the table and rolled dramatically from the room. Jean-Pierre Rives broke the silence. He is an orator as well as a wing-forward; he knows how to milk the dramatic situation as well as how to manipulate a wheeling pack. He looked at his team and he looked at Ferrasse: 'Garuet is a keen and honest player – he has been so welcome among us, his *confrères*. We dedicate this great victory of ours to him. Do not look upon this as a mutiny, but this young man must be told that his team is solidly behind him.'

At that Garuet came back into the room to applause from his colleagues. Later, he left, and probably he was leaving the scene for ever. Ferrasse looked at Rives and one quite expected the final item on the menu to read 'pistols at dawn'.

So the evening had quite overshadowed the afternoon. But that was not all that difficult. The aged Irish aged even more before our very eyes. France could have scored many more. I doubt if the Irish will dramatically pension off all the pensioners at one stoke. It will surely be done though in the next three matches. By the ides of March, the Irish will have a grand new team. Rives, however, does not quite believe that. As he said later in his speech, as he fondly held the gaze of his longtime friend and foe, Slattery: 'I guarantee to you that Fergus will be playing for Ireland still when my son is playing for France – and I am not married yet.'

* * *

A three-man disciplinary commission, comprising officials from France, Ireland and England, discussed the affair yesterday but the Federation office said no announcement would be made until today. Ferrasse said Garuet would not know any earlier himself.

Garuet, a 30-year-old potato seller from Lourdes, said: 'It

134

all started with a clash with O'Driscoll. He had already given me a few. When the game was stopped I wanted to take the ball from him and when he resisted, I laid my hand a bit violently on his head. The referee thought I had tried to stick my fingers in his eyes.'

## ONE-EYED DODS IS KING
*March 1984*

The main editorial in yesterday's top-selling Scottish Sunday newspaper, the *Post*, unrestrainedly summed it up in verse:

> Oh Flower of Scotland, when will we see your like again,
> That fought and thrilled us in every hill and glen
> And stood against the proud France's army,
> And send them homeward to think again.

I wonder if they had a tragedian's lament set up in type just in case. Certainly the poet's muse must have been working on something awfully sombre at half time.

After international matches, the Scottish dressing-room dungeon at Murrayfield has so often been locked and grim and silent with despairing curses making the only rustle. Now it was open house for a steamy carnival. In a corner Dods, the unlikely hero, had a lager in one hand, while the other cradled a massive champagne bottle. He took solemn swigs. He was in a delirious daze. The shy, gentle Galashiels carpenter and joiner had his right eye totally closed into a gruesome wink. His captain, Aitken, had considered changing kickers as Dods' eye closed fast through the first half – certainly Aitken had had another word once Dods had missed those two sitters immediately on the restart.

The faith paid off. A hush settled on the throng as, at 3-9 the pale boy plonked the thing down and measured his six, sheepish reverse steps, then put in that delicate, nervous sideways run. With only one good eye, he squinted up at the posts, then down at the ball. Finally, standing knock-kneed and with feet splayed at 10 to two, like Underwood preparing

135

to bowl, as always a deep breath, a nervous wipe of sweating palms on the seat of his pants, a tangling stutter of a run-up, then two smooth strides and a gentle, plopping wallop! That made it 6-9, a minute later it was 9-9.... We know the rest. The one-eyed man was king.

---

## MARK OF GENIUS TO FLY IN THE FACE OF WALES
### *November 1985*

I fancy the Welsh have been singin' and dancin' in the rain as it has ceaselessly slanted westwards across the hills for the better part of this week. Told you God wears a red shirt, they say. He is just setting things up, dead right, boy, for the powerful Welsh tight scrummages at Cardiff Arms Park today. Thus the theory that the electrifying Australian runners and passers will be fused: they might as well stay in the showers playing handball with a bar of soap.

It is always like talking to a post when you tell the Welsh not to be cocksure. It is worth repeating this time, for Mark Ella is calling the shots for the Wallabies. The aborigine is being generally rated as possibly one of the top 10 fly-halves of history. He looks out at the rain, and shrugs and smiles: 'Sure, at home we only play in the rain two or three times a year. But we have to continue telling ourselves that our running game is suited to all conditions. Okay, it's wet – so you play your natural game and we'll play ours.

'Of course, we'll keep running the ball and, you'll see, it can be done. You have to make an effort to play good rugby. So often in Britain I guess, three-quarters trot out and say, "Oh, it's raining, so let's just leave it to the forwards to slurp around." If backs don't try anything what are they out there for?'

There are more things in the philosophy of young Mark Ella than are dreamed of by the majority of greybeard clipboard screaming coaches in Britain.

The rain was already thrashing down when I met him last

week in Ulster. For almost an hour, the 25-year-old had sat on a table in the Malone RFC bar and talked without a note to an entranced group of some 60 or so of Ulster's leading coaches, schoolmasters and players. 'What I'm about to tell,' he began, 'is not meant to degrade your British style of play at all: I just think it is worth it to compare it with my own attitude towards rugby.' He was received in awed silence, except for the odd scratching of a pen as a coach scribbled notes. Talk about the infant preaching to the wise men in the temple.

His arms were folded across his green national sweater as he extemporised with insight and no little wit, his brown leather lace-up shoes gently rocking from the table. Behind him the usual clubhouse plaques in signwriters' gilt named the captains and the cups and the caps. The legendary Ernie Crawford played for Malone in the 1920s, Jimmy Nelson in the 1940s ... those old-timers would have been riveted by this young man.

The dark-skinned, handsome native boy from the aboriginal mission station was himself that missionary now. He was born into poverty 25 years ago in La Pérouse, which the rich whites of Sydney scornfully call 'Lapa – our Soweto'. They don't look down for shame when they fly into Sydney airport over Botany Bay. It has been an aborigine compound since Captain Cook hit land.

May and Gordon Ella brought up their 12 children in a shanty hut, which nailed-up plyboard partition turned into a two roomed job. The family slept on shared mattresses on the floor; no privacy, no sewerage; there was one cold tap; a bath was a communal trough in the yard; a shower was when it rained, for the roof was a sieve. Yet it was, the boy will tell you, a home with a lot of love and laughter. May was the adored, feared matriarch; Gordon, whose white grandfather had married an aboriginal girl, was the romantic who loved to catch mullet off the cliffs when he had time away from the factory night shift.

But at least – as ghettoes go – the compensation was the sea down the lane and the sun on their backs. And 'Lapa' had a junior rugby and cricket team, so the children knew more than the rudiments when they were admitted to Matraville

High School – since when Mark's brothers, his twin Glen and Gary, first inspired the Australian Schools XV to a thrilling walkabout round the world before graduating each one, to the full national side. Mark won his first cap in 1980. He was 20. The torch he carried has become brighter with every appearance. Last year, he was elected Young Australian of the Year.

I'm lucky, I once or twice saw the languid, arrogant outside body swerve of Richard Sharp; then there was the carefree, waiflike insouciance of Barry John; the hopscotch of Bennett; the vim, dash and control of young Gibson; the dozy skill and awareness of Porta. This boy, they say, is in the classic line. But he is a revolutionary within it.

He scarcely fits into the canon. An original. It is worth rereading the description of the old-time Australian player Cyril Towers. He wrote in the Twickenham programme a month ago: 'Ella runs from the shoulders down, with the fingers, hands and arms completely relaxed; he takes the ball on one side and passes before the foot comes down again; his concept of the fly-half position is that it is semi-restricted – the attack must begin further out; he is very difficult to think against – if you think ahead of him, he will slip inside, and it's no good thinking four or five moves ahead, because he hasn't invented them yet.'

Ella himself will admit to what he isn't. 'I'm not fast, I'm not a stepper. I can run a bit, but I've no idea of a jink either off left or right. And you know I can't kick for peanuts. At set pieces, no, I never run up in defence – simply because no one actually runs the ball at me; and in Britain they nearly always simply kick. A breakaway wing-forward has honestly never touched me in years – and I think that might be something to do with the secret.

'The crucial thing must be speed of the ball through the hand. The quicker you get it, the quicker you can pass it on.

'The nearer you play to the opposition and the straighter you run, the better. It's commonsense. Then, the shorter the pass the quicker you can decide your options. Then, you can think of varying the length of your passes.'

He despairs, you fancy, of the present British game.

'Kicking away possession is absolutely crazy. To score a try you have to have the ball in your hands. I say to my scrum-half, "I'm calling the shots, give me the ball however bad it is!" All this British business of kicking for 20 minutes to size up the opposition! If in the first 20 minutes my scrum-half puts up one kick himself, then okay, I suppose; if he puts up two, I'll go over and hit him. His job is to get the ball to me any way he can. I call the moves, I distribute to those outside me and then, with the ball in their hands, they can put the pace on it.

'I know a lot of our fancy moves cause us to make mistakes; we try everything and aren't quite getting the points on the board, but at least we try and we'll keep on trying. If not, isn't the whole thing totally boring for everyone concerned? How can you go out there and have the feeling "If I try something, and it doesn't work, we're going to lose"? No, you go out there and say "If I try something and it works, then we're going to win".'

It was still bucketing down outside and, no matter, Ella was smiling. I wished Carwyn James was still alive and thought of telling him Carwyn's definition of the great fly-halves – 'Some sniff the wind ... they create it.'

I think I know which side Carwyn will be on today come hwyl hymns, and Welsh high water.

---

## SCARLET FEVER GRIPS GRAVELL
### *March 1983*

The rub of the red has contrived two thunderous challenges for today's Welsh Cup Rugby Union semi-finals. Neath play Aberavon to log another ferocious chapter in their neighbourly civil wars, and east plays west in the ever-classic, timeless and definitive fixture between Llanelli and Cardiff.

For a forecast, it depends on the mood of Ray Gravell, Llanelli's favourite son. Like all the Celtic poets, there is a melancholy streak to his joyful songs. One minute he thinks the final is cut and dried, and the trophy is his tin-plate town's for sure; the next, he is black and sombre, certain the engraver has already been hired by Cardiff for the Cup.

Alas, the 32-year-old bearded prince will not be pulling on the scarlet today. He broke his shoulder in the third round when he was surely on course to appear in a record sixth Cup final. This winter, they say, he had been playing better than ever. He will watch the match today, broody, chain-smoking, hands deep in pockets, fearing the worst. 'It's purgatory watching, different from being dropped, but just as terrible in its way.'

He knows all about being dropped. Twice in the last 10 years the newspapers said 'Wales axe Gravell' and to be sure, he says, 'it was like having my balls chopped off.' Twice he came back and twice suffered the agony of rejection.

It was too much: 18 months ago he wrote to the national selectors and asked not to be considered ever again: the joy of being selected could not match the pain of being discarded. 'It was the country, you see. Dropped, I felt unclean, I felt I had a stigma. I could risk it no longer.'

Gravell played four times at centre three-quarter for the British Lions and 23 times for Wales. If Gareth and Bennett, J.J. and Gerald were, in Dylan's phrase 'the boys of summer', the honest cousin Gravell, in the midst of them, was the man 'of flint and pitch'. He would prepare the artists' canvas and shudderingly knock down the trespass. 'Nobody got through Fenwick and me.'

Ray Gravell's father would have been proud of his only child. Dad and the boy would sometimes on Saturday catch the Eynon's bus to Stradey and stand hand-in-hand on the 'tanner' bank to watch the Scarlets play. But mostly, they would hunt in the hills.

When the boy was 13 – he had failed the 11-plus and ended up with one O-level, in Welsh – his father injured his spine after an underground fall of rock. 'He was on the sick, on and off, but kept trying to go back to work.' One tea-time Ray came home from school. The ferret was in the hutch, Dad had gone shooting by himself. It was January.

'By 10 o'clock, in the pitch dark, we went out to look for him. It was a mile or two away from our usual beat, but oddly I

140

found myself drawn straight there. Dad was dead on the ground. He had shot himself.

'I remember, too, when I ran out for my first game for Wales against France at Paris in 1975. It wasn't so much that I even thought of Dad then, I knew he was just there, all around. Then they played *Land of My Fathers*. "Over freedom they lost their blood, The struggle still goes on ...". Yes, it was a natural reaction to cry. I was giving my allegiance you see. And to my father.'

The boy's beard was damp that day. He had the dressing-room telegrams from the village, and from his wife, the local golden girl called Aurona, and then his mother's – 'Chi'n gwbod pwy yw Toodles bois. Y gath!' Best wishes to my son, all my love from Mam and Toodles. Do you know who Toodles is, boys? The effin' cat. The effin' cat sent us a telegram! They all cried too, led by the coach Clive Rowlands.

To Carwyn James, Ray was the true and living, pre-medieval Prince of Wales. Gravell's one and only remains Delme Thomas. 'When Delme showed emotion the day in 1972 that the whistle went and we had beaten the All Blacks at Llanelli, only then did we know that we had done something fantastic.'

The boy came off the field a man that day. 'The weather had been gloomy black, dramatic, the crowd hemmed us in, it was fantastic, operatic, but the result was golden.' He did as he always did and felt in his jacket pocket for his Woodbines. 'I like a fag as soon as I'm in, to release the tension.'

He now works with school leavers, and mostly jobless kids, for the Llanelli Community Service.

I told him that I had looked up in the *Llanelli and County Guardian* of 18 April 1884, how 'the Llanelli team made their first appearance in full scarlet jersey and caps.' His eyes moistened again. 'Did we win? The Scarlets have just got to do it against Cardiff on Saturday.' And he took a long, long drag on his ciggie. Once again I didn't know if the dear fellow was going to laugh or cry.

# CHILCOTT, PROP WHO CAME IN FROM THE COLD

*April 1986*

I am glad Bath have made the final of Rugby Union's John Player Cup again – if only because, with today's official end of the English domestic season, it offers a last chance to get in some public retaliation on behalf of Gareth Chilcott, England's doughty prop-forward, whose appearance seems to have tickled pink, if not frightened, the uncommitted of the nation. When he's been on television, dowagers are said to lock up their dogs and daughters.

Certainly he is a forbidding sight. The brick out-house incarnate. He looks as broad as he is tall. In fact, the ratio is 17st 2lb to, as he puts it, 'five feet and a fag paper'. The Wormwood Scrubs hair crop fuzzing the bullet head does not help, accentuating as it does the two gnarled, mottled, cauliflower ears. When Chilcott played for England in Paris last month, David Miller, of *The Times*, whose son may be a fine artist, but who is no oil painting himself, loftily disdained – 'it is astonishing that in the 1980s anybody, even in rugby, can suppose that someone the shape of Chilcott can usefully perform at the highest level of any athletic, mobile, sport. Darts maybe.' The cheek of it.

The low-slung blacksmiths' forearms are attached, in fact, to ten delicate fingers. Gareth is a skilled French polisher enjoying work on the frailest of antique furniture. For the last couple of years he has worked as a Somerset lumberjack – logging through the summers and delivering in the winters. He loved the open air and it made the muscles mightier yet – but he is pleased to be back in the trade for which he was apprenticed 14 years ago when he was just 16.

In those days, it was the natural weekend activity for any unqualified laddo leaving Bristol's Ashton Park Comprehensive to be a Bristol City bovver boy. He and the gang travelled by train with their red favourites – 'everywhere, even as far as Carlisle'.

142

One day, a match at Ashton Gate was cancelled. Gareth was accosted by his old games master, Mr Ridgeway, who warned him that he was hanging about with the wrong sort. 'Why not come up to the Old Redcliffians rugger if you want to have a beer-up and then let off steam.' So unfolds the old tale once more. He started off as third team hooker. Then someone's car broke down so he moved to tighthead in the local derby against Clifton. Bath asked him for pre-season training after the Somerset Cup in 1976.

There had been working-class rugger in the blood somewhere for his father was a Welsh miner from the Ogmore Vale who had come over the water on the ferry looking for more congenial factory work. His mother is a Thomas. They brought up the family in Bedminster, one of Bristol's most crowded, sometimes troubled and occasionally troublesome areas.

'I think that's why, if ever I was asked to tour South Africa, I think I'd have to say "no". Certainly I'd have to think very hard. Bedminster's multi-racial. But it's a lovely, warm, friendly community. You know, "pop next door for a cupo' sugar". Everyone mucks in, in the pubs and the clubs. We're all working class, all the races. They tell me South Africa is a lovely place geography wise. But there must be something wrong when the law doesn't let different races play games with each other in the school playground.'

From the beginning of his career with Bath – and after recovering from two nasty knee operations – he steadily built a reputation not only as a hard scrummager, but as a hard nut fouler. When he was first chosen for England, against Australia in 1984, lilywhite hands were held up in horror and it must have pained the editor of the Twickenham programme to log that the new forward had been banned for a year 'for stamping'. At the time a girlfriend read that and asked me innocently 'What, he stamps on people's toes?' No, dear, much more malicious than that. That was against Bristol. He was banned for a year and then continued unprettily notorious even in Wales on wet Wednesdays.

Then another lay-off for 'a bit of fisticuffs'. Then six more weeks in the cooler for 'allegedly butting' someone from

Exeter. What do you mean 'allegedly'? 'Well, all right, just "butting" – that "allegedly" makes it sound a bit better don' it.' He has a lovely, warm, full-bellied laugh.

At Twickenham, that first day for England, what does he do? He not only clobbers the frail Aussie scrum-half, Farr-Jones but does it right in front of the press box. 'Don't I know how gormless I was? If you want to know, it was only a slap actually. Didn't really catch him right. Luckily. At the banquet affair, I felt so low. None of the officials would speak to me. The players tried to cheer me up, but I just knew "there it is then, I've gone and done it now, I'll just be a disgrace one-cap wonder for the rest of me life."

'When I got back home, Jack (Rowell, the Bath coach) sat me down for a wigging. "You've got one cap, you can still win another. You must simply stop letting yourself down, and the club, and your family. Your mother's very upset, you know." He threatened, bullied and encouraged me to see the light. I knew I was being stupidly hot-headed. But, do you know, my game suddenly improved wonderfully once I knew what I had to do – or rather not to do. Don't get me wrong, I didn't become no babby-ass. I still play it physical. You have to in the front row. But I began to look for the ball. Not the man. And it became much more fun, much more rewarding. I'd like to think now I'm known as a good prop and a good "fighter", but only in the right way.'

At the end of the matches, referees and opponents with beatific smiles would begin shaking hands warmly with the now chivalrous sinner who repenteth. That is why his recall to the colours this winter was so touching and satisfying. 'It proved my first cap was neither a fluke nor an aberration' – and he helped push Ireland all over the paddock.

Being recalled by England was the cherished honour he had prayed for – but he knows there is nothing to beat the comradeship of winning or losing in club rugby. This afternoon will be a case in point. 'Colleagues in club rugger are your best friends, too. You have been to hell and back with them. You drink with them and laugh with them and worry with them all year. You only do your best on the field for them, never for yourself. And you do it for the whole

144

club, and for Jack Rowell, who has had us out there twice a week at training in the dark and in the snow and the mud and the shit.

'We'll come up to the London hotel on Friday and perhaps play a game of pool or snooker. I'm not too bad, about third best, but not as good as Richard Hill, he's like a ferocious little Army boxer at anything he takes on. Or we might play chess.' Chess? 'Yes. I like a game when I'm in hotels. Usually I beat Dave Trick, too, for all his education and cleverness. I beat Halliday and Spurrell, as well. They think I'm a dumbo, but I usually beat 'em.'

This winter he's had 11 long weekends away from home. It is very wearing these days on top class rugger men. He is none too keen on that sort of life. Nor is his girl friend – 'I suppose I manage to see her every so often. She's inclined to play up like hell about it, bless her.'

---

# TWICKENHAM MOULD BROKEN FOR 47 SECONDS
## *January 1983*

'Well, it all went to plan at the start, Paul, what went wrong after that?' England's doleful captain Dodge rearranged his lugubrious face as he searched to frame an answer, but even while his mental gears were cranking into action, the coach Dick Greenwood – equally mournful beyond his soup-strainer moustache but far more practised at the post-match cliché and at talking an attacking game – jumped in to nail the question.

'Waddya mean "went wrong"? Why can't you ask what went right?' Er, okay, what did? From the very kick off England had dramatically run the ball back at the opposition to set up the first three points within one minute. And to be sure, that was a minute's more drama than against the Wallabies. Greenwood timed it at 43 seconds. A supporter butted in: that kick went over in the 47th second. 'There you are, then,' said Greenwood. 'It was a 47-second burst of mould-breaking for us and I find that quite encouraging, don't you?' Every second counts when you are clutching at straws in a gale.

'Come off it!' exploded a braver soul than me from the front row of the funeral parlour, 'England were simply and totally pathetic!' This stirred the Healey-eyebrowed gloom of the selector Derek Morgan, to break free from his festooning chains of black crêpe paper. He took the charge, as well he might, as a personal slight.

'You may use the word "pathetic," ' he said, 'but I think you should respect the position and feelings of 15 young men who have just played their hearts out for England. We play Ireland in a fortnight and surely the win today will have given the team confidence for Dublin.'

At that same moment, in another part of the old shrine, an Irish journalist was telephoning his story home. It began – 'So bare is England's cupboard that the Irish coach, Doyle, left Twickenham after his spying mission and must have giggled all the way to Heathrow. I can report that, as international fixtures go, this was well up to the standards of Monkstown Second XV v Powerstown Thirds on a wet Wednesday.'

Meanwhile the unaptly named Dodge, having organised his face into an even more brooding brown study, prepared to utter. England's new captain might be a dashing leader of men in the dressing-room, but public relations are not too high on his agenda, I would say.

Sure, Dodge had heard the jeers of the crowd – 'but you never take any notice of them – or at least I don't. I'm used to it, I suppose, but I dare say it got to some of the younger players.' Nice one, Paul. 'Anyway, I think we might be better off playing away from home.' The feeling may well be mutual.

It was time for another saving chirp from Greenwood. He couldn't wait to get back to that glorious, heady 47-second effervescence. 'I agree one swallow doesn't make the summer we are looking for. But, come on, straight from the kick off we had the scoreboard rattling, didn't we? And don't forget, the Romanians were hard to play against. They packed their side with seamers and we simply couldn't get the ball through the covers.'

At that, not only the already puzzled Romanian journalists found themselves closing their notebooks with relief. Anyway, we had already asterisked the quote of the day, long before, from the diplomatic and charming Romanian manager Morariu. How do you think England will get on against France in a month's time? 'If the French play anything like they played against us, I am afraid it will be not a question of rugby, but of mathematics!'

* * *

Afterwards England's last-minute recruit, David Cooke, said: 'We were very lost. There was no form of discipline in the sense that nobody knew where they were going. I found myself chipping in with advice and it ended up with about four of us having a say. It got out of hand. The forwards needed a dominant personality to lead but it wasn't there. It was very frustrating.'

---

# RITUAL ADVANCE OF THE THINKING MAN'S PLAYER
## *January 1988*

In the first three months of any year, I dare say, some of the most intense and (if you like that sort of thing) compelling live close-ups on English television are those that show the white-shirted goal-kicker of the national Rugby Union team as he frowns and fusses and frets, lines up and lays into his three-pointers in the international championship.

It is the plot within the plot, the tiny cameo that can alter radically the broadest canvas. In the manic higgledy-piggledy, haywire argy-bargy, the goal-kicker is the meticulous miniaturist.

Jonathan Webb will again play the starring cameo role at Twickenham today. He is a Bristol doctor and anyone less like a rugger-bugger hearty would be difficult to find. In the cauliflower-ear brigade, he is the clean-cut, upright young subaltern – a softly companionable, gentlemanly young man, beautifully mannered and modest to the point of shyness. His concession to flamboyance is a daffodil-yellow, two-seater MGB and a series of outstandingly brilliant games for Bristol RFC.

If, in England's continuing doldrums, he has yet to have his attacking potential realised or even understood by the national team, as last line of defence he has, nevertheless, been solely responsible, I would say, for the two most thrilling, momentary rearguard actions of the championship – his lassoing tackle of that darting, full-pelt peewit, Jonathan Davies at Twickenham ('Oh, I just had to get him, just had to, he's so brilliant, but so arrogant with it'), and his courageous catch, dodge and escape through half the Scottish pack under his posts at Murrayfield.

Then, the place-kicking, and if that has, to curdle the metaphor, left him with a curate's egg all over his face at times, then all the more intriguing to sit him down and talk him through it. In his overnight case today, as in all the internationals so far, will be packed the book, *The Inner Game*, that mystical mind-over-matter treatise on, you might say, 'sport as an extension of yoga', or vice versa, published a decade ago by the American zealot, Dr Timothy Gallwey.

I quote the good doctor, substituting goal-kicking for tennis: 'We learn goal-kicking element by element. If we learn it as a totality we could learn it in a hundredth of the time. Our biggest problem is ego, trying too hard. We all know how to kick goals, perfect goal-kicking is in all of us. You have to let the body experiment and bypass the mind. The brain acts like a sergeant, with the body a private' and so on and so forth.

Is the ritual all, I wondered, often being fascinated by the rehearsed exactitudes of preparing kickers down the years – Hiller's boot wipe, Peter Brown's sauntering turn-on-heel, Ollie's precise, split-second ballet dancer's 'points', Bennett's Moulin Rouge follow-through, Dusty's meticulous sort of agriculturalism.

Webb leaps to the theme and the bright eyes glaze over. 'Ah, yes, the ritual. No, it's nothing to do with superstition. There's logic to ritual. Because there are so many variables you could be employing, it makes sense to cut out as many as you can so that every attempt at goal has a pure and certain consistency about it.

'My ritual, my routine? Heel out the circle, then the trough. Always adjust the ball so the nozzle is slightly to the right, just so, then angle the upright torpedo just slightly towards the posts for more forward impetus. Eye alignment. Inner calm. Consider the wind. Stand. Left foot alongside ball, right instep right behind. Visualise the kick sailing over. Eye and foot aligned. Wipe hands. Four precise steps back. Stop. Check. Visualise. Then two-step chassé to left if it's a Mitre ball that we use at Bristol, one-and-a-half if it's a Gilbert at Twick, you must time them better though they go further. Visualise. How it will feel on your foot, how it will look going over. Lovely. Then stillness. Then a long, slow breath out, relax, keep as loose as poss, no tension, head down, swing cleanly, think of nothing, nothing at all to do with kicking a ball, from now on it's all sub-cerebral. Now just move in and do it.

'Just hit it, just reaffirm your system works, stop in their tracks those people saying "ah, shame his kicking's not good enough", but show them, "look, see what I can do when I don't worry what people think or what the papers will say tomorrow". Visualise, visualise. Stop telling your mind how to kick a ball. Goal-kicking is nothing to do with the cerebral. If you tried to write down on paper exactly what you do to kick a ball between two posts with absolute certainty, it would be totally impossible, you'd still be at it in a million years – but once you've done it just once, your body and mind has the exact formula stored and ready to be repeated.

'Yet it's impossible to explain. Like the last kick I took for England at Murrayfield. The match-winner. Uncanny, amazing, fascinating. I'd missed a couple, my nerves should have been really tight, but from the moment I got the ball, I hadn't the slightest doubt it was going over. A total certainty infused me, I just couldn't miss. Truly amazing. It sailed through – and I thought, well, if I could programme that feeling and switch into it every time, where might that end – but I know it's not as easy as that. Or is it?'

# UP FOR THE CUP WITH MUM AND DAD
*May 1978*

This Thursday morning England's national stadium changes character. At 10 a.m. Wembley starts erecting its crash barriers; the pitch is caged in with steel fencing; the police detention room is swept. A tale of two Saturdays.

There have been 4,000 more tickets sold for the forthcoming FA Cup final. The Rugby League people like to give their folk more room. They come early to sit down round mum's tablecloth spread out on the terraces. There are many more children at the Rugby League final – and many more mothers, lovers, sisters, cousins and aunts. They all know the words of *Ilkley Moor* or the *Lassie from Lancashire*. The rugby final represents – as that Eddie Waring of the 1950s, Wilfred Pickles, used to say – 'a spot of homely fun, bringing the people to the people.'

The rugby final must be what the FA final used to be like when teams like Bolton, Preston, Blackburn and Huddersfield stood a chance. On Saturday everyone on the terraces stood and sang *God Save the Queen* full belt and heartfelt.

It did not matter a fig that this particular game disappointed me. It never really crackled – though some of the tackling did. Widnes, explained a new friend, were too much on their best behaviour. If possession is nine points, then Wakefield were nine behind because they gave the ball away far too often.

It was good to see old names from the 15-a-side game like Smith and Lampkowski and Shaw. I thought Lampkowski played a treat. Come to think of it, when he had those couple of games for England at Twickenham he played then like a League scrum-half. England's RU mob could still do with Smith in the centre. As for Burke, the goal-kicker who was a Union man a year ago, well Twickenham should pay for him to defect.

Everyone round me was puzzled when seven old codgers

walked out in the distance to be presented before the game. It was all explained when I got home in the evening to my new toy, a video tape recorder, and Jim Reside's dear little BBC genuflection to half a century of northern pilgrimage to Wembley. The seven with bright new blazer badges and bright old moist eyes were the sole survivors, it turned out, of the 26 from Wigan and Dewsbury who had played that first final in 1929. Reside filmed them on an ancient steam train preserved by the Keighley and Worth Valley Railway and they re-enacted that first journey to London as Colin Welland interviewed them. There was Syd Abram, who scored Wembley's first try ('I didn't think about it till I got back to the half-way and two forwards said they were glad it were done by a local lad'), Henry Coates, who had to sell his loser's medal in the 1930s, and the RL gave him a replica only last Friday, Joe Malkin, Jim Rudd, Jack Woolmore, Tommy Beetham and Tommy Ring.

The first time the Rugby League final knifed its way into this soft southerner's consciousness was again thanks to the BBC on the last occasion Wakefield were at Wembley 11 years ago. Remember that last kick of the game, an absolute doddle under the posts? And Don Fox muffed it, fell weeping to the ground, and Eddie spoke for the nation when he said 'Eee, poor lad!'

Apparently Don Fox has never once talked about his feelings from that day to this. But he did on Saturday at last. Not to say this nice man does not still look shellshocked. He even admitted that he had had a premonition of this tragedy: 'When I were leaving on the Wednesday I gave my wife Mary a little kiss goodbye and all that and I said to her "I'll see you Saturday luv – as long as I haven't to decide the game with a last-minute kick." Me knees were like jelly as I went up to take it. We were on 240 quid each, which were a lot of money in them days.... Normally I would have back-heeled it over. I won the man of the match award, but no one mentioned that ever: they only remember me as "that lad who missed the goal".... Ah well, just one of them things.'

There was none of that sort of drama on Saturday. But it was nice to be there just in case. It was good, too, to see a football game at Wembley with vision uninterrupted by a wall of wire netting. It also helped the view when, long after the end, whole families stayed seated on the terraces as mum got out the thermos and passed round the sandwiches.

---

# A CODE WORTH CRACKING
*May 1985*

The comparison was chilling: after enduring in recent winters a string of tawdry, inept and sullen Rugby Union internationals, in which the standard of play and of the chivalry had scarcely done justice to either the occasion or its anticipation, one's faith in rugby football as one of modern man's finest minor inventions was fully restored on Saturday.

It has become worthless to bang on about the Rugby Union's patronising attitude to its brothers in the League. Surely every sane man agrees on that outside the blinds of south-west London's suburban bunker – but I must say you could twig after Saturday's salutary show why the Rugby Leaguers were dismissive in the autumn about Mark Ella, the Wallaby tourist who so inspired the state of the Union. He would not get a game for his country if he changed codes, said the RL boys.

Saturday's opposing half-backs happened to be blood-brothers. If Kenny deserved to be man of the match, his compatriot, Sterling, was president of the day. Kenny, at out-half, can sell a dummy with the twitch of an eyebrow. He stands on the periphery, uninterested, fingering his top lip, wondering what is on the television then, of a sudden, he can double-declutch about six times in four strides as he sweeps away from defenders.

Sterling was everything I have been told, and more: low-slung, straw-mopped, a workaday scurrier, you think, just perkily on the look-out for the odd quick single like a Clive Radley, and then outrageously he is drawing in two, three, even five great thundering tanks into the tackle, and at

152

the very moment he is clattered pops out the perfect pass, short, long or under-arm, and his man is in the clear.

The wingmen were set off on more fliers than a Biggin Hill bank holiday. If their Union counterparts in England like Underwood, Smith or Trick – who honestly tell you they go whole weekends without a pass – were watching on television, surely their applications will be in the post to somewhere up north with a first class stamp.

Gill, on one Wigan wing, riddled the spine every time he got going and, on the other, the aborigine, Ferguson, kept going off like an arrow. Like Basil D'Oliveira Ferguson is a leading sportsman late to the big-time. Like Basil, who stayed 34 for years and years until Bill Frindall, ever meticulous, blew the gaffe on his birth certificate, John is happy to remain 30. Some say he is coming up to his tenth 30th birthday. That obviously offends the Australian national selectors, who have yet to give him a cap, though he has long been in everyone's World XIII – with 99,801 more voters on Saturday.

It was a glorious day as well for some now less electrically charged old men. The 50th Wembley final was preceded by a touching salute to and parade of 49 of the game's epic performers – from Henry Coates, the tiny Dewsbury darter, who came down for the first metropolitan visit in 1929, through such as Markham, Risman, Bevan, Boston, Karalius and the wily old Foxes. As the proud 49ers stood there, bald and bandy, the hymn *Abide With Me* swept over them, and I looked down and thought how some even had been marked traitor to their caste – the likes who had gone from the Union like Arthur Lloyd, who left the bleak Wales of 50 years ago and more, his namesake, Reg, who defected from Neath in 1937, Trevor Foster, from Newport, right up to the legendary Lewis Jones and Dai Watkins.

# 7

# VROOMS AND FUMES

Sport can only be about winning and losing, never about living or dying. Motor racing is far more appallingly terminal than boxing – and that's a pretty horrific pastime in the name of leisure sports. Tom Pryce was universally presumed to be Britain's next world driving champion after James Hunt. He popped in to see me one morning. I recall it well, for it was the day my new kitten got stuck up a very tall tree. I said I'd rung the fire brigade for one of their famous 'mercy missions'. Forget it, said Tom, and shinned up the tree, just like that, and rescued the quivering mewler. Dear daring, zestful, youthful Tom. I said I'd call the cat Tommy – and we went out for a long lunch while his wife, Nella, did some shopping in Bayswater. At tea-time I saw them both off to Heathrow. They were going to South Africa, to the Grand Prix at Kyalami at the end of the week. That was Monday. On Saturday, Tom Pryce was dead, decapitated at 180mph. On Sunday, the office rang for my copy.

# SO SHY AND SENSITIVE
## November 1977

Tom Pryce had asked me not to forget to give him a full report of the England v Wales rugby international when he arrived back home today from the South African Grand Prix. But now he's not coming back. Just before the match started we were told that the young Welshman was dead. He is now just another tear-stained wail in the tragic litany of lives and loves lost in the name of his sport – Collins and Clark and Courage and Cevert; Schlesser, Spence, Siffert and Scarfiotti; Bandini, Birrel, and Bonnier; Bruce McLaren; Rodriguez, Revson and Rindt. And now young Tom Pryce, sensitive and shy, who didn't like talking about even the possibility of death. 'I'm not saying I don't fear it. But would I feel it? But I am frightened of it for what it might do to those I leave behind.'

I spent a lot of happy time with Pryce the week before he went to South Africa. And with those who are now left behind: his still blushing bride of two years, Nella, a trained teacher who wanted to open a riding school in the heart of the south-east's Thelwell country. And his dad, a police sergeant in rural north Wales and as proud as you can imagine of his boy. And his anxious mum who always 'knew, deep down', that it would end like this. If ever they went to watch him drive she would creep into the team caravan to pretend to listen to the radio commentary. It wasn't quite as bad as watching. His father told me last week: 'Crumbs, racedays are terrible up here. Our little house at Ruthin gets really excited. We closed ourselves in all day listening to the wireless for news of the boy. If I'm on duty Mrs Pryce telephones when anything comes through. But they don't give much gen, and the television's damned 'opeless, isn't it?' What a hideous way for them to hear the last news of Tom on Saturday.

Not that they called him Tom. His real name was Maldwyn, which is Welsh, see, for Montgomery, where the family originally came from. Tom speaks Welsh. 'Yes, we were very sorry when they changed his name to Tom. Very sad. But I suppose "Tom" is more catchy-like, more good for publicity. Maldwyn has always been reserved about publicity. I thought he should be much more forward. It is good for him. He keeps promising to be better. He always said he would, once he became a Formula One driver. After that it was "once he'd won his first Grand Prix". I wish he'd get better, 'cos I know you boys expect it.' No need now.

Sergeant Pryce doesn't have a clue what inspired Maldwyn to take up motor racing. 'Crumbs, it can't have been when we gave him that first trike, can it? His mam thinks it might have been the pedal car he had for his fourth birthday. And we used to have our fortnight's holiday on the Isle of Man, mind you. And for some reason it always seemed to be TT week. He would have been five I reckon when he saw his first TT – Geoff Duke won it, I think.' Tom Pryce couldn't remember much about the Isle of Man. But when he was eight in 1957 his dad took him to Aintree where Stirling Moss won a famous dice with Fangio in the British Grand Prix. Something must have rubbed off, although Tom only remembered clutching perilously with his father on to an advertising hoarding to see the cars pass, that and 'the terrible, terrible noise'.

In 1964, Pryce, the policeman, swopped his country copper's push bike ('I'm a country bobby – sheep stealing, none of this drug trafficking up here boy') for a Morris Oxford. Tom dreamed to himself at the wheel when it was parked outside their house. By 14 the walls of his little bedroom were plastered with posters of Grand Prix cars and drivers. He thought of being a farmer. But no money. He qualified to go to college as an agricultural engineer. There was nothing he didn't know about tractors. Certainly that they only went at 10mph. On Saturday they say he hit that poor misguided steward at 160mph. In 1968 Tom bought a mini-van. In 1969 he sold it to pay for lessons at Mallory Park. Sergeant Pryce went with him, bewildered but quite keen nevertheless. It was £12 for a test lesson, then £8 for each one thereafter.

Trevor Taylor, the instructor, told the policeman Tom was

very good. 'The rich guys did their course, wham-bang, and had finished it all in a month. It took me a year, I was working at a local garage to save up for lessons. I'm sure that gradualism paid off. I learned slowly, see.' So a year later he won a school competition sponsored by the *Daily Express*. In 1973 he won a Formula Three race at Monaco. The Formula One offers started to come in. His rise since has been sensational. So, in a sport where fast bucks sometimes seem faster than fast backs, has been his loyalty to the Shadow team.

Pryce's gentle shyness italicised his reputation as a bit of a loner on the circuit. But everyone accepted that he was easily among the dozen best drivers in the world. 'Of course, yes, Nella is marvellously good for me. So is Dad. But the thing about danger is that you must not talk too much to them about it. I know it is a factor but for them I only try to talk about the technical problems of the race coming up. It is not fair to try and relate to anyone else at all in terms of inner fear.' He said he never had nightmares. But his fingernails were bitten down to the quick, almost to the very knuckle. They were as badly bitten as the late Jim Clark's. His car was once badly hit up the backside when he was forced to stop at Monaco. He walked away without a scratch. In the 1975 German Grand Prix he finished standing up in his cockpit, bathed in petrol. It could have gone up any time, but didn't.

We had a long, laughing lunch together a couple of days before he and Nella left for South Africa. Just before he went off to continue his wickedly compelling, nail-biting blood-spattered sport he asked me to make sure I came with him to the British Grand Prix at Silverstone. 'There's no doubt about it, I'm going to win that one, and, come to that, I'll win at Monaco and Nurburgring too. I bet you. And don't forget to give me a full report on how Gareth and JPR lick the English at the Arms Park....'

# FAREWELL TO THE SHEENE MACHINE
*February 1984*

Barry Sheene retired from motorcycle racing yesterday after 16 seasons in which he won two 500cc world championships and survived two horrendous crashes. He said: 'If I continued it would just be for the money. I always promised that I would never do that. I leave the sport knowing I am riding as well as I have ever done.'

The 34-year-old had again been unable to organise a custom-built works machine for the new season. He might consider racing saloon cars, and will certainly drive for DAF in the occasional truck sideshow race. Barry's advertising contract with Brut is over; perhaps Yorkie Bars will now sign him up.

The engaging Sheene remains an extremely marketable property. He is as indelibly locked in the litany of his sports saints as Geoff Duke, John Surtees and Mike Hailwood. Sheene's courage – some would say fate-tempting – returned after his two dramatic accidents, made him a celebrity far outside the sports pages. Sheene was not at all a bad surname for an extremely bright little star.

I last saw him chirpily forecasting rain on the way, because his arthritis was playing up. He was sitting with his feet up in the sitting-room of his sensational 33-bedroom Elizabethan manor in Sussex. A couple of Mercedes were in the drive: somewhere on the estate the helicopter was on the pad. You wondered if it was a fair swap for two shattered legs, held in place with four metal plates and 23 screws, which were a souvenir of Silverstone in 1982, or a broken thigh, wrists, forearm, collarbones and six ribs, the reminder of Daytona in 1975.

There, he said, he had left enough skin on the track to cover a sofa – after falling off on a banked curve at 176mph when either the engine had locked or the front tyre burst. Nobody knows what caused it, but his squat little body was catapulted into a 150-yard skid. He came round in hospital two days later and his first words to the nurse were: 'You wouldn't by any chance have a cigarette, would you, love?'

A year later he won the world championship, capturing five of the six grands prix he entered. Next year, 1977, he did it again – only to have a number of the sport's olde-tyme adventurers attack him for funking the Isle of Man TT. Sheene smilingly Harvey Smithed them – 'say what you like, I don't give a damn. I'm a coward if you say so – but I'm an alive-and-well coward – and that's how I intend to remain.' When he was awarded the MBE in 1978, the Queen maternally made a point of telling him 'Now you be careful, young man' – and later that day he was in philosophical mood at the celebrations. 'I'm not a madman. I bring to my business all the judgement and skill I possess, and if something goes wrong I will have the consolation of knowing that it couldn't be my fault.

'You cannot get the most out of life if you are not aware of the possibility of death. I'm not morbid. I love life, girls and a drink. I like to see the sun coming up in the morning, but if I abandon the thing I do best, I feel that the edge might go out of the enjoyment that life gives me.'

You can always tell a motorcycle racer in a restaurant. He's the one throttling back his fork with the first two fingers of his right hand. Sheene has always been easier to identify – his left arm has almost permanently been around a willowy model they call Stephanie McLean, who first saw him crashing at Daytona on television and made the point of getting to know him as soon as he was back. She organised a modelling session with him and that was that – in spite of the fact that the photographer that day was also Stephanie's husband.

The ensuing gossip columns helped the image – they have been a glittering Dempster duo. Now it is a threesome with the birth of their first baby in November. Actually, the Sheene entourage has been a famous foursome for most of his career. For where Barry and Steph go, so have always followed his mum and dad – Mr Sheene with his spanners and as charming a nature as you could hope for, Mrs bringing up the rear with the oily rags and vacuum flask. Dad was a bit

159

of a racer and tinkerer himself, ace-man at a garage in London's Grays Inn Road. Barry left school at 15 and by 17 was riding one of his father's Bultacos – winning the British 125cc championship in 1970.

It was nine years later that he made one of my most stirring sporting memories – at the British GP at Silverstone in 1979. He had an intense duel with the American Kenny Roberts. With two laps left and the field of 30 left behind they banged elbows at 150mph, and were seen to motion at each other to get a move on. On the final turn Sheene, charging from behind, brushed the curve of the pavement and their leathered knees touched. Roberts came out a split-second ahead and kept the two-inch lead. They dismounted and embraced. Sheene and Silverstone did not smell of his famous Brut aftershave that afternoon.

The fumes have the whiff of genuine drama – as they always did when Sheene was shining.

---

## NIGEL OUT OF NEUTRAL CORNER
*October 1987*

*Mexico City*: He was, literally, left at the traffic lights, just like you and me in our Escort or Cortina. At the very start of the most important race of his life, Nigel Mansell saw the lights turn from red to green, thought he was in first gear, let out the clutch, found he was in neutral, panicked her into second – and jerked into juddering movement like he was old Mr or Mrs Bloggins coming back from their weekly shopping.

He had been a comparatively luxurious third position on the grid. A half decent race, and he was champion of the world. In the deafeningly dramatic couple of seconds that it took him to get his show on the road and his act into gear, he was 21st!

Because of his uncomplicated, straightforward British Midlands ordinariness in a smarmy jet-set world made up of self-styled beautiful people, our Nigel has long been the butt of the snide jokes. The Pershore hill climber who had for too

160

long been gatecrashing the wrong party. The Mexico Grand Prix, then, was going to be the crowning, crowing hour for the expensively moccasined mockers from Italy, France and South America. Here was utter proof of the funny old Englishman's provincialism.

'It was a nightmare. I flip the clutch, accelerate, and nothing happens. I've just got a bunchful of neutrals. I couldn't believe it. I pulled back into second and just chugged away from the line. What I should have done on the red light was creep forward a millimetre in first to make sure it was engaged – but the day before they had made a point at the drivers' meeting that any cars "creeping" on the grid would be penalised. I swore as they roared past, but I didn't panic. I said, "C'mon, patience, skills, dedication, give it all the qualities you know you have. Show the buggers that wherever you are you can still go as quick as the leaders".'

His resulting charge was electric. He left the grid in 21st place, was already 18th at the end of the first circuit and then stormingly picked them off to end in a dramatic fifth place, only one behind his Williams team-mate and closest rival, Nelson Piquet, of Brazil, who had been one ahead of him on the grid. Alain Prost, the other championship contender was second to the young Austrian Gerhard Berger, who won his first Grand Prix in his Bennetton BMW. They go to the season's final race in Adelaide on Sunday fortnight for a unique three-man shoot-out. Whatever the others do, Mansell has only to be third in Australia to take the title.

His Mexico race will be immediately remembered for the blushes of the Goodyear tyre company – on his rock-hard Pirelli tyres, Berger did not need one change, while all behind him on Goodyear's 'softs' were up and down on the pit jacks all through. It will be recalled as well for Mansell's tearaway tenacity. There was something heroic about it, and it was certainly worth a trip a couple of hours after the race to the airport to see him off.

He is wearing grubby sneakers, and carrying the most tourist-trapped see-you-coming three-and-a-half foot wide sombrero that you ever did see, all Sherwood green and silver bobbles and tassles. He checks in. There is time to order a

161

Coke and a steak. 'No gravy or mish-mash on it. Just a bottle of tomato ketchup, and an extra plate of chips.' The giant sombrero, like a docked space ship, is on the chair beside him.

'I was really feeling jolly ill yesterday, you know. It was honestly touch and go whether I would qualify for this race. I kept having to run to the toilet. As I put my foot down after the disaster today and started to chase I gave myself a few very hairy moments. It was not really the thing to do. This is a dangerous game, and I took risks today that I would not normally consider. I took chances, I overtook, I braked later than I should have, I was slipstreaming people down the track, which I wouldn't normally do. When I was charging Nelson at the end, I thought I was past him, then that car ahead blew up and put oil down. I went this way and that way to find the gap. I saw it, went for it, but that's where the oil was! I almost skidded off. Very hairy. That's why I thought "You stay back, lad!" Okay, I lost three seconds, but better safe than sorry, I always say. You must realise, you blokes, that these two men I'm challenging are unbelievably good drivers, great drivers, Nelson and Alain have got three world championships between them. I have never got near one.'

Before Australia he will have three days at his Isle of Man home playing some golf – and perhaps he might try staying up late watching videos and sleeping during the day, gearing himself to adjust his time clock for Australia – 'Just like I heard Ballesteros did in Spain the week before he went over to conquer the Masters, didn't he?'

---

# GRAND PRIX GRAND MASTER
*July 1987*

The welcome is so affable, so cheery, the face so animated, the brain (as you are to discover) so keen-sharp, that you totally forget yourself and stick out a mitt for a matey handshake. He grimaces and endeavours, wincingly and uselessly, to hoist his elbow or bend a wrist to crank himself up to offer at least a flicker of his hand in greeting. Frank Williams cannot shake hands. He was paralysed from the shoulders down 16 months ago when he drove his car off a minor road in southern France. It is an understatement to say he is lucky to be alive. But he does mention the fact.

Today and tomorrow, his wheelchair will be gently eased into place on the pit wall at Silverstone and a microphone placed at his lips and earphones clamped to his head, and he will be in direct, dramatic contact with his two drivers, Nigel Mansell and Nelson Piquet as they fume and vroom around the British GP circuit in Northamptonshire. When they cacklingly call Williams from their cockpits, he will be ready to tell them the score. Radio reception is perfect. The pitmen only speak if spoken to – 'There's no way we call up to say "Hi, Nigel, you've left your rear offside winker on"!' Mansell is far more talkative than Piquet. What sort of stuff?

'Well, about lap 10 last week in France, Nigel comes on to say he's picked up a bit of debris from another car and it was affecting his handling considerably, he reckoned. "I'm coming in, I'm coming in!" he radioed. We told him "Stay out there" because I could see his lap times were dropping only by a quarter of a second each lap.

'So then he asked "Can you change the front wing when I stop for tyres?" Again more discussion and he was given a definite "No – too much time and it could mean a gigantic cock-up." A new wing or nose can take 60 seconds – and then only if you get it spot-on. It would have cost him the race. So, a good decision, right?' Right. Really and truly, a fairly phenomenal fellow.

The Williams-Honda hurtler already leads the GP constructors' championship by a mile. It is becoming a habit. Not bad for a paralysed second-hand car dealer. His schoolboy ambition was to race. As a tearaway in the early 1960s he drove an Austin A40 in official saloon car hoolies before gypsying around Europe, cadging drives in Formula Three. Then he set up a stall as dealer in wheels and deals for clapped-out Coopers and Brabhams. Wanna banger? Go see Frank. By then he was sharing a flat in Harrow with the fast set which included Piers Courage, his first driver. Together they took to the circuit with panache. Piers won Formula Two

163

and was immediately a Formula One cracker in 1969.

In 1970 Piers was killed at speed. Frank Williams mourned and kept going in his memory. Williams is now the most famous and successful non-driver on the whole narrow-eyed, bread and circus, jet-set, merry-go-round. Life, however limp your body, must go on. Ten days ago, bound for the French GP, Williams revisited the spot where he almost killed himself. 'Just curiosity, I suppose.' Now he has to have somebody feed him 'like a baby' – and two men carry him into cars and on and off aeroplanes.

Sixteen months ago, lighthearted as he ever was, he had been in a rush to get from the Ricard circuit, east of Marseilles, to Nice airport, after a test session for the 1986 season. He careered off the little, short-cut B road at Moulinon. Now he had returned there. He was shown the exact spot. 'Totally my fault. I just cocked it up, didn't I?'

He knew he should have died. He survived. He has been to a lot of other people's funerals. His all-time fast-favourite Jochen Rindt, killed himself in 1970 at Monza. Courage, dashing charmer and flat-mate, went away the same year at Zandfoort in a black-orange plume. Suddenly for Williams, it was no longer public schoolboy fun, but business. And business is business.

'It was a major setback emotionally. And racing-wise it was pretty debilitating as well. But you have to carry on, don't you. I've buried a lot. I've been to a lot of funerals. But fewer and fewer, they're petering out almost, touch wood.' He makes to touch his wooden topped desk, but the hands can't feel a thing.

'I admit, I always had this passion to be a driver. If I'd taken out a racing licence and did what I did that day in France on the track instead, I'd probably have saved myself a lot of aggravation in the past 12 months. I had a go in the early 1960s, but I never had enough money and, anyway, was always too erratic, always flying off the track, literally. When I gave up it was only because I hadn't enough money. I always meant to return; never did.'

Tomorrow at Silverstone they will be watching him from every other pit-dungeon. He first set eyes on Silverstone in

1958 when he was 16. Holidays from his Scottish boarding school had just started and he hitched down from Nottingham. 'It took a terrible six hours for just 60 miles. But it was beautiful, beautiful. I arrived in the middle of the touring car race. Magic. And then Peter Collins won the Grand Prix. I remember being positively delighted that an Englishman won, but profoundly disappointed that it was a foreign car.

'Silverstone is unique. Well, think about it: there are only six corners. Only six. But by jove they're all so fast, except for the chicane and that's quite nifty as well. So we need total aerodynamic soundness and an engine that's extremely fuel efficient. The revs have to be so high that speeds at Silverstone just gulp in the fuel. We've got to get that right or we are sunk.'

It seems to be Williams v The Rest – but everybody knows, intriguingly, it's also Mansell v Piquet. 'Nigel's most obvious quality is also the most basic. He has become, simply immensely quick. Not that it was always evident to me I must say. In the two-and-a-bit years he's been with us it's been honestly quite thrilling to see him get quicker, and quicker, and quicker. On top of that, add his determination, his grit – not forgetting his application to the job. Mind you, the crowning quality is that he's an Englishman.'

Okay, okay, rule Britannia, but don't get too carried away. Surely there's no real difference between your drivers and anybody else's, it's just that some have faster cars and slicker tyres or more overhead camshafts or whatever? 'Don't you believe it. There are 27 guys on that grid and it really is a question of the quick and the slow. Some are born quick. Honestly, some have mountains more talent. And after that comes the absolutely crucial mix of experience-and-hunger. The fires have to be really stoked up for these guys to go as fast as they do. Do you twig? The more miles they do, the more they get better at simply going quick.

'But on the other hand the more miles some do over the years the more dulled and jaded they can become. So in the absolute A1 top guys the fires and the venom burns brighter from the time they announce themselves to the time they pack up – it just keeps on getting brighter, and I think in Nigel's case, he's just been getting faster, brighter and hotter every day since he joined us.'

To be first among equals, aye, that's the rub. Competition, he reckons, is all, even in your own team. As Piquet, nicely piqued, reminded Alan Henry yesterday, he had already won two world titles, while Mansell had managed only to lose one. What's Brazilian for touché? Frank Williams, being cheerfully enthused about his fellow Brit, now turns up both the brightness and contrast buttons for Nelson. 'So different to Nigel, not only amazingly quick himself but skilful too. Well, name me a more genuine contender for any championship in any year?'

What's 'skill' as opposed to 'speed'? Doesn't one mean the other? 'No, speed is speed. Raw, untarnished stuff. "Skill" is steering a GP car through, say, the right-hander at Ricard last week at 188.5mph, not lose one inch of control on your line – and do the very same, every single time for 80 laps. Car control pretty special, no? See my point?'

Okay, drivers vary, but why is the Williams invariably in the frame? 'Simply, we are competitive. Sure, we might win a particular race on a particular day because we have a car-chassis-driver-tyre-engine-luck combination that's simply as good as the opposition. I know that's a stupidly general answer and don't let it come out as over-proud and "aren't we Brits bloody good!" But the point is, like everybody else we are terribly fallible. Everybody must get 48,000 things right on the day. If we get one wrong, then we lose.'

This week the original and highly respected journalist, Keith Botsford, suggested that a ragged slip was showing below the hem of the Williams' span-spick turnout: Piquet, he said, was bellyaching about favouritism for the Brit.

Williams' crisp and comradely manner gets crisper and momentarily less friendly. 'I saw that. It is not accurate. I've ridden out far rougher storms. If my livelihood and success depended on what any given journalist wrote, I'd have sunk years ago. I'm not commenting any more on this matter – except to say there are two divergent arguments about any driver relations in any team of two: if there's an accepted No

1 and No 2 driver, the No 2 just has to do what he's told.

'But we are different, we have two drivers challenging each other hell-for-leather at the very top; so I agree while one driver can take points away from the other, which might seem bad management on the face of it, don't forget he's also taking points away from the competition. The less fast man on any particular week might have a bit of a moan, a theatrical niggle. Fair enough – but the crucial point is to say to yourself as team leader, "If we hadn't got that driver, then you can be bloody sure that McLaren or Lotus or Brabham would take him like a shot." If we want to win, we want the strongest team. It's as simple as that. We are in sport, I suppose. But, crucially, we are in business. And we are in business to win. Understand? Precisely. End of discussion, right?'

Right.

# 8

# RUNNERS AND RIDERS

Being brought up in Gloucestershire, you'd have thought that such annual four-legged fiestas as the Cheltenham Races and the Badminton Horse Trials would have been in the blood with my mother's milk. But I was more of a cricketing lad. It wasn't till I grew up that there was the stuff of real sportin' drama in them thar muddy fields near home. True, as kids we were taken once or twice in the old Ford Prefect to Chelt – over the top from Stroud past Painswick and Prinknash – but it all seemed perfectly innocent fun to me. The horses had nice comfy gymkhana names like *Prince Regent* and *Sheila's Cottage*, and in the paddock they looked like models for a Munnings' picture, all haughty, sleek and colourfully silky. Little did I know. Adulthood opened my eyes to Cheltenham and 'a day at the races'. The Irish even bring their own bookies over. Like the day a grizzled, holidaying farmer from County Cork put £100 on a horse at 8-1. The bookie's sign proclaimed him to be a Mr Finnegan of Bandon. When the nag obliged, your farmer had his £800 counted out, one by one, into his gnarled old palm. Halfway through, he looked up at his bookmaking compatriot, and declared softly, but with a smug certainty, 'Ah, yes, you've heard of *Finnegans Wake* to be sure – well, this is your fockin' wake, Finnegan!'

# A DAY OF DOG-COLLARS
*March 1976*

I've borrowed my dad's brown trilby and been to Cheltenham races. I knew it was cracked up to be something, but never anything quite like this. St Patrick's Day gone mad. The festival starts at Paddington, where first-class, non-stop morning specials leave on the half hour full of the buffeting champagne and cigar gentry, every man Jonathan of them smirkingly knowing a thing or three.

I caught the orthodox second class. More Irish. They know a thing or two of that as well. So they tell you. Our buffets were more scruffy. Brown ales and scarce a Wills Whiff to be seen. Everyone deep into the *Sporting Life*. All wide-eyed expectation as a cover for furtive, blotchy-faced despair. And, quietly, in corners, sheepishly studying *Timeform* as if a breviary, a host of Irish clergy.

And once at Cheltenham Station, in the long queue for buses and taxis you can't finish your count of the dog collars. Sunday clerics with the glint of midweek sport in their eye. And, I'd bet on it, twice as many again in civvy collar and tie and having told their abbots and bishops that they're off for their annual treat on the mainland on some unsuspecting convent school or whatever. Certainly Cheltenham's race-card could be printed in Latin and half the fancy could read it.

Mark you, Cheltenham races and the Catholic Church have long been hand in glove. A lively settlement of Romans was established there by refugees from the French Revolution. And when the merry Captain Berkley founded the race meeting below Cleeve Hill in the early part of last century, the Irish brought over their relatives, who in turn brought their nags, to join in the fun. Many stayed there and then. Indeed, 100 years ago Cheltenham had to build itself a new cemetery, for, as the old refrain went:

The churchyard's so small and the Irish so many
They ought to be pickled and sent to Kilkenny.

To the bible-thumper Dean Close, the horse-racing Irish of

Cheltenham were the pet hate ahead even of drink. 'Papists, gambling and profligacy' he ranted in 1835 'are essential concomitants of horseracing.' But he failed to wipe even a smile from their face and he stomped off to Carlisle. Cobbett failed, too. 'Cheltenham on raceday is the resort of the lame and lazy, the gourmandising and guzzling, the bilious and nervous....' Now that's the sort of thing I would have been thinking of if I'd caught the first-class.

Hey ho, but what a lovely jig the Irish give to the prim place. Not that the residents stir to wake out of their doze, unless they're hoteliers or traffic wardens or shopkeepers. One daft local grocer, for years now, has made a tradition of presenting a posy of jasmine and a packet of polos to the Queen Mother as she's chauffeured past his shop on her way up to the course. The Queen Mother has a horse called *Isle of Man*. 'Good luck to the *Isle of Wight*,' said the grocer in his blushing confusion. But the Queen Mother seemed beamingly oblivious as she accepted the gift.

Yesterday, bewildered but rubbing shoulders with the clergy, with shady Cockneys and nobs from the shires, I chanced across our film critic, Mr Malcolm, looking knowingly like everyone else, even more so in his porridgy oatmeal coat. With flamboyant confidence he gave me *Chekov* 'for classical reasons' to win the first race. It lost. He was certain about *Flitgrove* for the second. Not a flicker. Well, *Birds Nest* for the third. Nowhere. I consoled him with the posy I'd bought specially in case I met the Queen Mother. But he won on the fourth when I didn't bet. So I gave him the packet of Polos in celebration. To the uninitiated Cheltenham is no place to find the winner. But, now, if you are looking to be converted to the one true faith....

---

## LADY AND THE CHAMP
### March 1986

The Irish have been waiting for this one. The shamrock could be sprouting early. Even if *Dawn Run* completes her unique

Champion Hurdle–Gold Cup double this afternoon she will not be the most mobbed lady in the winner's enclosure. Most of the metaphorical sugar lumps will be for the mare's owner, Mrs Charmian Hill, who turns and smiles with a gracious sweetness even if you hail her the Galloping Granny. She is as genteel and piercing-eyed an Irish eccentric as to have stepped out of the pages of any deliciously evocative novel by that marvellous and mischievous Miss Molly Keane.

The widow of a Waterford doctor, Mrs Hill was the first of Ireland's women jockeys when they were allowed – riding against the men at Fairyhouse in Ireland's first official mixed race in 1973 when she was already 54 years old. At 63, her licence was withdrawn. The reason given was 'old age'.

In 1981 she bought herself a point-to-pointer in the November sales at Ballsbridge. She paid 5,800 guineas and, because her daughter Penny had just taken up jogging, she called it *Dawn Run*. She schooled the horse herself – and just three years later, uniquely, the mare was champion hurdler of Ireland, France and England. This afternoon she could make National Hunt history.

This Irish afternoon there is another decent quirk about Mrs Hill's being, after the Queen Mother, Cheltenham racetrack's most glamorous great-grandma. Someone reckoned this week how Cheltenham is 'The biggest Catholic congregation in England.' But Mrs Hill can be said to have sportingly 'ecumenicised' the Romans and the Anglos as much as Barry McGuigan is said to have done.

Dr and Mrs Hill were part of the two-and-a-half per cent Protestant population of the Republic. As a boy, the doctor – who died last year – was sent across the water to boarding school at Cheltenham's Dean Close, which specialised in Anglican parson's sons (which he was) and annual fiery, brimstone, springtime sermons to the scholars against the evils of gambling. Nothing like that any more. Or, at least, not voiced in front of Royalty.

Dr Hill's practice was appropriately down the road from the crystal-glass place. Waterford this week could be almost a north Gloucestershire suburb. When his wife brought home her strapping young 16.2 high mare from Ballsbridge on 7

November 1981, the doctor was none too sure – but his wife told him: 'Look at that long line right from her withers down over her quarters: that's what makes a jumper with speed.'

She schooled her on her own and the victories were notched up at the local point-to-points. She had already known that certain feeling beneath her as they learned to gallop. In Anne Holland's breezy, breathless little portrait on *Dawn Run* (Barker, £8.95) she reports: 'One day they were going a bit faster when they came to a muddy patch that would have slowed up most horses, but *Dawn Run* never changed her stride or altered her rhythm. Mrs Hill's hopes began to run high. Could this gentle mare turn out to be the one, the stuff that dreams are made of?'

She dismounted and rang the trainer, Paddy Mullins. She told him: 'There's just one thing: she's so placid that I'm afraid she may never make a racehorse. She cannot possibly be competitive enough.'

The rest is history. And by tea-time today there just might be a whole lot more where that came from.

---

# KING LESTER AND THE DERBY SET, A RACE APART
*June 1977*

The astonishing Lester does it again! Who else is there, bar Muhammad Ali, to lodge himself so relentlessly in sport's consciousness. The two of them never go away. Last year, Piggott won the Derby for an unparalleled seventh time. Yesterday, all arms, knees and bumps-a-daisy made it a doodling eighth. And it was a gorgeous sun-blessed English afternoon and, reportedly, the Queen jumped up and down with glee as Piggott passed the post.

My first Derby Day was *Sea Bird*'s a dozen sunny summers ago. I was there but not there, so to speak. For in all honesty I never saw a thing except seven enthralling seconds of a clustered, dusty posse riding past Tattenham Corner. It took half an hour for word on the winner to reach us. It was like being the loo attendant under the Centre Court at Wimbledon, a fellow very much at the heart of the day but one who has to get an evening paper to see what actually happened.

Anyway, I'd always since made a supper-party point of insisting that Tattenham Corner was the only place to witness the Derby: there you combine inner knowledge of both punter and punted. The one hand lets you commune with the sun and wind and grass and an England content, the other to witness the very nub of the race, note what is fifth and unstraining and a likely winner, see the frothing pant of the front runners who have already misjudged it, be at one with the jockey who, narrow-eyed, twigs the fractional gap at the very moment they pass you ... but in all the years, I've never really seen a thing.

Yesterday I wore a swank Press pass and suit and actually saw the race; more guffaws than jokes; ladies with cheeks of porcelain but voices of tin; suits fit but toppers don't, or vice versa; starlets holding hands with shiny chins. For a start, the jockeys, those tight-cheeked waxwork leprechauns. Most, when they walked the paddock, looked as if it were their gate to the gallows.

The fascination yesterday was to walk down with the *nonpareil* Lester alongside the fancied Frenchman Samani. Piggott on the second favourite, Samani on the top shot. Both stared ahead like little girl saints going to martyrdom. I asked Piggott, a smile blinking fast as a radar sounding, if he remembered the very first race here of the Queen's reign; he didn't deadpan remember. Actually, 25 years ago, Charlie Smirke won on the romping *Tulyar*. Piggott was a fast second on *Gay Time*, and it threw the teenager as soon as it passed the post.

Always near Piggott from first to last yesterday was that other small, cold pile of outrageous statistics, Samani. In fact, he had even more pressure on him than the housewives' choice, Lester. He had never seen the track before, nor had his horse. His third place might be seen to be a courageous effort. But in fact the day was all Lester's. The tiny jockeys piled into the weighing-room. 'Could you stand on a chair

173

Willie?' we shouted at the runner-up. But no Lester came. No need. He's done it all before and as much for the art of conversation as Richard Dunn has done for the world heavyweight boxing rankings. He wins, not talks, that's all.

When he won his record seventh Derby last year, apparently, Lester nonchalantly threw his whip into his Epsom locker, stretched his tiny, wizened frame and said to his adoring chums: 'I hope the next seven come as easy as the first seven.' It seems they do.

---

## WORK FASCINATES ME, SAYS GEORGE, I COULD WATCH IT ALL DAY
### *November 1988*

A mug's game? 'Well, let's just say you can't win them all. Never have been able to, though the trouble now is that you can't even see them all, get a look at them, you know. Over my time, Newmarket's become simply overrun with horses.'

Unlike those furtive hustlers with the fistful of 'spares' who smarmily refer to themselves as turnstile brokers, George Robinson is proud to call himself a tout. His is an ancient and honourable sporting profession. He agrees some of his mates have begun to prefer the phrase 'work-watcher' but that, he reckons, is the way of the changing world. And 'blimey,' he says, 'my world's changed more than most.' As the thoroughbreds have increased and multiplied, so have Newmarket's touts diminished. You have to take the eminent George's word for that, mind, for the name of the game has always been very low-profile indeed.

If you can look like a tree or a scarecrow, all to the good. Spotability is definitely not an asset. Anyway, you have to get up very early indeed to catch a wink of dawn's sharp Suffolk sun glinting off their distant binoculars. 'It's a fallacy that we just hide behind hedges,' says George, quite put out by my very supposition. 'Certainly, it's often so parky that we have to shelter behind windbreaks up on the Heath, or in clumps of trees, like that belt of beeches we had up there before last

174

year's gale did for them.'

The arctic nor'easterlies, ripping down past the Wash as unstoppable as *Shergar*, are real blighters, he says. 'Thermal underwear is one revolution I'm glad I've been in on.' George Robinson is 74 next month. He is just getting over shingles and recent days are the first he has ever missed in nearly 42 years at the job. 'Racehorses don't understand Christmas,' he laughs, full of the perky joys again. 'Thermals and a *real* overcoat, sure, but boots are also important. And gloves, yes, sometimes it's so cold up there you can't feel your hands holding your bins, let alone the pencil to write up your notes.'

He is back to breakfast and a warm-up by nine or 10, then comes a lot of work deciphering all his frozen and patented hieroglyphics against the form book, and then his 'information' is winging its way to Wapping. George is one of the élite. He is Newmarket's man for both *The Times* and the *Sun*. He is one of the last of the breed. Changes? 'Oh my good Lord, it's a different world since I came up here in 1947. First thing I had to buy was my bible – you know, *Horses In Training*. It cost me a bob. Now it's £8.50 in new money. There were 800 horses up here in 1947, if we were lucky. Now it's well over 3,000. How can we get to see them all? In 1947, Frank Butters trained 60, Jack Jarvis had 44 in his string, the Captain [Sir Cecil Boyd-Rochfort] had only 39, and look at this – unbelievable – that old Major Beatty who was always trying those coups of his, well, he only had 13 horses in his yard. Thirteen! For all his talk. And now Henry Cecil has 250-odd, Cumani has over 200, likewise Mr Stoute.'

A self-respecting tout cannot possibly cover the lot, so you have to be very canny. Like George. You've got to know your gallops, who's out and who's in, and who might be really stretching this morning. 'You've got to know exactly where to go for best vantage: too close and, one blink, you've missed them. You've got to see them jump off, say a mile or a mile-and-a-quarter, see the whole string, and then turn and see the next lot somewhere else. I'm generally a Limekilns man myself – good vantage points.' The all-weather gallops have changed the job drastically. And in the old days horses did a lot of winter roadwork 'to harden the shins'. You could 'see all you wanted to, then. But with today's traffic, no hope.'

Also, it seems, it isn't often nowadays that you see much more than a glorified canter, around three-quarter pace: 'In the old days, gallops were for galloping. Blimey, that old clerk of the course we had, Mr Marriott, he'd be out there of a morning looking fierce, and if he saw a trainer allowing his string to have a canter he'd be down like a ton of bricks, turning them off and saying, "If you want to canter, go over there." He'd tell them, "These are gallops and they're *only* for galloping, sir." And off they'd have to get, however famous they were. And then, at breakfast time, out would come the harrows and rollers pulled by those great big Suffolk Punches. Now it's all tractors, mechanised – and cantering on the gallops....'

If George Robinson has been a legend, however furtive, at Newmarket for over 40 years, it all really started when he was in the RAF. 'I began to run a book, all very underhand – it wasn't allowed, of course, couldn't write anything down, all kept in my head. Well, *Mahmoud* won the Derby in 1936 and I was away. I still remember the second horse that day, you know, had a funny name, trained by old Frank Butters [the horse was, in fact, *Taj Akbar*] – well, if he'd won I'd have had a heart attack. Went all through the war, then my brother-in-law asked me to come up to join him in Newmarket.

'It's marvellously rewarding, spotting a real good 'un, you know. And you look them up, and you realise you knew their mother or father. You knew *Shergar* was something when you first saw him; a bit of a handful, mind, always messing about at first. But the one to really make my eyes pop out was *Prince Simon*. The Captain [Boyd-Rochfort] had him. What a mover, big-striding, so it must have been like you were riding a bike in top gear, you know, you had to crank up the momentum. What a horse.

'In the Derby, Glendenning, the commentator, said at Tattenham Corner: "It's unbelievable, he's just cantering." Then up the straight he was just loping, hacking up. Then *Galcador*, somehow, came through and stole the race from him. We couldn't believe it. But look it up, "1950 Derby, second *Prince Simon*." That's racing. So it was all on the St

Leger, and 10 days before Doncaster *Prince Simon* does this secret gallop. I'd never seen such a wonderful, wonderful gallop; he must be a cert, I thought; unfair to take anyone's money for anything else. But no, he didn't win that either, must have ate something, or stood on something ... but what a horse.'

Sir Gordon Richards was the best jockey he has seen. 'Mind you, I've seen much the best horsemen among the work riders – oh yes, lots of them are better actual horsemen than the course jockeys. Just before he died I passed Sir Gordon, and he actually recognised this old tout. He raised his hat and said, "Hello, getting on okay, fit and well, are you?" That was nice, a real gent.'

It all gets back to money, he admits. He is a very cautious punter himself. Never bets when he is working – watching, say, the first-time runners at the spring meetings. 'Even if you only put a pound on, you'll be watching "your" horse, you won't be concentrating on the others.' Surely the adrenalin bubbled when one of his unlikely fancies stormed home and his hedgerow hours in the bitter winds were seen to pay off? He butts in: 'I went berserk in the *Sun* that day – 1981 or 1982 it was – when suddenly I had suggested a bet of 990,000-1. I had five winners on the trot and then a second in the ruddy third at Doncaster. I remember that day, one of Clive Brittain's came in at 50-1.

'You win some, you lose some. The biggest disappointment ever was that *Pholoptepes*, he was a racing certainty that first race at Yarmouth. They'd even timed the distance from the car park to the course bookies, you could have got everything on – then they delayed the start, the money got back to the course, and then the thing goes and gets beat by real bad horses. And then, after that, it goes and wins everything all round the country. Too late. Another was that *Prince Oleg*, trained by Noel Murless, a big black horse. He was riveting first time I saw him move. Crikey, I thought, people should put their houses on this. Thought we had a real coup – then one morning they gallop him against an old grey thing and, all of a sudden, you saw he wasn't worth a light. Amazing, that sort of thing. In this game you've always got to be on the

177

look-out for bold eyes, strides and general speed – but if they can't accelerate, then something that seems the cat's whiskers won't be worth a light. Acceleration is the whole key.'

With the end of the Flat season, the tout's year is just beginning. The heavy rollers of the Turf have all by now flown off to follow their fancies under the sun. The tout stays home. At this time of year, George enjoys 'the markings' when the yearlings are introduced to the Heath. Now that his favourite Beech Belt copse has gone, he might 'hide up' of a withering morning behind a Birnam-Wood type of portable windbreak, or another spot he quite fancies, 'on New Ground, behind a shed and just peeping over the roof'. His 'markings' are just that. He furiously squiggles his own sign-language into his notebook, whether such-and-such a new horse has, say, a white blaze, or a dappled chest, a couple of white ankles, a bobtail or a grey mottle – and then, when the trainers issue their January list for next season, he can check the names against his list of first-look markings.

Traditionally, the swank trainers resent the touts, sniping with their binoculars at form and future odds from their furtive, frozen hidey-holes. The present lot of trainers are as civil as any have been – Mr Cecil is 'a real polite gentleman' and Mr Cumani will 'have a laugh and joke and a banter with any man'. George supposes that the thinning ranks of his fellow touts, to just two or three, has made the trainers more relaxed. In the old days there were always more than a dozen, lurking, skulking, scribbling, and glinting their glasses.

'That Major Beatty, he was the old bugger always out to beat us. If my favourite beat was Limekilns, dear old Chippie Jackson used to fancy the Racecourse site. That was his domain, up in his haystack. One morning, Beatty brings four horses down for a real trial; or so Chippie had heard. He's up in his haystack for nearly two hours, frozen, till Beatty turns up. He just can't see the start, so Chippie slips down from the stack for a better view. Beatty sees him, holds up the horses and strides across to the haystack. "Mornin' Jackson," he says.

' "Oh, hello, sir," says Chippie, pretending he's all innocent, like. Now, Beatty knows poor old Chippie's blind as a bat without his bins. So he says, "Nice pair of binoculars you've got there, Jackson. What make are they? Let's have a look at them."

'Chippie has to hand them over. The ruddy Major clamps them to his own eyes, doesn't he, and barks out the order to begin the trial. Poor old Chippie never saw a thing.'

You never really bothered about that sort of thing, says George, because the 'utter beauty of this game is that there's always tomorrow'. Talking of which, I say, what did George fancy for the morrow? 'Funny you ask me that,' he says, 'but if I was you I'd be sure to risk a few bob on this *Sharenara* in tomorrow's one o'clock at the big meeting.' I did. It started favourite and finished last. Well, as George says, you can't win 'em all.

---

## DREAD OF FAILURE THAT MAKES SCUDAMORE JUMP
### *November 1988*

The Flat season ends in this Saturday's tea-time murk at Doncaster, and the high rollers chase the sun elsewhere – and leave the world to winter and a very different breed of hoofer and hero. Now courage comes into the cavalry charge. Not to mention more laughter. Well, National Hunt racing is really much more fun. Much more innately British.

If it has so rompingly been Pat Eddery's year on the Flat, with the bold little Irishman's Mr Punch profile hooking his nose in front at the post more times by far than anyone else, the National Hunt's opening cavalry charge has been led with even more dramatic *élan* by its champion jockey, Peter Scudamore, already faster than anyone in history to a half-century of winners. Last week he went past that 50-up mark with more than a fortnight to spare over John Francome's 1984 record. By the spring, barring accidents, he should easily beat Jonjo O'Neill's all-time record total of 149 winners in a season, set back in 1977.

To be sure, barring accidents again, Scudamore seems booked to be the name of his game for the next generation.

Though, of course, in National Hunt racing, the phrase barring accidents is one uttered only by lunatics.

Scudamore is one of the new breed. Hell-raising, jorrocksing cavaliers no longer become champion jockeys over the sticks. 'When I began,' says the man all racing knows and respects simply as Scu, 'the fun of it, the devil-take-the-hind-most, the simply "taking part" bit, was still uppermost. Now it's all about fitness, concentration, professionalism, and winning.'

Scu is different, all right. Not many other men are there to greet you, as arranged, dead on time – it was outside his handsome stone house, halfway up a hill in the plushest part of the Cotswolds of glitzy Gloucestershire – and wanting to apologise that it is not as heavenly as homely Herefordshire.

'Sorry and all that,' he says, 'I'd have given anything for a day back in Hereford. It's one of my few days off in the next six months, it's one of the sparklingest days of autumn and I bet the old county's looking sublime.' Spivvy Glos is also looking okay, I say, and it must be all the better for having the owners and racing's other rich and necessary 'connections' on his doorstep.

In spirit, Scudamore remains a son of less-fashionable Hereford. His father, Michael, is one of that county's celebrated sons, once a famous jockey and now a trainer. Dad first plonked Peter on a horse long before he bought him his first grey-flannel mite's school uniform to go to the Belmont Abbey prep school, just across the border at Llanarth.

By the time he got back to Belmont itself as a senior, the Benedictine monks had marked out Peter not as a horseman but as a demon wing-forward at rugby. He still looks as if he could be severe and darkly determined in the tackle. Funnily enough, though, he loved cricket best.

He still does. He had made us each a mug of tea, the phone had suddenly stopped ringing every minute, he had kicked off his shoes and he seemed relaxed and high-stirruped on the sofa at last, and so – with the likes of Cheltenham and Newbury in mind – I asked him about his very best day so far this year.

He did not need to think long. 'No question about it,

180

Worcester. Glorious day. Against Yorks. Hick comes in, that businesslike walk to the wicket, you know. He scored a hundred, of course. Sublime. Every ball. He just kept getting better and better.

'Bliss to be there witnessing greatness, knowing you were in on some sort of sporting beginnings of history.' With reflections like that, as if a blind has been lifted, Scudamore loses his taciturn, beetle-browed worry-pot image. You fancy he might have lived too long in the shadow of the onliest Francome, been too long the runner-up to a colourful pre-eminence whose name was a byword and whose vim and jaunty presence – and impeccable flair as a horseman – brought warm pleasure to the whole sport's remembrance.

Scudamore not only followed Francome as champion jockey, but also, like Dick Francis before both of them, as an author. He has two hardback titles on the library shelves, and his latest, *On Steeplechasing*, is as solemn, un-racy and, it must be said, unputdownable as a formula-ed Francis. But was he still in awe of Francome's genius?

'Oh, yes, I suppose, in a way. Who wouldn't be? He was a man apart, we all accepted that in the weighing-room. So did every man in the street or on the course. In a way John's retirement created extra pressures for me, as I immediately felt I had to be champion after him. If I failed when he left, well, there were no excuses left.

'I feel the memory of John in that privileged corner of our changing-room, the champion's peg, and it drives me on still. Once he'd packed up, I was never going to be totally satisfied with just being champion jockey twice, three or even four times. I must confess I want to be champion more times than John ever was, and more again. Not for any selfish reason, or wish to put his records down, but just for my own satisfaction. Success is my one driving force, you see.' Francome, he says, was 'a wonderful man and colleague'.

He added: 'Though John often accused me of taking life too seriously, of being too deep and intense, it never occurred to me that I was not enjoying life just as much. We only had different ways of showing it.

'I often wonder really what he thought of me when I

181

started trying to challenge him for the top spot. I dare say he thought me a bit dull, but once he'd got in his car to drive off for the next day's meeting, I suppose he never really gave me much thought at all.'

But it was a different breed of jockey that Scu had been brought up with, on his father's fields at Hoarwithy, near Ross. Terry Biddlecombe would be over regularly, passing on tips to the boy like he was handing out breakfast brandies and bonhomie. 'He'd say "Don't ride too short, lad" – and there was old Biddles with his ankles round his ears. But what a kind man and a hero, too, he was to me.

'Then there was Stan Mellor, tough and determined; dear Jonjo with his exceptional finishing drive; and Jeff King, who could drag horses over the line if need be. My father always said Jeff was the best rider who ever rode, but he never put himself out to try to be champion. Perhaps it was because he couldn't be bothered with ambition and ruthlessness, or perhaps he had an inner peace in him that didn't need to bother to read how good he was in next morning's papers.'

Scudamore now rides, first choice, for the stables of Martin Pipe ('an utter genius, no less') or the legendary Fred Winter. It makes for a long day, schooling at dawn with one or the other, Pipe down at Taunton, Winter at Lambourn. He is there before most of us are awake – head down, bottom up through the morning mists – before driving to the races in his long-hauler.

'Don't ask me how far Fontwell is in miles. All I know, like any jockey, is that it's two hours, 35 minutes, that Wincanton's two hours 55, that Ludlow is, say, two hours 10, and so on. We drive more hours than we are in the saddle racing.

'But we all have our music. I'd go mad without Springsteen, Dire Straits and the Eurythmics belting out. I'd love to be more classical, I suppose, but they could well increase the depression while I battle back along the M25 after that always fraught day taking on those dreadful slippery slopes at Plumpton.'

The two rampaging, much-loved sons are not back yet from the village school. Scudamore is not sure whether he will be able to send them one day to Belmont. But the phone has started screeching again: he does all his own bookings, though he has just appointed a 'brilliant' morning secretary since his wife Marilyn, a teacher, has found a job at some nearby stables. It is a long way from the Flat's champion-elect jockey, with his chauffeur, private Cessna aircraft and 100-acre estate farm in the Home Counties.

But there is not the slightest jealousy about Pat Eddery. 'He's a little wonder, no less. Even in my own field, never try and draw envious comparisons. Sure, they say I try to spend my life worrying about my own targets and standards. Well, what's wrong with that? Any professional man should.

'But just help others on the way, while always seeking out the satisfaction of the highest possible standards for yourself. At times I know I seem bloody miserable when things are going wrong, and I'm a candidate for euthanasia because the dread of failure is as powerful a motivator as it ever was. But I just want to achieve the highest possible standard for myself. What's wrong with that?'

We had another mug of tea. The kids charged in from school and, it being one of Dad's few days off for the next six months, I made an excuse and left. The winter was drawing in and the real horsemen of England were getting ready to go.

# 9

# SOCCER TO ME, BABY

It has always been a much loved game. Even at a rugger playing school, a bunch of us were happy to be regularly martyred for the cause – six of the best from the sadistic Fr Norbert for daring to play penalty area 'three-and-in' with a stupid oblong ball after rugby practice was over. My father and uncle first took me to see Fulham play at Villa Park when I was about nine. I can still remember the cataclysmic thrill that day gave me, the vast throng at one in spirit and delight and will. In fact, Fulham won and I have supported them ever since. But alas, has soccer become the first to inspire this middle-aged slob's tired old juices to curdle? The *Independent*'s brilliantly invigorating soccer writer, Paddy Barclay – as well as the more considered *Guardian* guru, David Lacey – are two friends I admire who have not become as jaded as me. So it's not a generation thing. Then why am I only enchanted now with soccer's olde tyme rhythms, the sweet airs of my youth? I saw Pelé, and Puskas before him; Charlton and Law in their prime; and Rodney and George. When those last two came down by the riverside a dozen years ago to play out their last half season as a farewell act at Fulham – well, after that, I knew I could take it or leave it, and do something else on Saturdays. When the incomparable Best finally departed an awful lot left with him. Except, of course, the memories.

# MOMENTS OF PURE TOSH
*April 1975*

Johnny Haynes was England's captain and unquestionably Fulham's finest footballer. But he was never what we reckoned to be your actual Fulham-type player. For one thing he was far, far too good. For another, he wasn't half eccentric enough. Haynes suffered 18 glorious, exasperated years for Fulham, carpeting out the world's most sumptuous passes to a motley crew of single-jointed unappreciative nuts; a Brylcreemed Schweitzer among the pygmies.

Going down to Fulham on Saturdays when Chelsea were playing away was part of the corduroy scene in the 1950s and early 1960s. They were, as John Moynihan said in his joyous chronicle of the times (*Soccer Syndrome*, MacGibbon and Kee), 'a Saturday afternoon team, offering a feeling of animated recreation rather than solid professionalism ... a side of happy, sometimes comic triers watched by garrulous actors, serious actors, pantomime players, band-leaders, stuntmen, starlets; tweeds, black leather, green leather, pink ankle-length knickers, baggy overcoats over armour-plated suede, cheroots between thumb and first finger.' They were days when a joint was a jazz cellar, LSD was a couple of Friday fivers, a trip was a moonlight bedsit flit – and dope, more often than not, was Bedford Jezzard's latest signing from the Hellenic League.

Liquid lunch, long walk alongside the cemetery past tiny, prim houses called 'Hazeldene' to marvel in wonder at Haynes – and to groan and wring our hands with him when the little men forgot to run on to – or even ran away from – those lancing, expansive long passes. He was too good for us, too; and really we turned up to love the fellows who forgot. What a litany: that loping trier, Maurice Cook, who could never quite fathom what Johnny was at; it was like Laurel and Hardy. Every resigned dismissive shrug by Haynes made Maurice simper with inferiority. And could it have been Maurice who ran out one afternoon with that high-stepping

185

dressage I'll-show-'em swank – and promptly doubled-up with a hamstring and was stretchered off even before the kick off?

Over the years they came and went. But mostly came and stayed: Arthur Stevens, grizzle-haired wigman, who'd be wound up at the start to run the full 90 minutes – but only in straight lines. 'They Also Swerve' we used to plain-chant at him. Arthur was the original subject of the legendary theatre-bill joke – 'This will run and run' – F. Cashin, *D. Sketch*. Then there was Jimmy ('Give it to the Rabbi') Hill – whom, of course, we still know and love. Jim, to be sure, scored many thousands of outstanding goals – but on double-checked reckoning he also muffed about 971 sitters (plus two half chances). One now famous actor said on the terraces that Jim only patented that piratical growth on his chin because he thought it might make him play like Charlie Buchan (don't strain yourself working it out, corny humour's changed too).

And what about Killer Keetch? Blond and butch, fancy in his pointed Eyetie patents, but a devil in boots, no shinpad had an earthly. Horrors, we even loved him that afternoon he got stuck into Bobby Charlton. He'd be jeaned and conspicuously casual down the Portobello on a Saturday morning – after a casual canter down Rotten Row – sniffing out bargains for his junk (sorry, high class antiques emporium) shop, outstanding headscarfed brunette snuggling into his armpit; at 2.30 (unless stated) he'd wickedly set about some unsuspecting and innocent No 9 shirt; by 6.30 he'd be downing a few swifties at the Queen's Elm, settling himself up for 10-ish and eyeball-to-eyeball confrontation with outstanding blonde over candles and white tablecloths of L'Ecu de France or some such gracious nosherie. (Why didn't Parky write a book on Keetch, for heaven's sake?)

Earlier, there was Eddie Lowe, the statutory baldy at wing-half alleged to have lost all his hair overnight, through the shock of reading one of Walter Winterbottom's coaching pamphlets on peripheral vision. Or Jim Langley, bow-legged back with convict's crew-cut who, astonishingly, played for England and didn't let us down (though we were terribly worried for him) and then taught that tubby antelope George Cohen all he knew about overlapping and George became the best in the biz.

Our last great joy at Craven Cottage was the young Rodney. In a way Marsh was more of a genius then, simply because he hadn't yet realised it; only we nobodies were telling him and he, sheepish then, thought we were taking the mickey. For one season, just about the final one of those lovely winters, we'd go and watch Marsh in the reserves. Once, the goalkeeper was injured and Rodney excitedly bagged the polo-neck and gloves for himself, but when the first corner came over the dear nut tried to tip it over the top with a flying bicycle kick. Own goal.

Rodney, as a teenager, rated self-education. His bible was *Pears' Cyclopaedia*. He carried it with him everywhere and learned pages by heart. On away train trips George Cohen would solemnly have to hear him – 'Right, ready: World's Longest Rivers. Ready?' – and he'd close his eyes and recite 'Amazon 28 billion yards', or whatever, 'Limpopo 19 billion ...' right down to the blooming Arno. When Rodney went deaf and almost had to pack up completely after he had nutted the crossbar with an almighty clang, it was sad, era's end – but it was also pure, undiluted Fulham.

But of all of them, most pure and undiluted Fulham was Tosh Chamberlain, winger supreme. It was Tosh who refused to get up after a hard tackle, saying he'd sit the game out 'until that bleeding ref apologises'. It was Tosh who once snapped the flag clean in two when he mistimed a corner kick (if the stick had carried we all bet that Maurice would have nodded it home). It was Tosh who once broke the ribs of his own goalkeeper, Tony Macedo, with a ferocious back-pass. Tosh was the only one who'd audibly swear back at Haynes – indeed once the referee, Mervyn Griffiths, Bethesda Chapel and all that, almost booked him for it.

The team's much slicker now. And there's an impressive grandstand covering the bank from where we used to watch the Boat Race – and invariably miss Fulham's one goal of the month. And they've got two ex-England captains now instead of one. But Tom Trinder, great stand-up comic, still sits down in the directors' box; and the thing to remember about all the foregoing list of loves is that, for all the memory of endearing incompetence, those sides were, more often than not, in the First Division – or rather, they were *quite* often there, and once in, it must be said, they spent all their time frenziedly trying to stay there. (Someone once tried to get a new nickname going for them, the Fokker Wolves – 'bloody miraculous how they stay up'.) But they finished 10th in the First Division once, in 1960. And they're no newts to FA Cup semi-finals. They lost in a replay in 1962, and in 1958 when Manchester United, rebuilt by Jimmy Murphy after the Munich crash, beat them by 5-3 with all the world praying for a Fulham defeat. The atmosphere was too much for Macedo, whose fine talent in goal had been instrumental (with Haynes') in getting them that far, but on the day he flapped and fumbled like a schoolgirl.

By and by, and hopefully not relevantly, Fulham's present goalkeeper, Peter Mellor has done more than most to get them to Hillsborough tomorrow; but he has been living with a reputation throughout his career as being prone to the most appalling gaffes – his colleagues cheerfully admit to calling him Teflon (non-stick) or Daffodil (he only comes out once a year). But he played a marvellous game in the sixth round, apparently, and if he catches everything tomorrow he will scotch the sniggering murmurs for ever. For himself. And for Fulham.

And if they do get to Wembley, unbelievable thought, the 1950s mob must have a reunion: laughter and memories. Who wouldn't pay a paypacket to hear J. Haynes rollicking Maurice again? Or Tosh showing Les Barrett how to take right-foot away, swinging corners from the left with the outside of his boot: 'The damn trouble is, lad, the damn flagpole makes it so damn difficult.'

# SUNSHINE AND BEST
*January 1977*

George Best exhibited another riveting little cameo for Fulham on Saturday, yet to the pedantic mandarins of Lytham St Anne's he is still on trial. Not until his probationary three-month period is up in two weeks' time, say these astonishing bureaucrats, will they give their decision on whether the Irish wizard will be allowed to stay and earn his crust in League football.

Just what can they be up to, when here we all are grasping and begging for the veriest crumb of quality? Even now, George Best remains one of the very, very few players with the ability to let the sunshine blaze through the dowdy, grey skies of our national professional game. Indeed, there is a case for the Lancashire pin-stripes to flop on their knees and plead with George to stay among us. We need him more than he needs us, this Huckleberry who really seems to have found his Mississippi down at the lazy, lovely old Thames.

On Saturday against Oldham – just as he had done the week before at Blackpool apparently – Best not only chased and harried with single-minded fervour on a skid-pan pitch, but warmed the very cockles with a collection of outrageously silky doodles that all the swank art galleries should have been falling over themselves to buy. He had some sort of hand in all Fulham's five goals, and in scoring the fourth himself, he put his signature to a glorious day with an exquisite flourish. Twenty yards from goal, and dead in front, he fastened on to a loose ball; no one to pass to, two pals ahead of him were offside. He lazily beat a man, sensed the goalkeeper straying from his line, so he chipped the thing over his head in the gentlest parabola. Like Nicklaus caressing his way out of the wickedest sand trap. The ball kissed the crossbar on the way, fell over the line and dropped dead, with the poor goalie on his backside and all of us beside ourselves with the marvel of it.

If that was the virtuoso's solo, the goal before it was,

collectively, almost as thrilling. This time Best, deep inside his own half, sold some slithering hatchetman a dummy de-luxe, released Mitchell with a stunning 40-yard pass and Maybank's forehead thundered home the centre. Maybank had already scored the second and Mitchell got the first and last. They both played very well, strapping enthusiasts each. Who will make room for Marsh when that worthy's pirouetting ankle mends? Neither of them on this form.

---

# BRIDGE OF SIGHS
### *December 1978*

Don't worry, they said, about the English national team. They do not reflect the strength and skill of our national game. Go on any Saturday to the English First Division to convince yourself that it remains the most competitive, the most attractive. It is still the envy of the world, they said. I took my biro to Stamford Bridge, but nobody asked for an adjective. Chelsea v Middlesbrough, Young Lions v Old Hands.

The first needless back-pass to the goalkeeper came after 38 seconds. Thereafter the end-to-end ding-dong clash went something like this;

Needless back-passes: Chelsea 10, Middlesbrough 16.

Aimless goalies' pass punts to centre circle: Chelsea 12, Mbo 23.

Inaccurate passes less than 22 yards: Chelsea 32, Mbo 18.

Accurate passes over 40 yards: Chelsea 4, Mbo 7.

Noticeable time wasting: Chelsea 10, Mbo 16.

Diagonal centres pumped hopefully into penalty area: Chelsea 33, Mbo 16.

Obviously considered ploys inside area: Chelsea 3, Mbo 6.

Free kicks pumped hopefully into area: Chelsea 14, Mbo 6.

Jersey pulling: Chelsea 14, Mbo 17.

Professional fouls: Chelsea 5, Mbo 9.

Amateurish fouls: Chelsea 10, Mbo 7.

Goalkeepers slightly extended (i.e. not fielding back-passes or catching said diagonal centres): Bonetti 2, Platt 3.

Triers: Langley, Ashcroft.
Talent submerged in mediocrity: Wilkins, Souness.
Terrace songs without noticeable swear words: 1.
Terrace songs with noticeable swear words: 6.
Crowd: 21,000.
Break even crowd necessary to balance book: 28,000.
Duration: 92 minutes.
Result: Chelsea 0, Middlesbrough 0.
Quotes: Neal – 'We were worse against Derby.' Shellito – 'We don't believe in ourselves.'
Television title: 'Match of The Day'.

---

## MELANIE'S DAD JOINS THE RED PILGRIMAGE
*May 1977*

The high spot of our day was going to the airport to meet the Liverpool team in the late afternoon. Till then we were happy to fill in time hanging around St Peter's making friendly Scouse jokes about the Pope and splashing boorishly around the fountains both to cool off in the sweltering heat as well as to annoy the thousands of tourists who, when they planned their pilgrimage, hadn't banked on having their Rosary upset by anthems and arias from the New Kirkby Hymnal.

The ancient old Bellini pillars that perfectly ring St Peter's Square have been witness to many a good and heartfelt tune over the centuries but none before, I warrant, that accompanied this sort of lyric:

We say to you Eyeties, give
    up your ice cream
Throw it away and come see
    you our team
If you don't bring your Pope
We won't bring you our Queen
Just come and give 'cheers'
    to our beautiful team
We know you'll admit it's a

191

        side very rare
And if you need another
        cathedral
We've got one to spare.

That was sung by a clutch of about 30 red and white
Koppites, aged from 12 to 50, yesterday lunchtime. And all
day more have been arriving. So far there's scarce been a
German to be seen. The Italians, meanwhile, continue with
warnings about the terrors of the English soccer hooligan. We
shall see. Certainly yesterday the whole temper of the visitors,
while ultimately becoming a bit of a bore, never went further
than that displayed by only slightly over-exuberant Blackpool
day-trippers. The Romans can't see it like that though.
Apparently tomorrow the police at the Olympic Stadium
promise more snapping dogs than Battersea could ever
dream of. Over 30,000 tickets have been sold in Italy and we
are promised that, to a man, they will be supporting Borussia.

To the airport to meet their team. On the way, halfway up
the Spanish steps a young red was sleeping off the night
before, but his banner still fluttered his message: 'Heighway
Sells More Dummies Than Mothercare'. And later, plans
were being made to spend the evening encamped outside the
players' hotel. Just to be near them. Young Joey Jones seems
the new Kop favourite. 'D'you know,' said one fellow in the
bar alongside St Mary Maggiore, 'he's been a Koppite since he
was eight; he had LFC tattooed on his right arm when he was
13. You ask him to show you.'

In the same bar, two older men grew misty-eyed. They see
tomorrow night as the culmination of Liverpool's 12-year run
in European competitions. They had travelled to the 1965
European Cup semi-final against Inter-Milan. Liverpool had
won the first leg easily but Milan had gone through after
walloping them in the San Siro. They still remembered every
detail. 'It was sheer bloody robbery. Their first goal came with
a free kick, indirect, which they scored from direct. Their
second was a blatant foul on poor Tommy Lawrence. But
their third, Facchetti scored it, made me burst into tears.
Never, ever, did that through the war. Do you know, truth,

when I got back home I never spoke to my Judy for three weeks ... not one bleeding word for 21 whole days.' Both of them had a great love for Liverpool's two present veterans, Smith and Callaghan. They were playing on that maudlin night in Milan. Both will be on duty tomorrow evening a dozen glorious years on. 'I only hope we can do it, not for me, not for any of us, but just for those two, Cally and old Smithy.' Not to mention, thought I, for his Judy.

Supporters paying their £100 and more range from retired dockers to Kirkby dole-queuers to a pretty 25-year-old Lewisham schoolteacher. Three hopefuls are due to arrive tomorrow morning after driving all the way in a Bedford van they only bought last Thursday for £70. Twenty years in exile, he usually hitchhikes to Liverpool's games in England. He told me about his family. 'My first son's called Ian St John. When our daughter was being born, I was there in the waiting room at the Royal Sussex. Nurse comes out and says "It's a girl". I had me two bob ready. I telephoned Anfield. I said: "I know Shank's old lady's called Nessie, but what's her baptismal name?" The secretary said she couldn't divulge it. The pips went so I said to the secretary: "What's your name then?" "Melanie" she says. So that's why my daughter's called Melanie isn't it?'

---

# TOTAL DESPAIR – AND NO RELIEF THIS TIME

*May 1985*

One more corpse was carried from the Heysel Stadium in Brussels last night. Soccer itself – draped in the Union Jack. It deserved to be spat upon. The game in Britain will certainly have a long, long time to mourn. Liverpool will certainly be made an example of, for sure. It is ironically tragic that, up to last night, they were proud at Anfield of their reputation.

The half dozen other clubs – certainly the English ones – who have qualified for European competitions next season will surely be missing from the respective hats when the draws

193

are made later this summer. The England team itself could well be struck from the World Cup to be played next year in Mexico – and Scotland, Wales and Northern Ireland, come to that. Followers of the England team have, if anything, hitherto been worse than those packs who follow the clubs that have rampaged through European cities for a couple of decades now. Even last week I was glad I was a second-man reporting the extra-mural activities of the supporters when England played in little Finland.

'Football is dead – the hooligans have won,' said Emlyn Hughes on the radio last night. The former Liverpool captain was in abject despair at the microphone as he and the commentator, Peter Jones, combined to produce a dramatic and harrowing war correspondent's dispatch, live from the stadium. Television might have had the pictures but they also had bland, weary public-relations spokesmen and the two radiomen were quite brilliant in describing the wretched scenes from the bunker hut.

Stunned, I found myself pulling my car onto the hard shoulder. It was going to be an extremely good day off – a sublime, silvery-blue, cricketing afternoon in the country, a drive back to base and a televised match between the two finest soccer teams in Europe. Jones and Hughes breathlessly pulled the black blinds down. 'It's no use,' said Hughes, 'fannying on about cancelling special trains or building higher fences – that sort of stuff is meat and drink to these hooligans.' For hooligans, now read murderers.

Mrs Thatcher must now show the mettle of her will – indeed, of her whole reputation. She will obviously wish this morning she had never thrown down the gauntlet with, which it seemed at the time, such little thought after the Luton–Millwall affair. Brussels, 1985, could yet mean more to her than the Falklands, 1982. If that war when many young men died helped make her electoral majority, then Liverpool's war in Brussels could well dilute it on the grand scale.

# I CAN FEEL IT COMING ON
*June 1986*

Shot of the week, according to the plonking, adenoidal East Ender, Trevor Brookin', was when the Russian, Rats, beat the groping gloveman of France, Bats. Rats and Bats – we'll come to these crazy names in a tick but yes, er, Trev, I agree with you there, er, it was one of the, er, few times so far that the, er, riggin' was really hissin'. Stephen Potter invented the word 'plonking' – that is, if you have nothing to say, or rather something extremely stupid and obvious, say it, but in a plonking tone of voice, i.e. roundly, but hollowly and dogmatically. The week has been full of plonking.

Personally, I preferred the commentaries from London when the sound broke down. Less frenetic. More calm. Do we really want a hysteric reading the Seoul telephone directory out to us after midnight for the full 90 minutes? But a million phonecalls wanted to know what was going on. 'Don't ask me,' said the urbane Brian Moore, 'I don't even know how a lawn-mower works.'

My Shot of the Week was Bobby Robson, having literally missed the team bus after Tuesday night's calamity, standing forlorn in the car park waiting for a lift while the Portuguese players V-signed him from their coach. A nation strained forward in their seats. Was he going to burst into tears? Bobby's been building up for the most convulsive blub for years. Was this the moment? Not quite, but it's on its way, I'm telling you. When they interview England managers for the job do they test them for the glycerine in their tear ducts? And for their resigned and rubbery lip movements. Greenwood was almost more of a Les Dawson landlady than Robson. At least Ramsey was always being more careful about the precision of his aspirates than the weeping collapse of his aspirations.

Yes, er, I agree with you there Trev, as they hit the road to Morocco, it was a bad week on the box for the Robson clan. (BBC Radio have even got a reporter out there called Mark

Robson, for heaven's sakes.) Bryan became the only World Cup captain to *arrive* at the match in an ambulance and as for Bobby I was fearing the worst even on Saturday night when he affixed to his face that smile of the most tortured optimism and told ITV: 'We've trained hard. We are ready. I will send out the lads with just two little words – "have some self-belief in yourselves" ' and nor did it add up on Tuesday – though if I hear anyone say 'it's early days yet' or 'at the end of the day' I'll have a little sob myself.

Scoop of the week was BBC's London Plus on Tuesday evening early when they wheeled in a Rabbi Romaine, from Maidenhead, to spout the Old Testament. If the sound lines had been working, Robson and Ireland's Billy Bingham would have got the message. For Bingham, prophetically, the good book warned 'Make ye haste to prepare a defensive wall'. For Bobby, from Proverbs, 'The net is spread in vain' and, for England's rooted back four, from Psalms, 'When my foot slips they magnify themselves against me.' Nice one, Rabbi.

I will also volley the set into the top corner if anybody else describes Shilton as the best goalie the universe has ever seen. That may be so, but only five minutes before our polo-necked Rambo in the lurex shorts was unravelling himself and the ball from the netting, Jimmy Hill was awesomely sermonising 'There's not an aspect of goalkeeping that Shilts hasn't got covered.' Oh yeah. The night before, Brian Clough, from London, had asked Shilton for his views on the Portuguese. 'Well, boss,' said Shilts, thinking fast, 'I don't know anything except that I went there for my holidays last year.'

Dearie me, the Panel. How dreary. It may be that Cloughie should be over there as England manager – but as a pundit these days it's as if he's turned up to do a turn on Spitting Image. Quite literally, warts 'n' all. He should stop playing the above-it-all weary, eyebrowed mandarin and get his act together. One expects something lucid, knowing and even provocative from him, not patronising, plonking, posing. Unless he has gone too far.

Of the others, Andy Gray is at least cheerful; Brian Hamilton looks dolefully like he's come from a hard day driving the hearse. On which subject, I enjoyed the line from the sage, Hill, after one of England's rare attacks had again fizzled out – 'Once more Bryan was in the box at the death.' Terry Venables is shrewd and foxy-sharp, but where's all that jaunty perkiness gone? Emlyn, too, seems to have been told to go easy on the natural effervescence. Keegan's hairdo is as old-fashioned as ever. I'm a Channon man myself; it's always refreshing to have a good old earthy Wessex burr talking sense; he still knows it is more difficult on the pitch than up there in the commentary eyrie, and his pronunciation of England's forward as LINN-ACRE must be retained. Orgasm of the week, by the way, was David Pleat's 'ooh, he's got a lovely composed left foot.'

'Be very brief, Trev,' said Moore to Francis in Italy, 'do you think Beardsley should play?' 'Very briefly Bri,' said Trevor, 'I've never ever seen him play.' Next question.

I remember spending days of my life during the last World Cup in Mexico, in 1970, travelling to Puebla and Toluca with Barry Davies, helping him learn the teams off by heart. Long parrot-fashioned, often hyphenated litanies of unknown dagoes and gringoes. He got them word perfect. But was anyone any the wiser? Poor old Barry's doubtless still at it this morning with some other poor sod holding the cribs – 'Oh Yun-Kyo, Parn Kyung-Hoon, Huw Jung Moo …'. When the commentators criticise these unknowns so knowingly, I'm reminded of the one-line theatre review by Dorothy Parker on a German actor – 'Guido Natzo was natzo guido.' In fact, only Brooking was prepared, as he would say, to 'take them on'. He just identifies his foreigners as 'No 17' or 'No 13'. Like any sane man.

Just before the Derby on Wednesday afternoon, ITV went over to the stunned England training camp. Sansom and Hoddle had pulled themselves together to run the Epsom Book. They all went for *Dancing Brave* – which lost, coming from behind too late. Omens everywhere. Jim Rosenthal suggested the team put a tenner on for the manager – on *Wise Counsellor*. They did. It came last.

I can feel it coming on, alas, and this Bobby blub could yet be the most apocalyptically soggy thing in the history of the handkerchief. Mind you, you have to feel sorry for the commentators. Training for years, fighting to make the squad. Before Sansom missed his man on Tuesday, Hill, tortuous as ever, apologised to the nation – 'I am sorry if you can hear me gripping this microphone so tightly. It's the tension. Not the tension of commentating. But the tension we are all feeling, for it's England's first match.'

---

# WHY UNCLE ROY IS DRAWING A VEIL OVER THE NEW SPROSON DOMAIN
*January 1988*

Just like the old days, it's a Cup tie Saturday in the Potteries. Us versus Them or, as we are allowed to say on these occasions, minnows and giants. Port Vale versus Tottenham Hotspur, the people against the gentry. Such matches were made for men called Sproson to get stuck in and do what a man had to do.

Phil Sproson, six foot bulwark of Port Vale's defence today against the strolling players of Spurs is a one-club man, answering over 400 League and Cup calls to the colours. But that's not half the matches his Uncle Roy managed in a playing career that, almost unbelievably, spanned 1950 to 1971.

While the passionate 'oohs' and 'aahs' and cheers and sighs this afternoon swirl all around nephew Phil in the muddy slop and slap and siege of the penalty area, some of them will be carried down on the chill winds from the bleak ridge of Burslem's Vale Park and be heard most certainly by Uncle Roy as he administers one of his three newsagent's shops down the hill. Roy Sproson will pretend not to hear, intimate in his affable, bluff and comradely manner that he doesn't give a fig for football any more.

When Roy Sproson was sacked as Port Vale's manager after serving the club, man and boy, for 25 years he vowed never to set foot in the place again, never even to glance up at the tumbledown old arena as he passes it time and again each

198

day. He has kept his resolution. This afternoon it will be tested severely, I fancy. Roy is in his greying middle 50s now, still a strapping man, as successful in business as he was down the years in his own half of a football field – more so, for when he drove away from Vale Park for the last time it was in a Cortina. Now he cruises about in a Mercedes.

'I never even looked back in the driving mirror. I'd worked there a quarter of a century. I've never set foot in the place from that day to this, and never will. I just can't, don't know why really. Other than Phil, I couldn't even tell you this Saturday's team. A manager can smell the end of his time, you know. The whole club reeks with an imminent sacking. Not that they actually say "you're bloody fired". It's all innuendo and muttering, you know, "things not going too well are they?" but you know they're after your blood – and if truth were told you already had your bags packed for weeks.'

C'mon, surely when you get up at five o'clock for the papers this Saturday morning, you'll make your cup of tea, look at the weather and think 'a good day for the Cup, eh?' and just get a bit misty-eyed and the old brain box will shuffle through a few of the memories?

'No, I won't.' Bet you will. 'I won't, promise.' I don't believe you, not even 1954 when Vale got to the semi-final? 'No, all behind me now, that.' Get away with you, fourth round of the Cup, 34 years ago to the very Saturday, Vale v Cup holders, Blackpool, all the stars and Stan Matthews back at the Potteries? The grin gets broader. 'Oh yes, okay, if you force me, I can't forget that.' The eyes glaze over. 'I was marking Ernie Taylor. No disrespect, but he was arrogant, jibing at me all through. When we looked like winning, I started getting back at him, "come and watch me in the next round, Mr Taylor". I was only a cocky kid then. At the end, Taylor just walked off, wouldn't shake hands. Stanley took it very well though, but I bet he was mad inside.'

When he was a sprog at Oakhill School before the war Roy used to wait every day at the bus stop at Trent Vale for a sight of his hero going to Stoke for training. Once Matthews had got on the bus, the boy would hare to school. When he grew up he had to mark him in the Cup tie against Blackpool. 'Stan was even more of a genius close to. I fancied myself as a tackler. Suddenly, he's coming at me down the touchline, jockeying, shimmying, his classic situation. Lo and behold he goes and shoves the ball too far in front of him: he's given it me. I smile to myself and think "watch this, folks, I'm bloody taking the ball off Matthews". Then bloody hell, unbelievable. Just as my toe was an eighth of an inch from the ball, he's found another gear, two ruddy gears, and his toe comes and sniffs it past me and he's skipping over my sliding leg and is away. I didn't just think I had him, I knew I had him – and now here I was flat on my backside realising genius is really genius, and the crowd all laughing.'

We are in one of his shops at Cobridge. A few hundred yards away is Arnold Bennett's old house in Waterloo Road. A few doors along is a mosque. Up there, Vale Park and its pylons looks damply forlorn, plucking up courage for Saturday. Outside sit the sponsored cars emblazoned with the players' names. Phil is now the big man at the back. Twenty years ago or so, he first went to watch his uncle play. 'It was against Brentford. I was so proud of him. Nobody believed he was my uncle till he came and tapped me on the head to prove it at the end. No, it's no matter he doesn't watch us now, he gives me advice whenever I've needed it.'

The home dressing-room is friendly, comfortable chairs and a carpet even. The visitors' room is like a barn. Cheerless, cold tiles, a slim bench round the walls, and one large ancient bathtub. 'This room's our secret weapon for Spurs,' says Phil, 'not forgetting their lukewarm pot of tea for half time.' His uncle chortles when I pass on the tactic. 'With any luck, Spurs might be in for a culture shock: out of their stockbroker houses and warm, snug luxury coach – straight into that huge cold room. There are omens too this week from that Blackpool match. It has rained all week, and our rain can chill the marrow.

'It chilled Blackpool. We'd spent days drying out the pitch with coal sacks, wringing them with mangles, even shovelling the water off, then forking and rolling so it looked quite reasonable till you trod on it and you'd sink in well over the top of your boots. Might be like that this Saturday. Then we'd soaked the leather ball in water for 24 hours – filling one of those screw-lid buckets with warm water and screwing the ball down into it for a day. After lunch on Saturday, out it comes, dry off the surface water, and then a coat of dubbin so it looked all right. But it weighed more than a cannonball. Then for the kick in we gave Blackpool a few old balls, dry and light and pumped up like balloons. After that they could hardly kick the match ball off the deck.'

So there you are, Roy, you see it took me no time to get you back in the mood for football? He grins some more and nods acknowledgement. 'Phil is a good stopper, more defensive than me perhaps, I started off as a wing-half of course, a left-sider who could run all day. People complain about the players today, but they're all right, pretty good. But no, you still won't get me up there even to see that Waddle or Ardiles, can't really explain why, but I'll never go again. It was already a younger man's game when I packed up at 41. But it had been a real good life. I came out of National Service and was suddenly earning £8 a week and £4 in the summers. That was more than my brother, Phil's dad, was getting as a skilled engineer.'

He played 761 League games. Only beaten narrowly by Trollope of Swindon (770), and Dickinson (764) of Portsmouth. 'Might have beaten them: one season I was off injured for 21 games.' At 41 he tossed his muddy kit into the laundry skip and tried life in a collar and tie as the manager. 'Any manager in football with a streak of reality or reason knows that sooner or later he's going to be crucified. I couldn't have been one of those blokes, good friends of mine too, you see at these annual get-togethers who just can't leave football alone. It's in their bloodstream like inky fingers are on news-agents' hands, and they scrimp and save for jobs scouting on wet Wednesdays on the Cheshire League and go round touching forelocks and cringing in front of directors. It's sad and pathetic, and there's an awful lot of them about I'm afraid.'

He will be up at five this morning and, okay, if you press him he might have a squint to see what the papers say about Port Vale's chances. By 9.30 he will be back home till the afternoon. Then, around four o'clock, he'll be driving back to organise the

201

evening rush. Won't he even glance up at the windswept paddock? 'I doubt it.' Not even switch on the radio for the half-time score? 'Yes I suppose I will, blast it' and he laughs at himself for his cussedness. 'Deep down, I really hope they do okay. I can't explain really why I couldn't bring myself to go, but like Arnold Bennett himself said somewhere, didn't he, "most things are to do with nothing, but in its way football is to do with everything".'

# 10

# FLAT EARTH SOCIETY

It takes a very, very special sort of fellow to hoist a gleaming, crisply laundered flag of chivalry over the sad and seedy, often corrupting and corruptible, cockpit of professional boxing. Some have managed it, a few with an heroic grandeur for good measure. Muhammad Ali did, and Ray Leonard. And far away from the television arc-lights and forests of greenbacks, honest men infatuated still by their 'game', like Winston Burnett, continue to run up a noble enough banner which even us cynics can rally around. Though not for long. The generation of mine that so wallowed in Ali's glorious talent and skittish capacity to out-Herod all the gruesomely muscled Herods who came at him with evil intent, will be for ever diminished when we know that our onliest champion of valour is now a shamed and shuffling figure with Parkinson's Disease – a disorder which is caused, as everyone knows, by taking too many blows to the head. If they banned boxing tomorrow, I'd be first in the queue to applaud the decision. While it's there, alas, its awful, awesome appeal brings out the worst in us, not to mention the adjectives.

# ALI SPARS WITH THE FILM MEN
*May 1976*

*Munich*: Having pitched tent here for a week Muhammad Ali's never-ending Flying Circus still swings about zanily on its permanent high. Its ringmaster managed to fit in a little light boxing and skipping between his everlasting round of spiel and promotion today. His main job, however, was to promote his forthcoming film, *The Greatest*, in which he plays himself and which, if he is to be believed, he will direct, produce and script himself, though the last three credits were hastily denied by the chalk-striped Columbia wide boys who had flown from London and Hollywood and whom the Great Nut totally out-spivved at their own game of Vapid Big-Time Charlies.

Meanwhile, those of us sent (almost certainly under false pretences) in the name of sport have to cast around desperately inventing, as that *real* Hollywood geezer, Goldwyn, put it, 'a few new clichés overnight'. So prepare yourself for a weekend of 'The Fight Is Off Horror', 'Promoters' Money Runs Out Claim', 'Stadium Closes Broke – Official', and 'Biddles Bid to Dope-test Pill-popping Champ'. The sum of it all must be something akin to *Le Monde*'s prelim on Agincourt: everything cut and dried in a boasting, presumptuous, glittery paraphernalia with an outcome so inevitable that actual battle plans are not worth a sentence. So, a film about him. We know that many have written books after years of research. Boxing apart, after five days one can only clutch simply at a definition someone once made of Edith Sitwell: Ali is a 'genuine phoney'. But the boxing, of course, is something else.

His henchmen (39 blacks plus Angelo Dundee) are apparently costing him £5,000 a day at the richest hotel in town. Well pressed dressers, they stand around a foyer like discarded *Times* Business Sections on a suburban Sunday eiderdown, until they are called upon to do their bit to boost the amazing Ego's ego. Nobody quite knows what their function is. As the fine US journalist, Wilfred Sheed explains: 'Even the hangers-on have hangers-on. One week a stranger shows up, by the next he will be on Ali's staff and complaining about other strangers showing up. It's like a political campaign; everyone wants to pull up the gang plank once he is on board.'

Meanwhile, the English camp upon the hill at the Hilton are bored ... but a great relief. There cannot be a sharper contrast. They are quiet – if not quietly confident. But Ali's menacing circus in the foyer does not bother Dunn's trainer and father-in-law, Jimmy Devanney. 'Of course we're not overawed by these black chat merchants, we've got far too many of 'em back 'ome in Bradford. Why, we're right used to seeing 'em dancing up and down Westgate with their tambourines on a Saturday.' It was 1.50 p.m. and Yorkshire's Dunn was resting in his comparatively tiny tent. How do you feel? 'Cheesed off as ever, mate, I'm telling you. Well, look at me, 10 to two of a Friday afternoon, it is, and I'm lying in a double bed all by myself reading *Reveille*. Look at me: if by any chance at home I wasn't working on t'shift, I'd be either taking King, me doberman, for a walk, or at least be doin' the washing up.'

'Aren't you just a teeny bit apprehensive?' 'Look, I'm telling you, it's shit or bust for me on Tuesday, I'm just going out there to fight. I've never been quoted as being scientific, like, but I'm telling you, I've got one or two ideas of me own and I'll be putting 'em into practice when the occasion arrives on the night. One of me plans is something that even George Foreman couldn't think of.' On Tuesday he is going to wear a dressing gown and shorts in the colours of his beloved Parachute Regiment. 'That'll do the trick if anything will,' he said. Then, having finished *Reveille*, this very nice fellow, far from the blockhead some have been painting him, turned over in his lonely double bed and got stuck into *A Bridge Too Far*.

# LORD OF THE RING
*October 1980*

A friend who had also lived through all the 17 sweet years, telephoned me first thing yesterday morning. 'I know he lost, but was he hurt?' he asked anxiously. I don't know, I said, but apparently they just helped him, mute and beaten, from the ring to his hotel room. 'I do hope he's not hurt.' We agreed that if you want to win something four times then the only way you are going to manage it is by trying a fourth time. That's the long and short of it.

'You're an old man. I'll give you talking lessons and boxing lessons and fighting lessons, but most of all you need falling down lessons.' Larry Holmes to Muhammad Ali at the weigh-in on Thursday? No. Cassius Clay to Sonny Liston at the weigh-in on 25 February 1964. 'Round eight to prove I'm great,' he recited. A round in credit, for Liston refused to come out for his seventh. Quit on his stool, a sullen, silent beaten-up old boy. Lordy though, it took a long, long time for the wheel to turn vicious full circle.

Incredibly, though he took on anyone in the world, from Joe Frazier to Richard Dunn, this was the first time he had lost inside the distance. Here's something for Mastermind. Who was the Ugly Bear, the Baby Bear, the Washerwoman, the Rabbit, the Mummy, the Beaver, the Peanut and so on and so on? And who, unquestionably, was The Greatest? Is there one of this century's sportsmen certain of a decently long entry in our grandchildren's Oxford Dictionary of Quotations? 'I am the Greatest! ... Float like a butterfly, sting like a bee! ... I ain't got nothing against them Viet Congs.... I'm so mean I make medicine sick.... Harry, you're not as dim as you look.... He's got two chances – slim and none.... Get out the guns, we're setting traps.... I chop wood, so it's like I borrow all my strength from trees....'

His first ticket-selling rhyme was as a young contender in 1963 when he fought Doug Jones. Pre-fight there was a long New York newspaper strike and no big build up. Cassius did the radio and television commercials himself. It remains my favourite:

> Jones likes to mix
> So I'll let it go six.
> If he talks jive,
> I'll cut it to five.
> And if he talks some more
> I'll cut it to four.

It was the first time in a dozen years apparently that Madison Square Garden was sold out for a boxing match.

When he slumped on his stool last night and the wise Dundee made his merciful move ahead of the blindly faithful Bundini, you sighed a big thankful sigh and let the roll of memories run through on the fast-forward spool from the day that Henry decked him in the year that Macmillan was still Prime Minister. He fought and won other battles which were even more genuine and deserve comforting. Eldridge Cleaver wrote in *Soul on Ice*: 'Essentially every black champion until Muhammad Ali had been a puppet, manipulated by whites in his private life to control his public image ... with the coming of Muhammad Ali, the puppet master was left with a handful of strings to which his dancing doll was no longer attached.'

And the day after he lost to Frazier on that epic New York night (pretty epic too, I remember in the Odeon, High St Ken., I can tell you) Ali said, 'I thought I couldn't lose, 'cause I was fightin' for people all over the world. If I win, people all over the world's gonna win. If I lose, they're all gonna lose. But you know, it's a good feelin' to lose sometimes. The people who follow you are goin' to lose, too. You gotta set an example of how to lose....' What a sportsman! What an epitaph! But it's not the one he wants. In a speech years ago to a New York college he said 'When I die, I want my tombstone to read – "No foolin'! No foolin'! But the name's been changed to protect the innocent." '

What a guy! Humour always there. And now, you listen to me, do you hear, you go right along home there and clamber onto that little ol' rocking chair young Larry Holmes kept talking about. But just one other thing before you go – thanks a million, pal.

---

## SWEET, SHARP SUGAR TAKES ALL
### *September 1981*

*Las Vegas*: It sure was one heck of a fistfight, and at times it got near even to living up to the outrageous ballyhoo that preceded it. In fiscal terms, Wednesday night's world welterweight fight at Las Vegas was certainly the richest fight in history in terms of fisticuffs; it matched its boast well enough and deserved at least to be listed as the first 'Fight of the Century' of this young decade. Sugar Ray Leonard, his pop eyes closing all the time into weasely slits, realised on exactly the right occasions when he had to be very, very good. And those were the times when Tommy Hearns, by comparison, seemed to me to be just slightly out of his depth. When the referee stopped the fight halfway through the 14th round with Hearns as laden with leather as a full cattle truck, the three judges announced Hearns slightly ahead on points. Well, as far as I am concerned that meant each of them was as daffy as Don King's barber.

The third round will surely remain logged as one of the most awesome three minutes of world championship fighting. Fire answers fire! And the sixth and seventh were not short of gruesome excitement either. Longeurs set in through the middle areas – Hearns, where he could not throw his jackhammer right hand for fear of the quicksilver left-hook counter, and Leonard, while cockily throwing examples of his full repertoire, seemed content enough to pace himself through a chess match now rather than a manhunt. Yet all the time Leonard's left eye – elbowed by a sparring partner in training – was getting uglier. His right cheekbone too was puffing up. Still Hearns remained tentative about mustering a concerted attack, just flicking out his left at Leonard's temples like a stinging wet towel and indeed by the 13th, as he admitted afterwards, Leonard had

208

just been circling the wagon, getting ever closer and twanging in the odd arrow or three. But then the burning faggots started flying and Hearns was a goner ... three minutes later the credits came up.

Hearns insisted afterwards that he was not as 'dizzy' at the end as the referee thought. He could have fooled me. He was in no fit state. After a quick shower and a long drink of water, Hearns seemed momentarily surprised when he heard he had been ahead on points – but recovered to say 'certainly I was far ahead – and I want a rematch'. But in real life Hearns is not cocky sugar or spice – he is the salt of the earth – so he shrugged and admitted with touching dignity 'The only problem was I got hit with some good shots. I fought my best and I think I gave a good show.'

Leonard, his face encased in huge black shades, said: 'I take my hat off to Mr Hearns. Sure, I knew it might have been close, but I always had it under control. I had to rely on my guts once my eyes started closing. Sure, I'll consider giving him a rematch.' At which, doubtless, the eyes of both sets of bank managers turned as well to slits behind their dark glasses.

All the preliminaries and then the magnificent challenge itself had been such that one felt deflated at the end. I don't mean the prelim fights – the usual insipid clutch of unknown junior lightweights from Mexico. Three hours of them was like dropping off at McDonalds, on the way to Simpsons in The Strand. Nobody watches them. You amble about the vast temporary amphitheatre, which is itself enclosed in a rim of desert mountains turning pink in the sunset. The sky is as blue as your Marks and Sparks underpants. The purple darkness closes in and the unknown Latins grunt on unnoticed. The buzz heightens.

The music is up, the lights down. Hearns is first in, his shining white gown bearing the legend 'Winner Takes All'. Leonard comes in dancing, a smirk playing about his mouth. He is in bridal white too, the gown edged with scarlet flames and the word 'Deliverance' scripted on the back. He looks far too confident. They both do. The bell, and at the same time total silence and a dreadful din. At once Leonard, a truly

209

thrilling operator, is on his circus trick-cycle – backwards and forwards and mostly sideways, left then right, always smiling, using the ropes like there might be a snakepit in the centre of the ring. Hearns looks menacing as he stalks the cocksure whisp. Hearns' confidence grows as he starts to connect. He seems so sure of his destiny at this time that the smile of his white gumshield has a grotesque certainty about it.

In the third Leonard stopped in his tracks and the two of them stood and traded blows. First one careered in, then the other. In turn some hundred glittering necklaces of sweat coiled up into the arc-lights from their fuzzy heads. Even the moths took cover. It was awesome. Neither man gave ground that he did not regain. Hearns' longer reach was telling, Leonard's superior skills even more so.

There was calm after that storm, comparatively. In the sixth, Hearns slipped. Leonard was on it with the suddenness of a mongoose. On instinct – and principle as it were – Hearns rode out the hurts, but he was never the same again, I fancied, after surviving another infinite variety of attacks in the seventh. Sure, his left was scoring points, but increasingly the hit-man was backing off now. It was unchartered ground for him.

Yet all the while the left jabs were closing Leonard's eyes. If the millionaire was pacing himself, was it wise to cruise in this way with his vision impaired, and with it his outstanding sense of balance and timing? Certainly Leonard's tactic allowed Hearns a second wind. Before the 12th the boy from Detroit conducted the chorus of 'Tomm-ee Tomm-ee', from his own personal Kop. The lefts were still scoring, still doing their nasty damage, and now his right-handers started catching Leonard in the face as well.

Leonard had to get cracking. He did, exactly on cue. Wallop! A roundhouse right caught Hearns on the ear and, simultaneously almost, a left hook hit the very button. Hearns' eyes rolled. Leonard crowded in with venom. He said afterwards he could see three men and went for the middle one. For a full minute Hearns was on the point of falling head-first down the cellar steps and turning the lights off on the way. He survived, engineering a push through the ropes which allowed him some sort of recovery, then he sat on the bottom rope and soaked up pain – his mouth still in that white, grotesque 'smile' that we now knew was no more than nerves – till an eight count and the bell gave him just one more time to unscramble his brain.

It was not long enough. At the 14th bell Leonard literally ran across the ring and speared Hearns in the kidneys. The blow turned the tall man's legs to old rope, but he courageously stayed upright as best he could, once sliding along the top rope in an effort to get away and keep his balance like a soldier crossing a river on a pulley. After one minute 45 seconds the referee mercifully stepped in and the judges announced their ridiculous, and in the event unnecessary, arithmetic. Both knew they had been in one heck of a fight. They both deserved, you felt, to be carried away on their shields, like warriors. Neither of them went to the Ball. But I dare say they sent their bank managers to lead the dance.

---

## PRINCIPLE OVERRODE CONTEH'S INTEREST
### October 1986

Whether it totally restores one's faith in professional prize fighting or not, for a host of reasons connected with goodness and integrity it remains a rewarding pleasure whenever you spend time with John Conteh. I last saw him walking for charity with Ian Botham in the Scottish Highlands. He is still only 34 and as trim and handsome as ever, still ready to crackle with wit, with intensity, and honesty. All the furies are fuelled these days only by Perrier water for one of his most challenging fights has been against the booze.

At his best, Conteh was probably the finest boxer from the heavier divisions that Britain produced in the last three decades. He fought seven world light-heavyweight title fights, winning four of them. Two huge money bouts he did not have as champion were those against Pierre Fourie and Victor

Galindez. They were to be promoted in South Africa and Conteh turned them down flat. When Frank Bruno first signed for tonight's fight against the white South African, Gerrie Coetzee, Conteh publicly advised the black Londoner against 'supporting the racist regime'. He has since had second thoughts.

'When I put my name to that letter to Frank I had really thought about it, I didn't rush at it,' he said. 'But in retrospect, I think I was wrong. It was me trying to impose my will upon someone else, which is precisely the thing I was against in the first place.'

It is now 10 years ago that South African promoters dangled their big money in front of Conteh. 'For a non-white to go down there and earn money was just not possible for me. Down there people don't even have the freedom to earn money.'

Conteh's own spirit has faced several poundings since he first arrived in London from Liverpool 15 years ago. Not only in the ring. Being cherished by his much-loved wife, Veronica, has been crucial, he says. The alcohol threw many a haymaker which he did not duck. He is determined now on the age-old cure of taking every non-drinking day as it comes and thanking God for getting through it. 'That first drink is like stepping out of a skyscraper window in the pitch dark and not knowing what floor you are on.' He has not boxed since his last world title fight in Atlantic City in 1980 (KOd, fourth – 'no feeling, no real hurt, like novocaine at the dentist's and all in slow motion'). He still works out in the gym and loves golf. He has the making of a superb after-dinner speaker and, as an actor, received enthusiastic notices for his performances in Willy Russell's *Blood Brothers* last year.

It was only a handful of years after leaving school and becoming a hod carrier that he was champion of the world – and suing with reckless but applauded daring boxing's establishment in the High Court. 'When I look back at that period now I see I was totally insane. I thought I was right at the time. I was causing so much trouble for myself by not continuing the way I got there in the first place with George (Francis), with Mickey (Duff) and the others.'

212

He thought he should have been getting much more money at the time but it cost him more to follow those thoughts through the courts than he'd have got anyway. The court cases were worth three big fight purses. He said: 'Maybe I was expecting too much, but I started to build up resentment instead of concentrating everything totally on my one ability at that time. A boxer's life is very short and I was in confusion, totally insecure and I was fighting two battles. But we live and learn, don't we?'

---

# BUGNER TAKES MONEY FOR OLD HOPE
*October 1987*

One of the longest goodbyes of all showbiz was mercifully concluded at last in the pokey little windowless referee's dungeon under the Tottenham Hotspur grandstand. 'Sorry about all the bullshit that's gone before, but you can take it I'll never fight again,' said the fat man on the bench as he dabbed with a towel at the grazes on his great squashed prow of a nose.

The official doctor had been first in, then the prize fighter's devoted moll called Marlene, who had watched the one-sided bore from an 'executive' box. They embraced. He said to her 'Sorry'. She said to him 'We are very, very proud of you.'

The cold white room was sparsely and eccentrically decorated in green and yellow streamers and those pointless little paper pompoms people put on present parcels. By the time he had lumbered, steaming, out of the shower, two perfectly formed crescents under the big fellow's eyes were already turning into the same matching colour scheme. By this morning they would be a painful, purplish mauve. Cheap at the price of £250,000.

Equally well-defined crescents were above Marlene's eyes and, just as methodically, were also man-made. She arched them, crossed long voluptuous legs, smoothed the creases in her expensive sequiny-dress and her equally rich made-up face and said 'Of course I was never worried. I had a definite pact with the corner men that at the first sign of the possibility of Joe being hurt they would throw in the towel. The end was sudden, so the towel came in. He was not hurt and I'm truly proud of the wonderful, wonderful job he did. He is a fine man, a great fighter and just listen at his chivalry in defeat.'

A caretaker-type wandered in and, stroking his chin, seemed to be considering the removal of the quaint wall decorations. He left them up while Joe, sitting under a strip of Elastoplast stuck to the wall with the word 'win' written on it, was fingering his own messed-about mandible even more tenderly, took up his girl's cue for a last cheerio (he promised most sincerely) to his public, mixing magnanimity with, as he put it, 'the end of this last bit of bullshit'.

Rather like Richard Nixon's first of his many goodbyes – 'you Press men haven't me to kick around any more' – Joe said he had been fired to stay on his feet only because he 'wanted to stick it to you Fleet Street guys'. He said the ultimate fall (only the third in 70-odd contests) must surely 'have marked the end of a great era as far as the legends of all boxing are concerned, for I go back to the fabulous era of Ali and Liston and Quarry, and all those people out there must surely realise that tonight was the end of an era for Britain and the world.'

Before he left to resume Marlene's efforts at button-holing the casting directors of the Australian film industry (a visit to his mother first this week) he paid generous tribute to young Bruno. 'Though I must say, I certainly suited his style tonight, I was so off-form, I was so determined but in the end I have to say he impressed me. Honestly he did. He was much better than I expected or planned. I was surprised how relaxed he was, and how effective his jab worked me over.

'We just had to bullshit to sell tickets and I think we did a very good job. If he's mentally right, Bruno could beat Tyson. But he'll have to get in quick because I think old Holmes will beat Tyson. Age doesn't come into it. I don't regret my age; I don't regret my weight; I don't regret anything – even if the referee was an idiot tonight at the end, letting him hit me like that. I don't regret anything. Life goes on, thank God.'

Spoken like the nice man he really is, and Marlene had by

now stopped arching her eyebrows, looked at him with love, resmoothed her dress for the umpteenth time, uncrossed her legs, and simply purred. The car was ready, she nodded the order, and off they went to re-read the cheque.

Meanwhile, away from this intimate tableau, in another part of the concrete jungle, Bruno was being fed by a hundred microphones and massed adulation. His tedious, self-humiliating rigmarole of gormlessly sending himself up does great – 'know what I mean, Harry' drones on as if scripted and so does the unending guff to any Australian of 'it's not cricket, old sport'. It makes me cringe, anyway, as though he either genuinely considers the world as simple-minded as he feigns to be, or is it that he is on a strategic course to end up as a presenter of Listen With Mother?

By the way Frank went on you'd have thought he had won the Booker Prize, not just taken an awful long time to out-jab an old man bullocking around pretty harmlessly in the pension queue. The fact of the matter was simply that for more than 200 grand it was well worth Joe's while to have bitten off more than he could maul. As I say, cheap at the price.

The last heavyweight sportsman to be flattened by anyone other than Dave Mackay on the centre-circle at White Hart Lane was Jack London by Bruce Woodcock on Saturday, 17 July 1945. That took six rounds. Many more, 38,000, watched it. Woodcock took home £995 to Doncaster and the fishmonger-promoter, Jack Solomons, admitted a profit of just £400. And, just like 32 years later, everyone went home happy. It was the result they wanted. Marlene and Joe included – unless the cheque bounces, it's goodbye from him and goodbye from her.

---

# THE SULLYING OF A ONCE-NOBLE ART
*September 1980*

British professional boxing's most tawdry seven days ends with the tragic young Johnny Owen seemingly on the point of giving up a last valiant challenge and – on its very doorstep at Wembley – the wretched aftermath of Alan Minter's brief reign as world middleweight champion when a section of the crowd were unable to comprehend that their idol did, after all the fuss, have feet of clay – and I don't mean you Cassius.

In the event, the hail of bottles (mostly plastic) and beer cans that rained down after Minter's vaulting ambition had met a sudden and terrible come-uppance on Saturday night did no more than douse the principals and ringsiders with beer. It all harshly illustrated yet again on worldwide television that you don't only have to be interested in soccer to know that British sport these days retains a collective, evil sickness about it. 'We were not fairly beaten, my lord – no Englishman is ever fairly beaten,' said the prophetic Shaw in *St Joan*. That line probably got a smug laugh when the play first opened in Shaftesbury Avenue.

Organised legal prize fighting is the last activity that can afford this sort of reaction from its supporters. Its very existence in a civilised society has long been the cause of reasonable debate. It is game, set and match to boxing's opponents if the crowds who attend are now to be allowed to get in on the bloodletting as well. The caging in of football crowds is pretty horrific when we care to think about it. If boxers now have to fight inside a cage it would be simply obscene. While he's at it, I wonder if Hector Monro's encouragingly nifty call yesterday for an inquiry into the Wembley fracas, might not be as good an excuse as any to examine officially and minutely all aspects of the business here. The horrendous story last year of the unlicensed US boxer Willie Classen – now simply a mound of earth labelled 'Range 59, Grave 52' at St Raymond's Cemetery in New York's Bronx – could serve as a starting point on the agenda with Saturday's little lot bringing up the rear. There is not much hope of it, however.

Nor did Minter have much hope after the first 20 or 30 seconds on Saturday. That's when I caught the flash of a savagely confident wolf's grin through Marvin Hagler's gumshield as he weathered the Englishman's first suicidal charge and then began to circle him, knowingly and greedily.

Thereafter, that grin was never far away and mercifully the 'kill' was fast.

On reflection, following the bloodbath two things may have exacerbated the beerbath. The guilty patrons up in the gods might not have realised the extent of their hero's lacerated fissog – and Minter's long build up to the fight (and I admit I chipped in my two penn'orth) had reached potty proportions of misplaced optimism. It seemed to be almost criminal, looking back on the unending stage-managed trumpeting chauvinism that preceded the contest: Royal Marines bandsmen led our boy into battle – plus conductor, I ask you – and long-legged, padded-crotched models pranced around helping get everyone worked up. Minter himself led the full-throated thunder for *God Save The Queen*, almost bellowing it into Hagler's ear. 'I thought it was disco music, man,' said the mischievous new champion afterwards.

British boxing's very own folk hero, Henry Cooper, was distraught. After taking off his radio earphone he shook his head: 'I have honestly never seen anything like it before. It was disgraceful. Do you know, tonight I feel degraded to admit I am British.'

If poor Alan Minter can't actually be blamed for the climax of the evening, I am afraid he must take it squarely on the chin for the anti-climax. He waded in suicidally geed up perhaps by the electric atmosphere. Hagler could hardly believe his luck. The boy from New Jersey was back in a teenage alleycat brawl in Newark. The dope was roped inside a minute. Hagler had brought a full toolkit of effective dismantling equipment to go with the two steam-hammer knuckles. He was able to lay it out at once. He did so with the workaday earnestness of a caveman unconcernedly setting about trapping his supper.

Minter has always cut easily. He kidded himself lately that the problem has gone away. Such problems don't, unless he had been on a bill at Lourdes and, sure enough, in that first half-minute Minter was slashed open under his left eye. In the second round, true to Olde Englishe, he turned the other cheek and that too opened up like a red letterbox. He continued the bull rushes and after Hagler had certainly taken two or three defiant blows, which nevertheless did not wipe away the wolf's grin, he scalpeled Minter's nostril as a parting shot at the end of the round. In the third, the tomato can burst asunder – to be followed at once by the beer.

Hagler's handlers had to shelter him with their human wigwam. The manager, Goody Petronelli said: 'It was the worst example of crowd behaviour I have seen anywhere in the world. We would never fight again in London. Why on earth Minter rushed us from the opening bell I will never know. We knew he would come at us for a few seconds, but he just kept it up.'

Meanwhile, surgeons, both plastic and otherwise, administered to the torn features of the fallen idol behind locked dungeon doors deep in the seedy old concrete pile – which cannot surely have seen seedier scenes than this time. At last Minter, apologetic and gracious in defeat, emerged to mutter: 'I trained and trained not to get involved, but to box him, to be clever. I reverted to type and I am sorry and have only myself to blame. He was too fresh.'

Well, Hagler was lots of things but personally I'd have thought 'fresh' too flimsy an adjective to describe this new champion.

---

# THE 69-TIME LOSER FIGHTS ON
*January 1988*

This morning, not long after Tyson and Holmes were mixing it in America for grotesque amounts of millions, a 28-year-old Cardiff man will be pulling on his trousers and preparing for a little light roadwork in the wintry dawn of Wales. Winston Burnett, light-heavyweight contender, has a very important fight at Bethnal Green on Wednesday. He is on the comeback trail.

As career records go, Burnett has the very best in British professional boxing. Or the very worst. It depends which way you look at it. No one has fought more, no one has lost more. So, in a way, he has certainly experienced much more than

Messrs Tyson or Holmes who, until this morning, had experienced defeat only twice between them, Holmes accounting for both. Burnett has been beaten 69 times in 88 fights. In 43 of his last 50 fights the referee has raised the other fellow's arm.

This week, the British Boxing Board of Control granted Burnett a new licence to box, provided he gets himself a manager and 'takes no further fights at short notice'. He has joined the London stable of Frank Warren and on Wednesday at the atmospheric little York Hall he fights Dave Owens of Castleford.

Burnett says, 'Six good wins and then Tony Wilson will have to give me a crack at his light-heavy title. Then I'll defend and then bow out undefeated at the end of my hundredth fight – a total no one can ever possibly match.'

I cannot recall a more pleasurable interview. He is a delightful man, bright, handsome, humorous and gently self-deprecating. He looks far less beaten up than many amateur rugby players. His new mood, he says, is to keep urging himself into determined optimism.

'When I do finally bow out I think I'll be remembered for a long time as a thoroughgoing professional. I will be sorely missed.' Many of his defeats, he says, were aberrations – 'many on the part of the referee', he laughs, fit to burst.

While Holmes returns to Pennsylvania this morning with another few million to add to his $50 million property pile, Burnett is content that while boxing has never given him more than £2,000 on one very special occasion, it has provided a new, spick little house which looks south across Cardiff docks and might yet fulfil an ambition to visit his birthplace in Jamaica for a visit – 'taking in a trip as well to Disneyland for my baby daughter'.

He lost his first 10 fights as an amateur but persevered heroically until he won two vests for Wales. He turned pro eight years ago – since when he can't think there can be many boxing rings in which he hasn't answered a bell. 'Not only in Britain, but all over the place, I've made friends everywhere I've boxed: there is no friend better than a man you have boxed, whoever was the winner.'

He has never made the top of the bill. Always either first on, before the main attraction, doing his utmost up there while the ringsiders come and go and get settled and buy programmes and chat among themselves. Or last on, when everyone's going home, seats tipping up, cleaners getting ready, and afterwards the hot water's run out in the shower, if there is one.

Gingerly fingering the bruises, or his thin little paypacket, as he drives the jalopy home from the fights down deserted motorways, he often thinks of the three or four nights when all the skills had come together, when the whole thing was oiled and polished and the crowd loved him – and only a decent rub of the green with the ref's scorecard might have set him on his way to be, yes, a genuine world class contender.

'In Cork once, January 1985 against this Canadian, Kid Morrison, ex-gridiron guy, built like a brick wall, massive. They were grooming him up, he'd flattened every previous opponent, a real KO artist. Sugar Ray Leonard was there. I got in off the boat the night before. Morrison came up and squared up to me, all brash and threatening and said he would murder me. First I cut him up and then outboxed him. I won on points and afterwards Sugar Ray said if I ever came to the States to get in touch.'

Such memories keep him warm. 'Another great night. Sheffield Town Hall, the place packed. I come in against Mick Mills, he's local and I'm black, and the booing for me was something terrible. They want Mick to rip me apart, but he can't, can he? By the fourth the jeers start to be aimed at Mick and by the end, though I lose the decision, they are calling my name and giving me a standing ovation. Wonderful. Then there was that night in Paris. Palais de Sport. Now that is really something. Tremendous. A real stadium. What atmosphere! And there on the scoreboard above the ring I suddenly see my name spelled out. My name in lights. It's all so worthwhile for times like that, isn't it?'

In fact, he must be quite a boxer for, incredibly, in 69 losses he has never been worryingly hurt or cut. His nose was broken for the first time last year – in a car crash. His worst cut, above the right temple, was inflicted by Paul Tchoue, of the Cameroun – 'a head butt, he catapulted off the ropes, ref stopped it in the fourth with me a street ahead'; and once, against Terry Crystal, who was a qualified doctor in the Hagler camp, 'I ended with a badly-cut lip and Terry came over at the end after he'd got the decision luckily, and prescribed four stitches: we had a laugh about that.'

His only knockout does not besmirch his record. The referee did not even bother to count. So it goes down as 'a stoppage'. It was, he says, the only time he has been off his feet. He blames the Boxing Board for that stoppage: 'They made me have a brain scan in 1985. Said they'd pay for it. Cost me £70. I'm still waiting to be reimbursed. Having to have a scan made me a bit apprehensive, like. So my first fight after was with Eddie Smith in Manchester, not quite concentrating, and at the beginning of the second, me already a mile ahead, he catches me with a right hand, I never saw it coming, normally I never get caught with a shot like that, but down I go and the ref said afterwards he never bothered counting.

'Yes, I agree, if I hadn't had so many defeats, I'd have been world champion. But I've been in there with a current world champion, the American, Frank Tate, last year. No trouble, all he had was a jab. All through I was making him miss. In the second I had him on the ropes, piled in hundreds of shots, he didn't know what to do. Then he gets on his bike and wouldn't come near me again, wouldn't trade a punch.

'Yes, I like a scientific match, but if someone wants to trade I'll trade back. Not Tate, just that jab and on his bike – and then all of a sudden with just 30 seconds to go of the last round, the referee jumps in and stops it in his favour. Thirty seconds. Incredible. Now Tate is world champion. Winning that would have been the making of me.'

He made £2,000 for fighting Tate – inflation, in real terms from the £40 in used notes he pocketed from his first pro purse 88 scraps ago when he set out full of hope at a north London hotel show in 1980. He was outpointed over four by Mike Burton, 'the only time I was ever bothered by butterflies and nerves'.

His last fight, a month ago at the Civic Theatre, Bow. Since when the Board have ordered him to take no fights at short notice. 'I was fit and 12.4. They'd told me this Rocky Palovnavitch would be 12.10. I look across at him. He's at least 13-and-a-half stone. Then they said he was a complete novice, so don't bother. A novice? He was a very powerful guy and I find out later he's the former kick-boxing champion of Great Britain. The bell goes and he catches me three shots – 1, 2, 3 and all below the belt. That really hurts.

'Third shot, I decide to go down just to get my breath back and ponder my next moves, and lo and behold the ref comes over and says "That's it, that's enough". I say, "Hang on, ref, everyone could see they were low." But he stopped it.

'Watch me go on Wednesday. I'm not selling myself short any more. Twelve fights to go to a century, and then retire as undefeated champion. Then it will have all been worthwhile, won't it?'

# 11

# RUBS OF THE GREEN

As a sports fan, I came late to golf. Tony Jacklin, chubby little Lincolnshire lad in his poacher's purple cardie, converted me on television when he won the Open championship at Lytham. Seven years later, glory be, I was sent to cover my first Open in person. My guide was the still revered, much lamented, Pat Ward-Thomas, of the *Guardian*. Talk about starting at the top. 'By the way, old boy,' said Pat, matter-of-fact, when I turned up scruffily awestruck to the Press tent that first morning, 'try and spruce up a bit, will you, we're dining with Jack tonight.' He meant Nicklaus, the veriest paragon of the game. The great man was, well simply, great. I asked him, tremulously, what he would dream about when he was retired and on a fishing trip in his dotage. He laughed at himself, and the blue eyes sparkled: 'I guess I'll be dreaming what I always dream about – making three pars and a birdie on the last four holes to win a major by a stroke.' Said Pat, 'Jack, that dream will stop once you go – and you'll only go the moment you admit to yourself you can never win another major.' 'Yep, 'spose so,' admitted Jack. And he is still turning out. But when he does go finally, not only golf, but all of sport and its attendant chivalries will be diminished.

# COTTON THE KING – 50 YEARS ON
*July 1977*

Romantics we all may have been, at Turnberry for the Open, but at the beginning we did not quite know where to look. We scuffed our shoes in the dunes, looked out to sea for the view, got to work on forearms with the suntan stuff ... for Henry Cotton, the one and only, had started his celebration lap of honour with some distressing, even almighty, gaffes. He was five over par after just two holes, 14 over after but seven. He turned in 50 and as the sun blazed down to weary him more it looked certain that the old man would ignominiously notch a new record – by making 100 in the Open championship.

But he did not. And long before his finish it would not even have mattered if he had. The grandstands rose to him as he nobly, hunchingly trudged to the packed grandeur of the 18th, his shooting stick swaggered across his shoulder as he drank fully his memories. He finished in 93. 'I'm disappointed, I was hoping for something around 80 or 82,' he said. 'It was an horrific start. But I was determined to finish and, whatever happens, I'll finish tomorrow too.'

It was a marvellous accident (if such it was) that paired with him was Arnold Palmer. They are the very two men whose personalities, even to a tyro, straddle the very heart and soul of this championship over half a century. For Cotton yesterday it was a famous jubilee. He first entered in 1927, when he was 20 and still working on his manifesto (*In Place of Snobs and Strife*) that was to change the very character and hitherto humble standing of any sporting professional.

Cotton won three Opens. His last entry was in 1960. That was Palmer's first, when he picked up an unconsidered gauntlet and inspired all the youth and strength of America and fired them to revitalise a wilting British Open. And with these two yesterday played Christy O'Connor, lovely man and lovely name and lovely land and lovely repartee. What a trio. No matter that Cotton was round in 93, he cannot wake up this morning without a warm gleam for young Schroeder's 66.

Yesterday the old man, in grey flannels, Aertex vest and silk grey-green shirt flapping over his hips, and looking for all the world like a pasty-faced Somerset Maugham, did his stuff. At the sixth his ball into the rough singed my eyebrows. At the seventh he took a terrible nine. At the famous ninth, when every man was given a cooling Pepsi, he took one annoyed sip and gave the can back hastily to his caddy and, waiting to drive on this noted Lighthouse hole, he looked out to sea over the high railings, looking for all the world as proud, grand and withered as Lord Mountbatten, another grey face, keeping up spirits on This Is Your Life. But he hit a good drive. Arnie put his arm round him and said: 'Well done.' And as he went into the distance and we thought he would hit a terrible century, the fact is that he did not. And we cheered him down the length of the 18th.

---

## THE BEAR WITH A SORE HEAD
*July 1977*

By an absolute fluke, he actually sat next to me in the first of yesterday's early morning shuttle flights out of Glasgow. It was a jam-packed scrum, every man, woman and child for themselves. His son, Steve, was marooned in the last spare seat a couple of rows back; his wife Barbara was three rows up and immediately game for a chinwag with an unknown neighbour.

The big fellow didn't want to talk about it much. He had awakened on Sunday morning more disappointed than he had gone to sleep. 'Tom just played better ... yep, I think he's really getting it now ... but no, you cannot measure "greatness" in a sportsman till he figures a lot in the records – it's not technique or guts or flair, "greatness" can only have one yardstick, and that's to be always winning, then winning some more. You can have a classic swing or the best competitive nature, but nobody remembers you if you haven't won anything, if you aren't in the records.... Now, will you excuse me, please, I must try to finish my book....' He said he

225

would have rather gone to sleep, but he dug into his battered executive's case and flicked through the paperback *The Rhinemann Exchange* to find his place from last night in bed at the Turnberry Hotel. He was into it at once. About 60 pages to go.

The back cover screamed out the unattributed reviews ... 'All Intense Action ... Intriguing Suspense ... Nerve Wrenching International Thriller' – and no fellow hack could surely think of a better blurb for the drama that he himself had played out 15 hours before. Jack Nicklaus escaped into his book. Escaped from the day before. And I relaxed into awe.

In the row ahead of us three Scotsmen, oblivious, read their Sunday sports pages. One said 'Watson Makes His Dream Reality'. Another was 'Watson Muzzles The Bear'. The third 'Jack Blows Up Again'. He had looked at them, but hadn't seemed to read them. So he got into the book. About us, on this bleary pyjama flight, were men who had lost far more badly than Nicklaus. Though every one of them knew that he was the only loser. Johnny Miller yawned a lot and fidgeted, trying to entertain his little son. Last year when he was champion, Mormon Miller had said he had missed his children. Golf wasn't as important as to make you miss your children, was it, he had asked. And all of us had refused to look him in the eye when they gave a throwaway answer. And a year later, last Thursday, he had told me blunt that he was of the opinion he doesn't much like big-time golf any more.

A bronze Ben Crenshaw, but he had lost too, though of course he was pleased with his showing. He knows, we know, he'll win it one year soon. He slept like a complacent babe through all the flight. I may have been in awe of my neighbour, gentle Ben is still in awe of history. When he arrived a week ago, he had asked his driver to take him straight to the Prestwick course up the road from Turnberry – not for practice, but 'I had to play there, just because it's history isn't it?' He just had to play on the ancient greens that Tom Morris once mowed. That pilgrimage, one fancies, meant even more to him than the following week. What an outstanding, touching champion will Crenshaw be one day.

226

We crossed the Pennines ... then Manchester ... ahead of us was bleary Ballesteros, another doe-eyed youngster who snoozed the flight through. Mrs Nicklaus chattered charmingly on ... incidentally she's now a celebrity too. She does television commercials, one for bicycles and another, nationwide, for Magic Chef ovens – 'Hi, I'm Barbara Nicklaus. I'm Magic. Buy Me.' The name of all games is 'Endorsements'.

And Mr Nicklaus read on. By London and seatbelts, he had 20 pages left. He said he was spellbound. I said *we* were yesterday. That's the way it goes he shrugged. 'I've never remembered shooting two last 65s and still lost. Tom played better, that's all. He really did.... Yes, I'm still disappointed. Up to 17, I thought I was in, but apparently Tom was on heat, he said to his caddie "we've got him now", even before the last two holes. And he did get me.'

But they left the final green and it was Nicklaus who put his arm round the still young Pretender ... but yesterday he admitted he was feeling sick. He made a generous and noble speech to the Coliseum at the prize giving. Eleven years ago he had won his first Open at Muirfield. He admitted he had cried tears then, saying 'Excuse me, friends, do you mind if I weep? You see, I just want to enjoy this moment.' And I know now he was near to tears on Saturday.

At Heathrow he herded up the family for the transfer flight home. En route he signed autograph after autograph. Rough or well-mannered applications came alike. 'Thank *you*,' he said to them all and signed the bits of paper, asking if a porter said 'for my nephew,' 'what's his name?'. And writing 'to Dave, Best Wishes, Jack Nicklaus.' As someone said, there's Muhammad Ali, Lester Piggott, Pelé and Jack Nicklaus ... we're alive and so are they so we should realise how lucky we are.

I hope he finished his thriller on the Atlantic flight. Especially if it took his mind off the sadness ... it probably did, because it was, wasn't it, 'Intense Action ... Intriguing Suspense ... Nerve Wrenching International Thriller'.

Sometimes losers can actually be winners. The outstanding and deserving champion, Watson, who looks like Jimmy

Carter ('Mah name is Tommy Watson and ah'm runnin' for champee-on') knows that on Saturday golf's loser was also sport's Victor Ludorum and at this stage he doesn't mind, I fancy. From first to last the affection and esteem for Nicklaus at Turnberry last week was something to savour in a thousand tiny ways, let alone the big one.

Alistair Cooke's fine words long ago about Bobby Jones, an acknowledged great champion, sit well on my aeroplane neighbour of yesterday morning: 'What we talk about here is not the hero as golfer but that something Americans hungered for and found: the best performer in the world who was also the hero as human being, the gentle, chivalrous, wholly self-sufficient male. Jefferson's lost paragon: the wise innocent.'

---

# JACKLIN'S FAITHFUL FEW
*July 1979*

There were about a dozen of them. A straggly bunch, most aged around 40 and carrying their sandwiches and woolly cardigans in plastic bags as they scuffed their feet on the first tee at noon yesterday. They were waiting for someone. None of them actually seemed to acknowledge each other, but it was seen that they shared some common bond the moment Tony Jacklin was called up to start his practice round.

Crack! Soft sad eyes brightened suddenly and they rhubarbed approval to themselves as their deadpan hero pinged the tiny infuriating missile at the very core of the faraway green. Jacklin picked up his tee, jauntily tucked his glove into back pocket and strode off on stocky little legs looking neither to the right nor left. Outside the ropes the devoted dozen picked up their clobber and followed their once and future champion into the distance. Silently they would see him round the full 18 holes and at 1.30 today they will be back to nurse him around another 18 when it will be for real. They will have one hand in a pocket so as not to show they're crossing their fingers, that's the way to spot them.

Jacklin has given them many a long day lately. Indeed, many long years. Those who follow Jacklin are not the kind of folk to run to shooting sticks. Tony Jacklin remains unquestionably the People's Choice. A million British housewives who cannot remotely even pronounce Oosterhuis' name let alone spell it, and believe that Faldo is some sort of Spanish dance they saw on holiday, will ask their husbands tonight 'How did our Tony get on?'

Ten years ago, same time, same place, those same chunky legs carried him up the last Lytham fairway and into the legends. Lytham and St Antony! At 25 that day his life was irretrievably altered; so, I fancy, did it change the lives of many more than that doughty dozen of cockeyed optimists who trudged after him yesterday. The higher you get the further you fall. And oh, what a clatter he made when he fell.

A decade ago: 'As I came off the 18th green, Jack Nicklaus was there.... I said to him "Jesus Christ, I never thought I could be that nervous and play golf." He laughed and replied "I know. Isn't it great?" He was the only man in the whole of the British Isles at that time whom I knew would understand what I was saying – I couldn't have said it to anyone else.

'After that I was numb for 24 hours. I was spent, elated. You win the Open, but you don't go out, go up to someone and say, Hi, I'm Tony Jacklin, I won the Open yesterday. It's personal. It's something which is yours alone.'

But it was not allowed to remain his alone. Not on your life it wasn't. The English nation got out the hymn books for months of Allelujah and clamoured for a slice of the triumph. For a few years young Tony continued to feed them the goodies with abandon. Tossing them out of the electrically-operated windows of his Rolls or off the battlements of his very own country mansion. Then the taste started turning nasty. Headlines became not so much Nicklaus Wins but Jacklin Fails. He had enough money for life but even he realised, did the lorry driver's son, that money wasn't everything. Suddenly he thought he was not very good at what he was best at. Mostly he could not putt, but when the putts dropped he could not drive, and when he could the bits in between were falling apart. There were suddenly too many bunkers on golf courses.

He tries too hard, said some. He doesn't try hard enough, said others. Wrong agent. Wrong clubs. Only interested in money. Not interested in anything. Practises too much. Doesn't practise enough. Desperate, he enrolled in an expensive course in Scientology. He took pills to sleep and pills to wake up. He went to America for the good of his game – and came back to England for the good of his game. He tried hypnotists. He returned to the same clubs and clothes he had used in his glory games. They only ever worked for three rounds in four.

Always harking back, beginning with the vivid boyhood dreams of the 15-year-old apprentice at the local steelworks: 'I got to work at 7.30 a.m. and filed lumps of steel standing at a bench all day. It was awful. You could spend three or four days working on one bit of steel. It would be one-hundredth of an inch out, and a fellow would chuck it away and say, start again. I got £3 11s 3d a week for that. One hour for lunch. I would rush through my meal, cycle three miles to the golf club, have 15 minutes' practice and cycle back in time to clock in again.'

Jacklin was 35 last week. Before he was 30 he had had lunch with the Queen and dined with Frank Sinatra. He has got a thing about Sinatra: 'Sinatra had two careers. He was way up, and then he was down. Then Frank went way up again. There must be a hell of a lot of satisfaction in that somewhere.... I think I'm capable of that. I wouldn't bet against my winning another Open if I get the bit between my teeth. When I get it rolling, I still feel exactly the same as I did at Lytham in July 1969.'

That's the why and wherefore as those 12 anonymous good friends and true traipse after him praying it will soon all get rolling again.

# HOW I BEAT ARNIE AT BALLYBUNNION
*October 1976*

Irish sport, they asked? Well, nutty gamesman that I am, do
you know the first thing that leaped into my brain? English
games. I thought at once of 15 madcap men in the green
mounting one last warming winter's charge (win or lose, they
always end with a flourish, bless them) in the misty, murky,
musty atmosphere of that dear old stadium alongside the
railway tracks at Lansdowne Road.

Tell a few yarns, I reckoned, about Liam Brady or Eamonn
Dunphy. And why not tell a fib or three from the legend
about Irish fighting men, tales all as jaunty, long and
unchecked as Rinty Monoghan's nose, like the timeless one
when Jack Doyle was doing his usual Caruso bit after a
typically hilarious fight in which he was up and down like an
O'Otis elevator and his manager turned to his trainer in the
corner and whispered 'Sure, he can sing Mother Macree, but
I wish he could fight her!'

Or even Irish cricket. Did you know the Gentlemen of
Ireland once bowled out the mighty Sobers-sided West Indies
for 25. The Black had been beautiful the night before,
apparently, and well after the 10 o'clock news some
hospitable cricketing Pad from Belvedere had wheeled in a
kindly crate of rum, just for a wee nightcap, you understand.
And it was served by smilin' redheads with freckles.

Then I thought, hey! Irish sport is not about that sort of
thing at all at all. Rugger and soccer and cricket and
Queensberry are organised games foisted on them (willingly
enough to be sure) when the rules were writ by Victoria's
muscular Christians, bods in quads with haughty high collars.

No, for the real sport of Ireland go away down the green
and soggy till the drizzle dampens your Long Johns and the
nice crispies that are Atlantic winds make your cheeks puff
purple with exhilaration and your ears tingle red. (Come to
think of it, I'd always thought west Irishmen had big ears
because of short haircuts; but perhaps it's all that tinglin'.)

231

Anyroad, down there is where you get to grips with the real sport of the old place ... the fishing, the riding, the boating, the golfing, and ah yes, the hare coursing, a beastly centuries-old pastime that a knot of the lads with a cap on their heads and a quid in their pocket go totally potty about.

I have long supped out on the story from a waiter there in the Clonmel Arms. During the Coursing Festival he got an order one morning from Room 152: cornflakes, bacon, egg, and sausage. 'When I knocked on the door and took the tray in, the man was on the floor and the dog was in the bed, and be damned if he didn't feed the whole of the breakfast to the animal.'

It's the golf I love. Not that I'm any cop at all (I play half-hearted cover drives at golf, and delicate out-of-the-sand-to-mid-on chips at cricket). But you don't have to be any good in Ireland. There's a grand welcome in most every club. Green fees are low and lunch is often followed by cake. Mind you, the Irish middle classes can be fearful boring but most of them gallivant up to Dublin sooner or later so needn't bother you at all. Out in the wild green yonder it's just us and the aristocracy.

In my time I've swiped at the little dimpled onion right up that Atlantic coast. I actually holed out in two at the blissful, lakeside 18th at Killarney; I can't think what I did at Skibbereen, but the name rings a bell; I remember Tralee for my daisycutters; at wild and wondrous Ballybunnion I took four on a hole where once Arnie Palmer, they said, had lost a ball in the sea and taken eight (that's the beauty of golf: there's no way I could bat in a Test match at Lord's, but at Ballybunnion I once beat Palmer by three!). I've played in a manner of speaking at Galway (it was the morning after the oyster festival), bought a glove and a cap with a bobble at Westport, and lunched with the captain and parish priest (one and the same man) at glorious Clifden.

A week up the west coast for golf can't be more highly recommended. Aer Lingus have some marvellous short weekends or long fortnights on offer. Start at Waterville and work up to Westport. Or vice versa. It'll be zigzag all the way. Like my round at lovely Lahinch where once Patrick

Campbell's father, I was told, got to the Irish Closed final only to cut his hand on a glass jug just before the off but devised a method of hitting the ball which came to be known forever after as 'the Lahinch dunch with tuck-in'. Thus, one-and-a-half handed, he won. Later his son, in the funniest essay I've ever read on golf, won through two rounds of the Irish Open. He was drawn both times against the doddery old fathers of two prime American champions, so beat them charitably and easily, unbeknown to the Dublin sub-editors who only had the scorecards to go on; so that evening the headlines in the city rang out 'Brilliant Campbell Sees Off American Challenge' or somesuch.

At Killarney, after the golf, we rode horseback. All fixed again by Aer Lingus with the Tourist Board man playing ostler. Now sometimes I connect at golf; on horseback I connect all too often: when he came up I came down; and again the other way round. It was a funny way to have a walk, but if you like that sort of thing it is very cheap compared with fees in the English livery shires. Every centre has recommended stables which welcome everyone from Cauthen to Keatings. Dobbin and I roamed with increasing rapport over the former acres of Viscount Castlerosse, who was Beaverbrook's Dempster of his day; he built the sensational golf course and, when he died in 1942, left 300 monogrammed silk shirts and pyjamas to the nuns of the nearby Convent of the Presentation who, I'm told, wore them under their habits in winter for a quarter of a century; they are yet seeing service as dusters for the high altar.

The purply views around the Lake were sumptuous even from my precarious perch. 'Himself, he owned every blade of grass as far as your eye can see,' said our instructor. I was reminded to look up an essay by Henry Longhurst (a lamented old purply view himself) of a dawn he spent with the Viscount at stalking. Single file up the mountain years ago, just like Dobs and me now: 'Castlerosse led the way, followed by myself, two retainers carrying rifles and telescopes, and in the rear another man carrying only a pail. I did not like to display my ignorance by asking the significance of the pail. Later it turned out to be the ice for his Lordship's whiskey and soda.'

I've never fished in Ireland – but again it's all laid on. There are miraculous tales – gerraway! – in every bar of the blighter that gorraway, but there remains a heavily backed rumour that the Irish are, in their mad dash towards industrialisation, turning fishes into bread ... i.e. the rivers are starting to be a touch polluted or blocked. Certainly the deep sea fishing off Kinsale remains an adventure and popular. When rivers flow into lochs it means trouble. The Tourist Board should be worried. Really.

But still they flock across, the grandchildren of those haughty wing-collared English public schoolboys of last century. They've paid well for their 'stretch' and their tackle. The waders they still buy in St James's. Like one, who fished for a week till he finally landed his solitary trout. As he gratefully basketed it he confided to his boatman, 'Patrick, that fish cost me £2,000, y'know.' 'Then yer lucky' replied Paddy, 'that ye caught only one, sor.'

# 12

## HIT PARADE

Cricket is a game beloved by swots who find orgasms lurking beneath frindling facts and figures, as well as more uncomplicated devotees who don't need *Wisden*'s long logarithmic columns to tell them a player is made of the real stuff or not. More often than not, however, the two come together. We have lived in a triumphant cricketing age – of Chappell and Border and Lillee, and Sobers and Lloyd and Richards, Hadlee and Kapil, and Amiss and all. Plus, of course, Ian Botham, the only Test all-rounder surely to match Sir Garfield – and sometimes with knobs on. And I wonder how Graeme Hick, Botham's *confrère* at Worcester, will measure up when the next generation come to contribute to this series of essays? (I will, of course, tell my grandchildren that I saw Hick's 405 at Taunton, though I was there only for the first 170-odd: the office, damn them, sent me next day to the Badminton horses). But I must make the choice and state, without equivocation, that the very best two of my time have been the batsman, Sunil Gavaskar, and the bowler, Malcolm Marshall – and, I'd bet on it, of all time. Though some favourite, personable and doughty triers run them close in cricket's unending charms.

# SUNNY FORECAST FOR INDIAN SUMMER
*June 1987*

It was only that this winter was slightly worse than usual. From the cream of England's batting, the league table of centurions against the West Indies over the last 15 years reads pretty limply – Amiss four, Greig, Gooch and Lamb three apiece, the rest nowhere.

In that time, India's Sunil Gavaskar, brown-eyed, baby-faced and less than five feet five inches in his cotton socks, has, alone and almost incredibly, hit the fierce and relentless West Indian barrage for an astonishing 13 hundreds, three of them double centuries. Hall, Holder and Sobers were playing when he first took guard in the Caribbean: since then he has seen off Boyce, Julien, Daniel, Clarke, Roberts, Holding, Croft, Garner, Marshall and all.

Gavaskar is Test cricket's most prolific batsman of all time. His 9,192 aggregate is already a thousand more than anyone else's. With his last undefeated double century against the West Indies, he overtook Bradman's record of 29 Test hundreds. In Australia earlier this year his two not out innings of 172 and 166 took that total to 32. It seems inviolate: all other contemporaries lag far, far behind. The purity of Gavaskar's technique matches the placid fearless-ness of his temperament. But he is no deadbat Dan; his stroke-play can at times be quite voluptuous.

Another reason it is good to have him back among us this summer is that he is a warming, companionable man of, in turn, solemn humours and fanciful flights and sharp insights: he has integrity, a catching chuckle and he is devoted to family, friendship and cricket. It might well be the last time to hurry along to watch him, for he will be 37 the week before the third Test ends in July. He only comes to supper if you promise not to offer him a curry. Everywhere an Indian cricket team goes, good hosts dish up curry. 'It's worse,' he says, 'in Australia, where they even serve it to us for breakfast to try and be friendly.' This time he has roast lamb followed by chocolate pudding and just one glass of medium sweet white wine. And, oh yes, he would like to be back in his hotel room in time to watch Miami Vice. Television at bedtime makes him sleep better if he is batting in the morning.

He is too steeped in his native civilities and good manners to whinge about touring accommodation for cricketers in England – as do English teams, loudly and inevitably, when they visit India. But by a flicker of assent from his eyelid you can tell he does admit that things have changed for the good since he first came here in 1971 – when the British boarding house mentality reigned and after the game sometimes all 20 of the rain-drenched squad had to share one bathroom at the end of the corridor, would miss their meat and two veg if they weren't in by eight prompt, and would shiver all night under two moth-eaten Witney blankets.

What I want to know first, of course, is this – does a teeny weeny opening bat of five feet four-and-a-half inches get just a little bit scared when he walks out to face West Indians who are all six feet tall and savagely quick? 'Scared? You can't be scared. Thank God I have never been frightened. Sure I might go out there feeling worried – but only about my form, about my feet moving the right way, about being certain to get behind the line…. But scared? Of course not.' But he doesn't even wear a helmet? 'I could never wear one – only, sometimes, my little plastic skull cap that I put on under my floppy white sunhat.' Before he pulls it on he looks like a Pope.

'The Caribbean is a lovely place to play cricket. I like the light and the sun on my back and the crowds and everyone's so involved and passionate. And all the West Indian players, they're so very, very friendly chaps.' Friendly sure. But not when they're bowling? 'I have had one or two that did glance off my head,' he admits, involuntarily fingering a particular area just above his right temple. 'Michael Holding, Guyana a couple of years ago: that was a blow. No, I didn't fall down, and as all the fielders rushed up, all I could think of was "get away, you're stopping me going for a leg bye." So, it didn't throw me from my rhythm although it hurt. I was about 38 or something then and went on to get 140 not out.

'But I suppose you asking about it brings back the realities, which is that however technically capable you might be, at this time one has to be on guard always against that only delivery which can mean a serious injury. When the odd ball takes you by surprise like that the danger is that you might jerk your body out of the way without thinking. Very noticeable in my time is how the art of playing back has changed; not many these days go back and across, sideways on, as the books would have you do. I am lucky I learned on good wickets. Now people open up their guard – and suddenly the West Indies are upon you and you are into big trouble.'

Had he heard of this new debate about a line halfway down the pitch? 'How could that happen? Marshall now, Thomson and Holding in the 1970s, those boys could get the thing up at your head from a perfect length – far more dangerous than what they call a bouncer, which gives you an extra yard to see it. But perhaps we have reached the stage where some might be getting a little bit carried away – and when people like Marshall and company find a bit of resistance from the bat they're bound to, you know, pitch it short again, so as to wear down your temperament even more than your technique.

'So in a way perhaps it does boil down to more a game of courage than of skill. How long can you keep going at fending the ball off your face? It's only a matter of time perhaps till you're going to be playing an involuntary jab that lobs the ball up into the air – so before that happens you want at least to try some attacking shots don't you?'

Since 1971, England bowlers have only seen a ripe handful of the famous 32 centuries, but surely the cascading glory of his 221 on the last day at The Oval in 1979 was one of the finest Test innings of all time? 'Do you know, I honestly don't remember much about that innings. The only thing that keeps recurring is the memory of just one delivery: Botham came charging up at me and bowled a slower one. His varieties are the very devil. What is coming next? His intentions are always good: when he tries to deceive you, he really tries to deceive you.

'However, this was one of the most miserable slower ones that have ever come to me in all my life, and I whacked it away for four past point. It was so miserable I can never forget it! The only ball I can remember in the whole innings. I suppose I was concentrating so much.'

His regard for Botham is evident, cemented by a very happy season with Somerset. Memories of the big boy's japes however turn the complexion a whiter shade of pale. 'Ian knows I have a phobia about dogs. Any little dog makes me scared even if it's on the other side of the field. Once at Taunton I went to a phone-box to make a call. Ian tied a dog to the booth. I could not come out for one hour. There was a big queue waving their fists. Old ladies hammering at the glass. I could not venture out. Perhaps I am getting better about the phobia after that.'

Like Botham, Gavaskar does not believe in net practice. 'Each to his own. My routine preparation the night before an innings is to be ready for bed around 10.30. If not television I will read a book to help get drowsy. I always have two books in my bag at the ground. This time I have already bought my two big novels: a Nelson de Mille and a Robert Ludlum. They are my insurance for an early dismissal.' Surely that's bad luck – why not say 'For a rainy day'? 'No, no, a rainy day is different. Then you pass the time with the other blokes with no tenseness. You can have a game of cards, lark around, pull each other's legs. In a Test match you have none of that, everybody is so serious in the dressing-room, so keyed up and tense. I don't have the brains to do crossword puzzles. So I always have my books ready for an early dismissal.

'When I am out early I am no longer livid with myself or sulky. It was one of the great changes of my life in 1981. For about six years till then I had had no season of absolute failure; although I don't wish to sound immodest, it was the case. But that tour to Australia was miserable: six Tests, just two 50s. It was not Lillee so much – Pascoe kept getting me. I was dreading to get back home. I thought my friends would not like me. Nothing of the sort! They were just normal. They all stood by me and I said to myself "Never ever do this to yourself again, never get worked up about being successful at cricket." It relaxed my whole attitude to life. Even more I enjoyed the game and my family and my music.' Music? 'Oh, anything that sounds good on the ears. It could be Indian film music; something you call Casals – yes, Pablo Casals is the man; it could be classical, or pop, Eastern or Western.'

When not humming, batting or reading, he's standing at slip for hour upon hour. Boring? 'Boring. Never. It is concentration all the time. It depends too who is wicket-keeper. With Farokh (Engineer) it was like being in the front row at the all-day concert: he'd have you in splits, all the jokes in the book coming thick and fast and much quicker than the edges were coming. Don't forget as well, at slip you have the grandstand view of all the world's good batting or good bowling.

'In Somerset, Peter (Roebuck) and I were in slips; we'd pass the whole day picking our best teams – you know, World's Best Good Looking XI, or Most Ugly XI, or Our Most Hated XI.' Botham was usually bowling at the time: did he make their Handsome XI? 'Ian? Handsome? No chance! He is not bad when he smiles, I suppose, the good fellow.'

Out there in the fields all day, does he contemplate the ending of the story? 'Yes, the very word "retirement" keeps recurring to me. I think one only needs a lot of guts to call it a day, a lot of courage to say "that's it, you're finishing with the game you love". It can be easy to deceive yourself at my age and think you're playing better than you are. I will leave the decision to the selection committee for them to tell me I am dropped and that's it.

'In Detroit, America, last year a lady came up to me and heard my name and said "I knew your father very well when he was playing for India all those years ago in 1971." Honestly. She did not believe it could still be me. Now, I can understand someone saying that to Clive Lloyd, but not to little me.'

---

## A 'WIMP' IN A HURRY TO HURT
*January 1986*

'Macho'. The nickname seems sinisterly apt. For to be sure, out there on the cricket field Malcolm Marshall's machismo is at full throttle as he looks to prove his virility by violent domination. He goes about his work with a cold-eyed, businesslike, unsmiling, scary relish. He seems in a hurry to hurt. It is one thing to be acknowledged by all opposition batsmen as the fastest in the world, quite a different kettle of cower to be the most dangerously lethal. Test batsmen have genuine nightmares about Marshall these days – only their wives wake up with worse sweats.

Suddenly, like a revelation, the game is won or lost and Marshall's features crease in a crow's feet network of laugh lines. He is much liked around cricket's dressing-rooms. People enjoy hanging their hat on the peg next to his. For one thing he whistles only the most cheerful reggae tunes. He is a whole-hearted, keen and confident comrade.

On Monday, in his home town pavilion at Bridgetown, his infectiously giggling delight bubbled all over as he cuddled, and was cuddled by, his Barbados captain Joel Garner after the two of them had laid Jamaica to waste to bring back the Shell shield to mighty little Barbados. The Colgate-smiling, hand-slapping glee went on for an hour or so and, of a sudden, the nickname Macho had become convivial, endearing, and totally untense. Just as the gold chain around his neck with his name on the pendant did not look half so, well, macho, or not as dangerous as it does when it glints ominously like a hired assassin's gun in the sun – or does when he turns from his mark to scud in on his toes with that short sprinter's hostility and that cruel and nasty narrowness to his eyes.

His loins girded with only a towel, Marshall looks almost ludicrously small-boned and slight; certainly he looks more of a spinner with cunning than a devilish and upsetting fast bowler. Botham calls him the 'skinny wimp'. When you talk to him, even my plump five feet 11 inches tower over him by at least an inch. To Wes Hall's Larry Holmes, Charlie Griffith's Frazier, Michael Holding's Muhammad, Colin Croft's Foreman, and Garner's, say, Carnera, he looks as small, tiny, loose and angelic as Sugar Ray Leonard at 160 lb. It is dotty to believe that Malcolm Marshall is less than two stone heavier than Barry McGuigan.

For all that, mind you, Marshall is in the whippy physical

image of other legends of the fast ball – Martindale, Constantine, Gilchrist and that long ago founder of the faith and man of the people, George John, from some 60 years ago, who was but five feet nine inches and, as C.L.R. James said: 'All power is in proportion ... pace and body action, he hits many a poor batsman on the inside of the knee to collapse them like a felled ox.' This new welterweight is even lighter. Marshall's half dozen summers so far with Hampshire have delighted him to make it his second home. But in truth Bournemouth's balmy breezes and corporation – imported palm trees patently cannot match his very nature's affinity with the bold primary colours and jangling, carefree good cheer of Barbados.

'Malcolm's real strength,' said his captain Garner above the hubbub of Monday evening, 'is that he has never given less than 110 per cent for any side he has ever played for – from school, club, Barbados, Hampshire or with us fellows in the West Indian team. Pulling his weight for the side just means everything to him.' Garner and Marshall slapped hands in a last and poignant intimacy that we hangers-on had no business to dare even understand. On Monday evening they would meet later, sure, for celebration drinks, a little music and much more laughter, but the team was off from the airport first thing in the morning to prepare for this weekend's lap of honour in Guyana so they would, they promised themselves, be early abed.

Now, nattily, crisply, and casually dressed, Marshall eases through the throng to rev up his sleek car and go home, perhaps for another change of clothing, for organising the evening. He revs up at the first traffic light. His countrymen recognise their silky bachelor boy hero, and shout 'Hey, Macho, you showed 'em!' or 'You lightnin' man, Macho,' and there was not the slightest tremor of resentment that his cricket was building him one of the loveliest homes on the island.

If the Big Bird, Joel, is the working class hero's prime minister, then Marshall is very much the one true Minister of Culture. Garner, for instance, has built himself, appropriately, the highest and most substantial house on the very foundations of the wooden shack in which his mother brought him up. There is no surprise, when you delve into it, that Marshall loves Hampshire so. He supposes it might have started as his favourite English county when he was a ragged urchin at primary school. The Barbadian cavalier Roy Marshall was the southern counties' most dashing import when the young Malcolm was first at school, and had learned to read.

He would look up Marshall's scores, just because of the same name in the paper. Then, when he was 14, the other hero, Andy Roberts, joined Hampshire didn't he? Again he would examine in *The Nation* the English scoreboards every morning. When he first came to England it was almost natural that he joined Hampshire. In his debut game in April 1979 it snowed. Nevertheless, with three sweaters on he took seven wickets when he was not embracing the dressing-room radiator. Sorry, 'ragged urchin' was pathetically romantic. But it is not right. Marshall, they say, was always beautifully turned out for school by his mother and grandmother. First at St Giles primary, where he is now challenging Wes Hall as A1 Alumnus, then at the Parkinson Comprehensive, where he was always immaculate in his khaki shorts and shirt. He was, teachers said last week, a model pupil, a team man.

Like Gary Sobers, from across the way at Bayland, Marshall's was a matriarchal boyhood. When Garfield was six his merchant seaman father's ship was torpedoed. When Malcolm was still in his cot his policeman father died in a motorcycle accident. Dad had played for the police team. Uncle was a cricketer as well, but it was his grandfather, Oscar, who would bowl to him in the backyard every evening or on the beach on Sundays. The boy loved batting then, and he loves it best now to tell the truth. He would, he admits, dearly enjoy to match Botham, Kapil or Imran as a match-winning Test all-rounder.

It is touching that he gives thanks to the fortune of having a steady apprenticeship as understudy after his Packer-induced introduction to Test cricket in 1978 after, incredibly, only one first class game. It followed his debut for Barbados when, just like this week, a set of pallid Jamaicans treated him like sheep for the shearing and his seven wickets got him picked for the tour to India. Marshall was deputy then to the quick quartet and, says Joel, he was always the most cheerful and willing of twelfth men, ready with the drinks, the hot bath and laundry. A few years later Colin Croft sold his soul to South Africa, then Roberts retired ... now Marshall is in the very pomp of fire and evil on the field. He will be 28 in April, and is possibly still short of his prime.

There was a perfect example of his awesome, awful talent on Monday. It was heightened by the baying of the crowd. It was like they were at an execution. Tyburn stuff. With only an hour left and still six Jamaican wickets to fall, Marshall threw in a startlingly nasty bouncer from scarcely short of a length that reared from his ribs to graze Davidson's helmet and, taking off in a screaming fizz, cleared the gloves of the wicket-keeper standing a pitch length back, though he leapt like Shilton. It went at one bounce for four byes. The next fearsome ball seemed exactly the same length and pitch. This time Davidson, scared and weary, ducked his head to the level of his shins, but the ball skidded straight on, hit the nerve that joined his left bicep to his collar bone. As the batsman writhed in his crease, white-faced, he was given out. Plumb leg before, even from the pavilion it was frightening. Poor Davidson rolled away looking drunk with fear and holding his badly bruised, limp arm.

Marshall cannot explain his knack, except to say he is an athlete, with a supple, rubbery physique. He says he has worked hard to balance himself through his short run-up, so he is always at top speed as he delivers. He looks like Roberts from the ropes, and from 22 yards, they say, he has discovered the value of the three-speed bouncer. 'Give them a few first-gear bouncers and they might get confident: throw in three times as fast and they appear in no position to play it: they are not ready.' Purists at the old game of chivalry would say there is something sickening, even sadistic, about Marshall's bowling. He is confident about his defence: 'Simply, I am a professional. I play to the rules. I am lucky to have my fitness and aggression, but I do not lack sense. I am a fast bowler, this is my job; if I bowl dangerously and I'm told I intimidate, then the umpires are empowered to stop me. When they do I will think of bowling differently; till then, I can only play to the best of my ability, such as it is. I am simply a man who loves cricket and happens to be a fast bowler, a keen professional and a working man with obligations to meet and a new mortgage to pay. I am a man who wants to do his best for himself and his team every time I go to work.'

The first Test in Jamaica is racing towards the English tourists. Sabina Park will probably be the fastest wicket. Yet Gower has scored a Test century against Marshall at Sabina. 'I can think of better things than facing him: he is a brilliant bowler, but it is not very nice,' says the England captain. Gooch has also hit a hundred against him at Sabina, 'but he is definitely nasty as a proposition'. Lamb has scored three hundreds against Marshall in England – 'He bounces you at will, and Malcolm must be the nastiest of them all.'

Last summer at Taunton Botham walked in at 50 for five, called for his white helmet, and though peppered by ferocious stuff from Marshall, answered fire with fire in a blazing innings of 149 in 106 balls, first dismissing Tremlett and then driving Marshall back with skimmingly crazy two-iron shots over long-on or long-off, or hooking him off his whiskers into the car park over fine leg. Exasperated, that cold-eyed look and beady fury on his brow, Marshall finally clean bowled the blond baron of beef, and then went down the wicket with the broadest of grins, embraced his opponent, and clapped him all the way back to the pavilion.

As Botham said earlier this week, as he vanished up into the Bajam Hills, and into faraway, devious, late-night haunts with his pals Garner and Marshall: 'Of course we are friends. Malcolm and I relish the contest. He is a magnificent bowler, but he's a cricketer too. He is an athlete. I always say to the skinny wimp when I get to the wicket, "What have you in store for me today?" Malcolm is unquestionably the quickest and most dangerous man about today. He is no Lillee yet, but he is swinging it and plays it just as hard. But the point with him is everyone has a laugh and a joke afterwards.'

I asked Marshall if he would remember Botham's Taunton innings when England faced him in Jamaica this month. 'I am not sure if I will be selected,' he said modestly, and at that, from the highest corner of the dressing-room, Garner stood up and laughed so much that Marshall had to join in, giggling, and slapping a few nearby palms. Macho, sure, but a jolly nice sportsman as well.

---

## FOR SERVICES TO ENGLAND ...
### *July 1980*

By chance, we had lunch in an olde Englishe place not far from Lincoln's Inn Fields where he started work as a solicitor's office boy at the age of 14 in 1932. The ageing, aproned English waiters recognised him, which was nice. He didn't even look at the menu but simply ordered roast beef and greens. For a split second I even fancied he hummed a snatch of Gilbert and Sullivan 'When I was a boy I served a term as office boy to an attorney's firm ...'.

The Englishness of it all was appropriate. Alec Bedser, at 63, may be a successful something-in-the-city now, but he is still the great big-eared English yeoman of a long and ancient and trustworthy line. He bowled his boots off for England. He hung them up 21 years ago. In 1962 he became a Test selector and for the last nine years he has been chairman. Peter May is to succeed him.

I had thought that the England team at Old Trafford tomorrow was effectively the last one to be picked by Bedser and that May would be co-opted to help choose the side for the last Test and the tour of India. Not a bit of it. Alec's last list will be the touring team – 'And anyway,' he says, 'I dare say they'll ask me to help 'em out again soon enough.' So it meant I couldn't get any secrets out of him, though I did sniff the teeniest, accidental hint that Keith Fletcher will be the touring captain. We will see.

I met a young first class cricketer the other day who honestly did not know even that his chairman of selectors had himself played for England. He just presumed Bedser was one of 'them' up there at Lord's. 'I dunno,' moans Alec, 'these youngsters today ...' and he shakes his head and his eyes colour a sad grey-blue and he is at a loss for words till another, 'I dunno, they don't know how lucky they are.' He loves a good moan does Alec.

You sometimes think he blames it all on school meals. Well, Eric and he had to walk four miles a day to and from the Monument Hill Central School, Woking, didn't they, with sandwiches in the satchel and just a cup of water in the lunch hour. This lot don't know how lucky they are. At 14 he and Eric would get the train to London at 7.30 in the morning and get home at 8 that night – at 10 on the three evenings a week they studied shorthand and book-keeping at night school.

Their father was a bricklayer. He died at 89 three years ago. The two beloved bachelor boys still live with Mum, 88 last birthday, in the little house at Woking that the family built, brick by brick, in 1932, the boys labouring and Dad laying. Mother went to work, even though they were once down to their last shilling for the gas. Dad always said he would earn the money if she looked after the boys. She still does and is as lively and active as a cricket round the hearth.

Eric was born first by a few minutes. If they are not quite identical now, Eric being slightly plumper, there's scarcely a wrinkle in it. John Woodcock, the editor of *Wisden*, once played golf with them at Worplesdon. Same outfits, same shot off the first tee with identical No 2 woods and identical short swing; the two balls ended up on the fairway kissing each other – 'Eggs in the same nest'. They both joined the Surrey ground staff in 1938. They served together throughout the war, long, dusty, dangerous days in Africa and wetter ones in Italy. On the resumption of fun Alec started taking wickets by the hatful.

At once he played in the 1946 Test trial and though he had damaged a thigh he secretly strapped it up in the lavatory. 'Where d'you field?' said B.H. Valentine. 'Slip,' lied Alec. Then he winced, took a deep breath, and got out Hammond and Hutton and was chosen for the first Test against India. The great big boy walked to Woking station with his great big cricket bag. He took the tube from Waterloo to Baker Street, then a bus to Lord's. Wally Hammond gruffed 'Good luck'.

247

He took 11 wickets in the match, then another 11 in the next one. In all, he was to take a record 236 wickets for England. On Hammond's tour of Australia he toiled heroically for more than 500 overs. It lasted from 31 August 1946, to 17 April 1947; he was paid £295, plus 25 bob a week spending money. At Adelaide in 104 degrees he had to go off to be sick, then bowled Bradman with a ball that the Don still says was the best that ever got him. 'Yeah, and I bowled a lot more like it since,' mutters Alec, tucking into his greens.

He loves Australia. It's just that he likes England better. He still writes very regularly to Bradman, Arthur Morris, Ron Archer and Keith Miller. 'Keith, of course, has never replied, but always rings me first thing whenever he arrives in England.'

Brown's next tour of Australia: 'We could have won easy, but old Freddie stupidly wanted to be surrounded by youngsters. If we had taken the likes of Keeton, Langridge, Edrich, Gimblett, Brookes, Ikin, Jackson, Robertson or Watson instead of kids like Dewes, Sheppard, Parkhouse, Close and Berry, we'd have walked it.'

The end came in terms of the big-time, for the second Test of Hutton's tour. Alec had shingles and should never have played in the first match. England were slaughtered. Alec, sickly, took one for 131 ('seven catches dropped, mind you'). So they let the Typhoon loose. 'No sour grapes, Tyson got plenty, sure, but I would have got 100 wickets on those pitches. Arthur Morris put us in 'cos he didn't want to face me that first morning.' But when the captain pinned up the team in the dressing-room Bedser was not on it. Hutton had not even mentioned it. Alec felt humiliated. 'Funny bloke, Len. Do you know, when I was ill on that tour I was in bed for a fortnight. He was in the next room, but never once did he pop in to visit.'

He is a more kindly selector. Either he or the captain is always in touch with the team on the phone. Alec's first chairman of selectors was the late R.W.V. Robins. Snobby Robby. 'We would meet at his flat or his St James's Club on a Sunday morning. He never really watched any cricket. Just went on what he read in the papers or heard from his cronies.

He would turn up to the first day of a Test, but on the second day, after lunch, he'd sometimes clear off and go to the pictures.'

Boycott has loomed large over Alec's own chairmanship. The self-imposed exile started around the time Geoffrey kept getting out to the Indian, Solkar: 'a real toffee apple bowler'. Then he sulked something rotten when Denness was made captain. At the beginning of every season Bedser would ring Boycott. The rum Yorkshireman was convinced 'public school blokes at Lord's had it in for him'. Alec would patiently tell him that the selectors, Bedser, Barrington, Hutton, and Elliott had all been to elementary school.

When Geoffrey telephoned that he might be ready to return in 1977 he was playing at Northampton. Alec said he'd come and see him. 'No,' said Geoffrey, 'not here at the ground, man!' 'All right,' said Alec. 'I'll see you after the game in the corner of the foyer at the Grand Hotel, Northampton.'

'No,' insisted Geoffrey. 'I'll be in the car park at the Watford Gap service station. No, not in the snack bar, in the car park. We mustn't be seen together.' They sat there side by side for two hours. 'At least he was on time,' mutters Alec. The truce was worked out and the glorious comeback determined. To have to coerce a man into playing for England must have been extremely distasteful to Alec. It was probably something, he thought, to do with free school meals. 'I dunno,' and he shakes his head and his eyes cloud over. 'I dunno … these young blokes today....'

---

# STAKING ALL ON THE TURN OF AN ACE QADIR
### *June 1987*

Even from a distance there is no mistaking the most distinctive bowling action in Test match cricket. Abdul Qadir, possibly the very last of history's regal line of leg-spinners was practising to ensure his entrance at Lord's today – and so, quite simply, this summer's Test series can truly begin in earnest. Time for olde tyme – and what treats may be in store. Certainly Qadir was worth waiting for. Such a singular mystic must be allowed his licence. I fancy even more of his Pakistani colleagues will not really believe he has come to the aid of the party till he marks out his run today with those riveting eccentric hops and steps and jumps.

After nursing his sick wife in Lahore for the first 50 days of the tour, Qadir arrived at Heathrow on Sunday since when he has been practising at Lord's. It is more than two months since he had a bowl, but he has 'kept supple with exercise,' he says, 'all my bowling needs is suppleness'. As well as, you mischievously think, an umpire who understands the lbw law. But you resist the quip. Qadir is one of those interviewees whose actions speak louder than words.

He looks longingly across the stately old London ground from the Nursery end. 'Is the pitch bouncing? Is it hard?' He needs bounce, always, for his full repertoire. In his last Test match here, he reminds you, he took six English wickets – 'some with the new ball to give me more bounce'. You did not need reminding. He's so bamboozled any number of the English batsmen – some stretching till they stretched too far, others scurrying back into their stumps – that a historic match was won and a series set alight. The scenario could be the same this time.

His wife, it seems, has suffered a nervous breakdown – though when such sicknesses happen to foreigners, English Sunday papers blaze out with cruel merriment such headlines as 'Cricketer's Haunted Wife' and 'Mrs Q Possessed By Spirits'. Which was the sort of guff that greeted him when he arrived in London. He will pray for her many times each day. 'Of course, the Maker is our guiding light.' He prays too, for success at cricket before every match. 'Sometimes, like Lord's last time, before every ball. Yes, of course, I still carry my prayer mat in the cricket bag.'

Then, with a soft smile, he wheels away to his marker at the top of his run, turns, eyes now alight with concentration, ball in his right hand, and sways back expansively on the heel of his left foot. Now a fierce looping whir of the ball as he spins it to his left hand, then displays it to the batsman in the distance like a tennis server to an opponent, or as a conjuror does an orange to a schoolboy. Finally, at the end of a crabby, sideways two-step shuffle, the ball is transferred back to the right hand and, arms now like flailing windmills, he prances into first a lollop of a trot, then just before delivery one springy bound of menace and over she comes. Out of the hat might come an orthodox leg-break, a googly, or a flipper, a top-spinner or, most devastating of all, a substitute top-spinner bowled with an extra twirl in the follow-through that makes the bat play for an orthodox googly. Or is it the other way round?

That is only the first act – for the appeals and the anguish, the pleadings and poutings, the joys and intrigues, the agonies and ecstasies follow every ball. At Lord's last time, I seem to remember, he was warned for 'over-appealing'. Sometimes he was almost on his knees in supplication before the great white god, Dickie Bird. In real life, Qadir seems a serenely detached young man: only an enquiry for lbw can inject him with dynamic obsessions. Away from the crease the kestrel eye is un-beady and he seems of a calming, even studious bent. He learned, he says, by watching – and being apprenticed to – two of the game's last exponents of the dying craft, Intikhab Alam and Mushtaq Mohammad.

The massive Inti rolled his shoulder to put the ball on the spot, the tiny Mushy was all wrist. Uniquely, Qadir rolls them over with both shoulder and wrist. Qadir alone in the big-time now carries the torch for such maestros as Marriott and Mailey, Grimmett and Benaud, Wright and O'Reilly, Hollies and Hobbs.

After street cricket in Lahore, the puppy-fat plump little son of a leading religious preacher in the great mosque, developed at school as a batsman; from Government College he joined Javed Miandad's Habib Bank club and immediately announced himself with 12 wickets for 74 in his first two senior matches of 1975.

His first Test series was against Brearley's tourists in 1977, and in the Hyderabad Test he took six for 44, at one point getting Randall, Roope, Taylor and Edmonds in 16 balls for four runs. The wizard was off and away for a consummately

251

fascinating career which (thus far anyway) was voluptuously crowned last winter when he took six for 16 in nine overs at Faisalabad to rout Viv Richards' West Indians for just 53.

For all such rewards he offers gratitude, simply and with a shy smile, to the Maker. It can be no sacrilege to surmise that the Muslim nature embraces the leg-spinner's mystique. Thus it is a pity that in terms of cricket England's national religion inspires bowlers mostly to be, as another crafty and joyous 'letter', Ian Peebles used to complain, 'just good old straight up and down, no nonsense, military medium, Church of England trundling.'

Yet while there's Qadir there is hope that the ancient art that was fashioned and matured on the green grass of England is not completely dead and buried and obsolete somewhere in the world. One of England's best leggers of the legend was Roley Jenkins, of Worcestershire, who ran up rather like Qadir in slow motion, a crab in dancing pumps. One Saturday afternoon, against Sussex, Roley had the young Rev. D. Sheppard scuffling about in embarrassed trouble for over upon over. But still the good Lord looked after his own.

At last, exasperated, Roley rolled down the wicket to suggest, 'Reverend, if I had your luck, I'd be ruddy Archbishop of Canterbury!' – which at least gave the young Bishop-to-be his pulpit text for the morrow, which was: 'Never go back. Religious faith, my dear brethren, is like facing Roley Jenkins. No hesitation: if you decide to go forward, go forward all the way.'

We will see today at Lord's how stands the religious faith of Englishmen. The series starts here.

---

# MACLAGAN: THE BOWLING OF A MAIDEN OVER
### *May 1986*

Nicest present the Women's Cricket Association could receive in this diamond jubilee year would be for Lord's to let them play for a day on the hallowed male preserve when the

Australian women's team tour next year. The Long Room mandarins have agreed to pencil-in a possible Thursday next July, but many of the girls have heard that before and are none too hopeful that the promise will be honoured by MCC's male chauvinists. Women cricketers have been allowed to play there only once – 10 years ago, and grudgingly.

Meanwhile, the WCA celebrations this year are open to all. Yesterday they marked the jubilee with a match at Gosden Common, near Guildford, scene of the first ever recorded match between 'Eleven maids of Bramley and 11 of Hambleton' on 26 June 1745.

'Look it up, I think you'll find it was the very same week the Young Pretender arrived back on the coast of Scotland,' says Myrtle Maclagan briskly. She is 75 years old and in the 1930s was the pioneering England all-rounder of Bothamesque achievement and a shorter hair-style. Over half a century ago she scored the first ever women's Test match hundred – versus Australia in Sydney.

You fancy she knows her Scottish military history. She is, literally, an old soldier, being a pre-war major in the Auxiliary Training Corps, woman's first 'regiment', and later top brass in the WRAC. She thinks Mrs Thatcher is getting a rotten, unfair Press. For all that introduction, you know really she'd prefer to be laughing and if you pass muster the fierce blue eyes turn readily to jollity and the chuckles tumble on. Her last great innings was in 1963 – 81 not out for the Combined Services at Aldershot.

The newly-formed WCA had sent down a team to play the school. As a result, she turned up to cricket week, still an annual hen-party, at Colwall, near Malvern. 'Would you believe, my very first day, a senior match, I took all 10 wickets for 22 runs. Never did it again, but couldn't have chosen a better moment to crash in on them all, could I?' The memory makes for much laughter. 'Off-breaks, me, with a few leg-breaks chucked up. Later, I learned all about flighting and that sort of thing. They didn't know I'd come from bowling for hour upon hour at my brother in the garden. Then I made myself a batsman.'

Maclagan and Snowball became the 1930s' Hobbs and

Sutcliffe in pleated white gymslips. All the country knew of them. A master at her brother's school, Haileybury, had said 'Give it up, gel, no use cricket for women.' It gave her pleasure to come back to him a few years later and say: 'Cricket? Well, it got me a world tour.'

That first ever England tour to Australia left in the late winter of 1934. 'On the SS *Cathay*. There was me, seven teachers, two secretaries, one art student, one lawyer, two or three who "did nothing"; most of us were under 24. We paid our own fare out, then we were guests of Australians. We were amateurs so could not accept any gifts of bats or blazers. We stood on our own two feet. Nowadays they seem to expect to be paid for everything.'

The team was unbeaten. In the first Test, at Brisbane, Australia were bowled out for 47 – Maclagan seven for 10. In the second at Sydney, Maclagan's was the first ever Test century. She cannot remember much about the innings – 'except the stroke I did it with, because the Press gave me a photo afterwards: it was a cover-drive: Hammond stuff, you know! No, I don't think it was all that good a stroke, to be honest, though many years later I had the director of the Army Sports Control Board round for coffee here and I showed him the picture and he said "What a good looking stroke!" '

In 1951, she captained England and was awarded the MBE. She is devoted to gardening as her sumptuous borders at Camberley colourfully testify, even in this soggy spring. But most beloved of all, are her brothers, nieces and great-nieces. On the coffee-table the knitting bag covers two glossy picture books – on *The Archers* and *Princess Diana*. Her old Gunn & Moore Autograph bat, teak-brown and twine-bound, leans next to the front door, ready to repel.

A great-niece asked the other day why she had never married. 'Never met anyone whose face I wanted to see at breakfast – nor him mine, I dare say.' More chuckles. 'I told her, look here I've had the best family, the best country, the best fun. Do you know, I've really been darned lucky. Now, do have some more ginger cake and tell me the inside story of this Botham business....'

# 13

## EXTRA TIMES

It has not by any means been a question of swanking and swanning around the great and grand amphitheatres of the world. Most fun perhaps has come from the unconsidered, knocked-off, day-out jobs which I dare say have contributed over half the three million odd words that I've banged into the *Guardian* alone over the last 15 years. My first ever sports reporting was for the *Hereford Times* and *Stroud News* back as a cub in the 1950s at hedging and ploughing matches! Ooh, yes, I knew all about straight furrows and hazel whipcord. After dipping into this little lot, many of you will think I should have stuck to ploughing and hedging.

Tell you what, I wouldn't half mind getting back to it one day. Fresh air – and the beer tents stay open all day.

# CLOTH OF GOLD
*April 1985*

Jarndyce v Jarndyce was never so drawn out nor dramatic as a case as Taylor v Davis. All this considered, I dare say Charles Dickens himself would have approved: he always reckoned he was a man of the people. The third episode of BBC 2's classic serial Bleak House which swam mistily into view in the early hours of Monday morning – put off by the continuing saga of Dennis Taylor's unlikely snooker epic – will be repeated this evening at six o'clock, replacing Laramie.

It was well past midnight and the lights were still on all over England when Taylor, the tubby little Ulster outsider with the tubby, glinting, bright-moon spectacles, sank the fortnight's very final black to take the world championship from the cool kid and knowing metropolitan, Steve Davis, the nonpareil. It was like Sergeant Bilko beating Ali over the full 15.

And it was more than just the stuff of sport. An unlikely winner had an even more unlikely army behind him, witness half a nation of sons and mums, nobs and nobodies, debs and plebs and proles in shoals who blearily set off for their differing Monday morning shifts with bloodshot eyelids rimmed with red – or rather, pink, blue, green ... not forgetting the black.

An initial guess from the BBC yesterday did not quibble at my suggestion of a phenomenal past midnight audience of over 12 million. Even Dickensian scholars must have stayed hooked. Quite a few of these one-off live dramas of the television age have involved not only giant steps for mankind but nice little sporting extravaganzas. The World Cup final in 1966, of course; snooker itself once or twice, certainly when the Hurricane blew into Sheffield a year or three back. I remember a provincial high street crowd almost blocking the traffic around Multibroadcast when Botham was batting against Australia one Saturday afternoon – or even the midweek morning when Willis was bowling in the same series.

Or the Gillette semi-final at Old Trafford when Lancashire beat Gloucester and David Hughes' sixes just saved the nine o'clock news being put back.

This Sunday night drama was italicised for taking us so by surprise. For two weeks the moving wallpaper has been gently unrolling in everybody's sitting room – a softly clinking kaleidoscope of colours over there in the corner, accompanied by a crew of somnolent whispering Ovaltini old-time hypnotists. You could take it or leave it, flicking back and forth when Newsnight got too schoolmasterly.

By Sunday lunchtime there seemed the certainty that the fortnight of watching green-baize grass grow had turned into a dreadfully sad anti-climax. Taylor was 0-7 down and the only interest was to watch the waistcoated executioner narrow his eyes and lay out the corpse. The Sunday papers were almost ripe with obituaries.

Slowly through the day – clink, clink, pot, pot, glint, glint – Taylord fiddled with his spectacles and eked his way back. The climax, off the last ball of the last shot of the last gasp, was tumultuous in its almost dotty fulfilment of dramatic unities. Alan Clark, the director, has filmed a Trevor Preston script into a hugely anticipated musical – *Billy The Kid And The Green Baize Vampire* – and reckons nobody backing it would have believed his ending of a title determined on the final black of all.

I rang a friend in Belfast to offer him some sort of second-hand congratulations. He had been unable to watch the last frame and had locked himself in another room. Rather like boxing with McGuigan, snooker in Ulster has crossed the sectarian divide. It is the working class pastime. Higgins is from the Donegal Road, Taylor from Coalisland, in Tyrone, hitherto best known as the scene of the first reverberating Civil Rights march in 1968.

Taylor's parents named their tubby Dennis with two Ns after Dennis Haughey, the SDLP politician whom Mum thought 'a fine wee lad'. His mother died last year and he seriously thought of packing up the game. He had only won £16,000 last year and had Denise, Damian and Brendan to educate. He rang his father Tom in the middle of the wee hours on Monday and could hear the bands playing down the street.

Next week Taylor, who has since settled in Lancashire, returns to his beloved Province where for two nights in Antrim at the Riverside, he takes on the locals who have been battling for months to play him in the *Sunday News* competition. The cheers from the beleaguered old gap-toothed bleak houses next week will match those across the water well after midnight on Sunday. And the bloodshot eyes at work next day will be coloured the same.

---

# LISA OPIE AND THE LADYLIKE ART OF KILLING ON COURT
### *November 1988*

Squash is no game for a convent schoolgirl. For a start, 'game' stretches the point somewhat. Anyone who has played the sport even to reasonable club-league level knows it is more like seething martial combat, a case of GBH on the mid-court T.

The knack in squash is not so much to score points, of course, but to sandbag your rival's will and spirit into submission. Sweat flies about this sneaker-squeaking snakepit in bucketloads, but it could as well be blood.

So what's a nice girl like this doing as the best woman player in the country? Last night in Bristol, Lisa Opie set about winning the British national championship for a record fifth time. She is 25, gymslip gorgeous and occasionally giggly, and looks as if marge would not melt in her mouth. Not so. She has to tell you that she is by no means demure and Persil-white, and that venom lurks when her racket-dagger is in her hand.

Another dramatic thing is that her deadly rival and the woman she is seeded to meet in next Thursday's final, Martine le Moignan, went to the very same convent school on Guernsey, and both of them learned the rudiments of the game on what was then the island's only court. They now travel the globe, being paid to stop off here and there in windowless dungeons and let the crowds watch them try to scratch and tear each other's self-esteem to shreds. There are now only a couple of more formidable women squash players in the whole world than these two hot-blooded, tight-chested Guernsey sweaters.

Lisa came from softer stock than her present calling would indicate. Her father is a potter on the island, and she learned to throw clay at five and then to paint and glaze. The home beach that this incipient tomboy romped on was old Renoir's much-loved seascape stretch at Moulin Huet.

Squash then came only in a bottle, and she was all set to go to art school on leaving the Sisters of Mercy at Blanchelande Convent. Somehow she found herself next to Martine, who is a year older, as they were coached in the game's rudiments by a local mathematician, Reg Harbour. She was hooked. So was Martine. The duel was forged. 'If Martine did well, then I had to try for better,' she says. 'If I was playing well, it served only as a spur to her. The rivalry got us going, and in a way it still keeps us striving to be the best.' Sisters of mercy, indeed.

As any woman will tell you in an unguarded moment, if you can handle female rivalry then that of macho men is comparative peanuts. Lisa, by now, is used to chauvinist taunts on the squash courts. 'Like, a few months ago the Derbyshire county player, Nigel Millington, who comes from a leading squash family, said I might be able to beat him when he wasn't really trying, but that if we put some money down on it I wouldn't be in with a chance. I slapped £10 down and he matched it. I beat him. It got very aggressive in there. Very tense. A real war of the sexes. Then he slapped £50 down: I matched it. The gloves were really off. Hammer and tongs, furious, competitive stuff. I beat him in the end.' She has a marvellous laugh.

Journalists describe her career as turbulent. Once she V-signed a referee on television. She has thrown rackets and been fined by governing bodies even more than – when they check up – their rules allow. 'I know it's no excuse to say that it can get pretty tight and tense in there, but your concentration can get you into real turmoils. The psychological side is the one I've been working on, and I really think I've improved and become much more relaxed about it. I've got into meditation and imagery – you know, imagining a match from start to finish, every aspect of it; say winning it when all has seemed lost, or even losing one against someone you don't like and then not getting uptight about it.

'Of course, I still get uptight in there, but I can control the demons now, I think. Jonah [Barrington] will be pleased, won't he? When I was training with him, he was really good for me with coaching, discipline and diets and so on – and if he might have been a bit intense with me at times, he was nothing like his colleague, Bomber Harris. I'm afraid every time Bomber's temperament collided with mine, the whole thing just erupted.'

She thanks Jonah still for putting her on a diet. 'Five or six years ago I was really overweight for the circuit. He cut out all fats. Now it's just toast for breakfast and, four hours before a match, a plate of pasta for energy and stamina. Afterwards, pasta and potatoes.'

Not that good old Jonah is really entitled to talk, I told her. He once told me that his sadism more than his fitness had sometimes carried him on to victory, saying there was 'a savage, fantastic and unrivalled satisfaction, the moment when, in a long match, you look into your opponent's eyes and see defeat and degradation staring back.'

Oh sure, lovely Lisa knows the feeling. 'Yes, on court you've got to be aggressive, challenging. Sometimes, mind, if you're playing someone you don't like anyway, you can get too fired up. Not that there's much bitchiness or butchiness on the circuit; there are about 30 of us regulars and on the whole we get on very well indeed off court.'

Some outstanding juniors, such as Lucy Soutter and Alison Cumings, are coming through determinedly, but the rivalry of the two Guernsey players still lights up the women's game with jangling tensions whenever they take the court together.

'They aren't "grudge" matches at all,' she says, 'though there's always been this amazing rivalry because of our background. It was much worse when we were juniors, I can tell you. Now Martine lives in Germany and I'm in

Nottingham, so we don't travel so much together.

'And then, our games are so very different, a real clash of styles. Martine's a big girl relying a lot on her strength and reach, and her amazing unorthodoxy – she can conjure up shots that I think take even her by surprise. If she's hot, she's very hot; so she just goes out and plays her own game and sees if it all comes together. I'm totally different. I think I work things out more. Okay, when I go on court with her I do my damnedest to look all confident and perky, like. However the match progresses I've got to keep that up, keep looking unbothered, keep mixing my game up, doing all my good, delicate things in the front court, relying on my determination and stamina, and not forget to lob and drop her when she keeps trying to force me into the back corners. Once her head starts to drop I usually know I've got the match.

'You're wrong if you think aggressive players are the ones who hit hard all the time. Properly channelled aggression, to be really worthwhile and destructive, is not thumping the ball but being sly and controlled – plus not getting exhausted first. But the best match I must ever have played, I can't remember a thing about. You're sort of in a trance when you're playing really well, on a high. That was against the Australian Vicki Cardwell in the world team championships in New Zealand. She'd won the British [Open] title four times and was now playing for her country, which makes her trebly full of aggro. We were love-one down. This one I was going to win.

'I might remember the first service, but that's all. I was in a trance of concentration, a cocoon of invincibility. I came off, and still don't have a clue about the score. Except that I beat her. You play by instinct, by autopilot, and you win famously. It's uncanny. It's also excruciating the morning after you've lost a match that you should have won. That hurts cruelly.

'I curse myself horribly then for being too like my father. He always likes to try different things in the pottery – he goes from ovenware to tableware to casseroles to tourist mugs to porcelain, always something new. Like me on court, sometimes: getting bored with this match and looking to diversify, playing too many shots, trying to impress myself with something really great instead of just winning the point.'

261

She has to look up what she might win for taking the national title next week. It is, comparatively, very good wages: £2,500 to the champion. Much more than most titles she goes for. Endorsements keep her going: Reebok has just signed her in a £30,000 three year deal covering shoes and clothing; Formula Sports gives her another deserved wodge for using its rackets and bags.

A long way from Renoir's sublime beaches, let alone Daddy's pottery. Hard work, sure, but does it take a ruthless streak too? 'What, me ruthless?' poutingly ponders the champion. 'Not fair at all!'

Nor is it. But nor, on court, is she a Sister of Mercy.

---

## ALL IRELAND SET TO TOAST THE MATCH OF THE CENTURY
### *March 1984*

*Dublin*: Heard the one about the Irishman who thought the English had a cricket team? Such was the greeting as I ducked into dark and dingy and convivial bars to escape British soccer supporters from Glasgow and Liverpool who were the wretched marauders in Dublin this week. Fortunately for the old city, the most worthwhile bars are always the hardest to find. You pop into one to see who's having a jar, have one, then both move on to the next. The pub crawl becomes like a schoolgirl's crocodile, and they print the route maps in the guidebooks.

In Scruffy Murphy's upstairs bar, just off Lower Mount Street the talk remained on sport, but none of your blithering soccer. The two midweek matches were just tasters for Sunday. Tomorrow at Croke Park takes place the Gaelic football All-Ireland final – the very Centenary match no less, and, as luck will have it, to be contested by the classic rivals of history, Dublin and Kerry. The Dubs v The Kingdom.

Scruffy's was full already of sportsmen. It was The Match to be talked about. Anticipation was already crackling. Sport can embrace the nation in Ireland like nowhere else.

262

Especially the Gaelic, which is at one with the Captains and the Kings, the poets and the Little People. More than 60,000 will be packed in the park tomorrow – but no hooligans. One man in Scruffy's raised a long black glass. 'Kerry for the Holidays, Dublin for the Cup.' Charles Haughey, the former Prime Minister, smiled his raffish smile at that. At University College Dublin he was a demon at the Gaelic. After Sunday he will be back on the campaign trail.

In the group was Ron Delaney, one-time Olympic champion and still bald and still beaming, a man who once marked Stanley Matthews at Dalymount Park; and Ulick O'Connor, the playwright and biographer of both Oliver St Gogarty and Brendan Behan. And the two eminent doctors of medicine, Karl Mullen, who captained the Triple Crowners of the late 1940s, and Kevin O'Flanagan, double international who was asked one Saturday by Arsenal what his expenses were – 'Fourpence,' he replied, 'I came up to Highbury on the Tube' and there was the golfer, Tommie Campbell, who once drove a golf ball 392 yards, the longest non wind-assisted drive ever.

Ulick says he once took a taxi to play a round with Campbell. Said the taxi driver: 'For Jesus' sake, that drive of his bounced off a stone.' That's Dublin for you – the only city in the world that has produced three Nobel prize winners for literature and where every yobbo thinks he can do better, and where they tell you that their only record holder in golf bounced the ball off a stone to make his great drive.

If poets were really immortal they would have all been here talking of Sunday. Beckett was hot stuff at cricket and boxing and his school magazine at Portora said he was 'a brilliant scrum-half'. Sean O'Casey would have looked in for sure: his eyesight was too narrow for hurling, but he was match secretary of the great Dublin Gaelic football side, O'Toole's, whose ghosts will be cheering the Dubs tomorrow.

Jack Lynch, another former Prime Minister, was all for the Gaelic and a double all-Ireland medallist at both hurling and football. Eamon de Valera would never miss a game: when he was president, even instead of a bishop, he was asked to throw the ball in to start the final. One time he did it and in a glorious passage of sustained imagery, a barracker shouted at him: 'Valera, why don't you throw your own two in after it, and then you can make a pawnshop of the game like you have done to this country!'

O'Connor explained the game. It seems a compromise between Association and Rugby. You can punch the ball, pass forward, kick-and-run with it. The nearest thing might be Australian rules, which was founded by press-ganged Irish soldiers and gold-diggers over there in the middle of the last century. It can be, by all accounts, thunderously exciting and I am assured that if we watch the transmission tomorrow on Channel 4 the intricacies even will soon be reasonably apparent. Certainly the drama will.

The English in Ireland tried to stop all indigenous sport, thinking it was a cover for freedom fighters' training. 'All artisans, mechanics and labourers' were banned from organised Gaelic sport. Indeed on 21 November 1921 – Bloody Sunday – the British army opened fire from above the terraces and killed 14 people and wounded 62 soon after the All-Ireland final had begun that year in Croke Park.

That is something else old men and grandchildren will be remembering in the same arena tomorrow – and remembering too that group of Fenian patriots who secretly made a rendezvous 100 years ago, on All Saints' Day 1884, in the shuttered billiards room of Miss Hayes' Commercial Hotel, Thurles, where it was formally decided to found secretly 'The Gaelic Association for the Preservation and Cultivation of our National Pastimes'. Mr Haughey had to leave for an art exhibition and the meeting was breaking up, but as Joyce might have said had he been at Scruffy's: 'We will now read the second chapter of Guinnesses!'

---

## FOR JUMPS, READ HUMPS …
*April 1985*

*Dubai*: It was not exactly Aintree. The races were being televised, but at least we were spared David Coleman's titfer and Julian Wilson's vowels and ears in the jostle of the unsaddling enclosure. In fact this Persian Gulf racecourse was just holding a warm-up meeting yesterday morning; the Grand National of camel racing does not take place until next week. Many of the leading entries for the 700-odd camel race festival are still making their way to Dubai from all points of Araby, led by their four-stone jockeys, who all look like blanket-wrapped seven-year-olds from a distance, although some are already on the Phyllosan and have probably banked a boodle of prize money.

Dubai's ruling dynasty, led by His Highness Sheikh Rashin bin Saeed al Maktoum – who is also Prime Minister of these United Arab Emirates – and his sons and nephews, were giving sumptuously generous patronage to the tribal sport of their desert forefathers long before they started pumping pounds into breeding their winners for British horseracing. In recent years they have been even more keen on revitalising the long line of their heritage.

The sportswriter from *Gulf News* has never changed his descriptive writing since the Old Testament, let alone the New. 'Energetic local jockeys showed good control,' he wrote. 'The ships of the desert sailed fast along the sea of sand to vie for the valuable cash awards.' Then came the results and starting prices. It is rather like Newmarket transferred in a dream to Weston-super-Mare. The wood-fenced track stretches interminably to a sandy, distant heat haze. Binoculars are no good. You can spot the field's progress only by its snowballing, rolling cloud of dust. Outside the fence, as at Aintree, is a parallel track on which the race is followed by a fleet of cars and vans, travelling at about 12mph, I estimate. The television camera truck leads the parade; it is the only vehicle clear of the dust. The races themselves are as interminable as a Bedouin's patience: they distance between eight and 20 kilometres (about 13 miles).

'Come on my son!' sounds roughly the same in Arabic. If you're not following by car, you swan about the enclosure of a modern grandstand and nod to stately white-robed head-dressed men and their beautiful, voluptuous, lip-sticked, ear-ringed women in the *shalwar-kameez*, those elegant

Muslim pyjamas of dashing primary colours. Few really watch the distant roll of dust – the television monitors tell a better story as the long-necked necklace unravels in the sandy distance.

Round the back, the 'stables' are as the world over: a busy, jabbering babel with the clang of buckets and the smell of tack and manure and hay and annoyance and industry. I was told a racing camel's diet consists of cows' milk, butter, maize, green grass and hay, in carefully monitored quantities. Drugs, they say, will never be used.

The midget jocks don't seem to bother what colour sheets they sling over their shoulders. Nor are racecards printed. Everyone seems to know who is who. The Sheikhs put up exorbitant prizes – but other sheikhs seem to own all the winners. The cost of one classic racing camel has reached the equivalent of £1 million but the average are bred and change hands at something above £100,000. There is a local breed, the 'Hisani', they are working on, but the best racers originate from the Butan region of the Sudan, two breeds more sleek than the friendly things you ride in the zoo: the 'Boushary' strain is dark brown, the 'Anafi' honey gold or sometimes white.

For speed, the rounded bulbous curve of their chests is further from their front legs than looks possible. The jockeys perch almost on their tails and carry a large bamboo stick which mostly they rub on the side of their animal's neck at different speeds as if to generate rhythmic gearchanges – which indeed, you can see they do. But very, very slowly. The skew-wiff, wonky-tabled gait of a camel, let alone its lugubrious, buck-toothed expression, make their racing comic to an outsider. The length of the races and the comparative lack of overdrive until the end – which can be exciting enough – makes it no surprise that suddenly this neck of the world's woods has taken with such enthusiasm to cricket. Both sports, some would say, have the appeal of watching grass grow.

# FROTH AND SMILES AMIDST ROCKS AND WILES

*October 1987*

At Bourg St Maurice, high in France's Haute-Savoie today a 27-year-old Englishman, Richard Fox, looks to become the world singles kayak canoe champion for an astonishing fourth successive time. No one before has even done it twice. Coes and Crams and Bothams hog the headlines, but probably only Daley Thompson might match Fox for the simple untarnished perfection of his international results.

When he was 11 and about to start at Verulam School, St Albans, Richard's parents gave him a canoe kit. That single act did more for the sport than any, I dare say, since 1866 when one of legend's most eccentric sons, John McGregor, set out from the Star and Garter at Richmond to paddle his famous prototype 'Rob Roy' kayak across the Channel and through the waterways of Europe to generate interest in his 'newly invented and codified' racing pastime. Also to sell his boats, no doubt. The amazing McGregor pottered about on comparatively flat waters. Fox's speciality is the slalom, equivalent to steering a bobbing cork through 25 gates in strictly numbered order down an almost sheer chute of boiling white water totally enclosed by sharply jutting crags. He wears a lifejacket and a crash helmet. If he so much as touches a gate he's a goner. In the world championships you have two runs and that's it for another two years.

Fox, a handsome man brimming with health and with a ready smile, is an honours graduate in PE from Bill Slater's 'academy' at Birmingham University. He is a full-time canoeist inasmuch as he coaches and lectures, and is sponsored by canoe builders. He gets a £5,000 grant from the Sports Aid Foundation. His first competition was at 14 on the Ouse at Bedford, his first slalom a year later at Duck Mill. Within two years, in 1977, he was in his first world championships in Austria. Two years later, in north Wales, he was world champion. 'The strain of the build-up and then the emotional release at the end was considerable but not all that euphoric, I must say if I am honest.' In 1983 he won again – 'very dull; sure, I performed, but it just came and went. I just did the job.'

But in 1985 at Augsburg, West Germany, he retained the title, and this time the cup overflowed. 'The sensational feeling at last: 15,000 people, incredible; dancing water, a buzz and a hum and everything on the knife edge; I'd never experienced anything like it. On the first run I thought I'd blown it, trying too hard, no rhythm, no timing, not really getting anywhere, not panicking, but just a dull blank.'

He was fifth at the end of the first run and presumed he was out of it. He crept away to a corner. 'I checked my run on the video: quite a good top half, but a couple of gormless mistakes at the bottom. "That's it, too defensive, not natural, too tense and hesitant." I told myself that this was the best time of my life and if I did not do myself justice now, I never would. Suddenly it was like waking out of a nightmare. It was all crystal clear, and I wasn't uncomfortable, dull or scared any more. I'd never experienced that before. All of a sudden I wasn't trapped in the shell, wasn't restricted to the dull grooves. I had a drink of water, I remember, and clear as anything I revisualised the strategies for the second run. Wondrously, it all clicked, and from then to the very end I was on a high, in an incredible trance. And I was world champion three times running. Amazing.'

Tonight, for the last time, he will run through the course yet again on his pillow. 'Three, two, one – allez! You're on automatic. It's simply instinct. At Bourg the approach to the first gate, wherever they put it, is devilishly tricky. If you get a good run through the waves from the off, you're on a flyer. But if you get a couple of waves immediately that slap on to your chest, you know you're in big trouble. Even a quick roll and you know you've had it. Even the quickest roll loses four seconds, so with your rhythm in tatters and your energy being shredded you'll never settle again.

'I've never capsized in a big event but it can happen so easily. The top half at Augsburg is very shallow, so you must watch your paddle on those rocks ... look, can we talk about something else, please? You just cannot allow yourself to think about those things. The top half is so fast, so steep, the cascading water whooshing about so much, the eddies so strong and the gate so intense you are not thinking about anything, except, blankly I suppose, putting trust in training and instinct and, if you like, plain survival. All wrapped up into this intense concentration, willing and willing for the ultimate run.'

For the week the build-up will become more and more intense, good friends not catching each other's eye, becoming more introverted, more tense. 'Then comes the day. You look across at your competitors, seeking for a clue as to how they're feeling. The water is cold and refreshing, the sun always hot in Bourg, the crowd hemming you in, chatting, pushing and craning for a view. It is all hubbub and you look at your rivals again. It's you against each of them, but in a bigger way. It's also us select competitors, the little band of us, against the rest of the world; intense rivalry and intense comradeship at one and the same time.

'There we'll all be, ready to go, old hands and doubtless a new pack of young bloods. All in an odd confraternity ... the two West Germans, Michelor, silver medallist last time, and Prijom, very dangerous. Then the four Yugoslavs, all very good, all going for it ferociously on the basis that one of them is bound to get it; then the Czech, Hilgert, always the dark horse, a real big guy who looks ungainly, clumsy, and awkward, but is so strong that suddenly he's down and clean through everything and terribly, terribly fast. Funny, isn't it, top level sport? Is there really an "ultimate"? How do you know if it's actually worth all the time and effort and sweat? Will we look back and think it was all a bit of a waste really?'

He laughs, 'I don't know. What do you think?'

---

## DRESSED UP TO KILL
*November 1979*

Imagine: it is 8.55 on a weekday morning at Victoria Station in London. The whole grey world, it seems, decamps from suburbs to City. Glazed-eyed, they hack their way through with umbrella and briefcase. *Telegraph*-man at his most grey-faced pompous nasty. The *Sun*s and *Mirror*s have long gone, the *Times*-ites are still to come.

The lone unshaven shaver brandishing his *Guardian* and his gumboots against the frenzied tide of workers was little me. I was going the wrong way and panicking that I should not get the 9.02 to Dorking and the Downs. But, hang on a tick! What's this? Through the seething pack, looking neither right nor left, heels sparking, spurs tapping typists' ankles to clear a path, marched – tum tara tum – an amazing figure in his late 70s, with bulbous nose and a fearsome mien above broad-bottomed beam. He wore a black top hat, a scarlet tailcoat, gold tiepin, white breeches and clanging fiery boots. And he was carrying a cellophane packet of three cheese rolls. I slipped into his slipstream as grandpa Moses parted the sea of dowdy charcoal-grey and sallow, sniggering secretaries. Raphael de Sola was goin' huntin'. And so was I.

Mr de Sola enacts this gloriously loony, incongruous panto almost every winter Wednesday. A 24 bus from his Mayfair flat, the 9.02 to Dorking, a taxi to his livery stables where groom is waiting with saddled nag and then a few hours with the old Surrey Union Hunt. And what, I ask this morning on Sports Pages, is wrong with that? Just footslogging for me, of course. Sheer funk. Hunters are hellish huge. I once sat on a docile enough chestnut in Gloucestershire preeningly posing for pictures, when suddenly it bent down to nibble some grass – and muggins went flying between his ears, didn't he?

The thought of walking above Dorking on a cold and frosty morning appealed from the start – especially in mind of the hoo-ha stirred up last week when Bridgnorth Technical College opened courses for huntsmen which caused Gerry Fowler MP, to rabbit on and on about dumb animals and privilege and 'educationalists pandering to strange groups hung over from the nineteenth century when they don't realise there are pressing problems in Telford.' Come off it, Gerry, you have more anglers in your constituency than nearly anyone else. But fish don't squeal. For all Wilde's 'unspeakable in pursuit of the uneatable,' for my money Shaw was near the knuckle when he suggested you go anywhere in

England 'where there are natural, wholesome, contented and really nice people; and what do you always find? That the stables are the centre of the household.' That is the sort of feeling I had with the Surrey Union.

I met a dozen or so fellow footsloggers by 10.30-ish, high on the North Downs above Ockley. There was an expectant tingle in some glorious, freezing chapped-lipped air. Hipflasks were passed about. In ones or twos the horsemen arrived. My first surprise – they greeted us pedestrians like old pals. 'Mornin', Jack,' 'Mornin', Mabel.' Colonel Thing and Major Who, Farmer Giles and Mrs Everyone. Some of the girls were devastating. At 11 on the dot the huntsman arrived, with some 30 hands (they call them 15 couple). The dogs were twitching. It was a superb sight. The huntsman and his assistant (the whip) are paid servants of the hunt. 'Agricultural wages – but the perks are pretty good.'

No discussion is heard, but they decide to first try the copse up yonder. Already you realise that for all the criticism of the people it is the hounds that are the very fundamental element. Riders are just mounted spectators, who can go as fast or as slow as they like. Indeed my friend, Mr de Sola, never seemed to raise a trot all morning. At once, from the wood, a fox passed not 20 yards from me, going hell for leather. The cry of the hounds changed key as they picked up the scent. The huntsman's job was now to sense where Reynard would make for and to get the dogs and his followers there with a minimum of effort.

That first fox ran to his earth about three miles away after a tooting, whirling chase and a clatter of hooves. I and my gumboots brought up the rear panting proud. They sent a terrier down to chase him out, but the fox laid low. Had he escaped the huntsman would have shot him humanely. Throughout the five-hour day with scarcely a halt to catch one's breath, one fox was shot and another turned into the pack and was dead in seconds. Four got away. That first one was the only fox I saw all day. Many of the riders did not see even one.

About 50,000 people ride to hounds each winter in Britain, behind 200 packs. Ten times as many are closely associated as

271

regular supporters and footsloggers. It has been a patiently enduring sport through history. The bodies against cruelty are only the latest of hunting's headaches. Canals, railways, the Baptist church, motorways, have each cut a swathe through their necessary enjoyment. When wire fences arrived in 1862 it was surely the end of the sport, but even the invention of the loathsome barbed variety in 1888 could not keep a good nag down.

Mind you, huntsmen are on the defensive. The well meaning 'Antis' nag away at them with conscience-stricken, disruptive, effective and even felonious tactics. The Surrey Union, for instance, never nowadays announce their meets in the local rag. The hunt supporters are very quick to offer dreadful and often practised alternatives – there is a new trade in fox pelts which brings good money for snaring the animal and meaning a long self-strangulation.

As I lay content and weary in a piping hot bath after a crumpet tea I knew I could not remember when sport had given me such a warming exhilaration. And I mused on the words of Trotsky (for it was he, that very same bearded weirdo) – 'field sports act on the mind as poultice does on a sore.' And later, changed and in the pink and surrounded by the same lovely ladies as in the morning, an acting master poured me another nosewarmer, and I even heard myself dredging up Aristotle: 'If some animals are good at hunting and others are suitable for hunting, then the gods must clearly smile on hunting.'

---

## BARRELS OF FUN …
*August 1978*

Remember that story last year about Sheikh Zaid Ben Sultan, the ruler of Abu Dhabi, who decided to try his hand at the gentry's sport of popping off the odd cartridge at frightened feathered friends, on his luxurious new English estate – and how distressed the gamekeeper was when his new squire turned up with a machine gun? It is a story that didn't go down too well when I told it this week at Ruislip, where Holland and Holland, the celebrated gunmakers, have their shooting grounds. I was there to see preparations for today's big competitive shoot for the Famous Grouse trophy, for which most of the leading clay pigeon shots in the country will be banging off.

On first consideration of the Ruislip grounds, where all year you can hire tuition and time for practice (other Arab sheikhs have signed on), it seemed to me that clay pigeon shooting was a very nobby, upmarket sport. Yes, said someone, wrinkling his nose, you can buy an imported gun for £100 – 'but an English gun will cost you £500'.

A random glance at the bookings list in the pavilion showed that that day's shots were a colonel, a knight, a peer and an 'A.P. Huntington Esq. and friend'. All the officials wore tweed suits and plus-fours. Even though the grounds are off the Ruislip High Street, once in the pavilion one felt an immediate whiff of the grouse moors and Speyside as narrow-eyed, bearded Scots watched that you did not mishandle your weapon. There are 10 commandments framed on a wall. No 1 is 'Don't point your gun at anyone'. No 10 is 'If in doubt don't shoot'. Quite. Actually, clay pigeon shooting takes in all sorts. It is not necessarily a snob's pastime. Simply put, it is a simulated walk in the wilds. Hidden traps are dotted about the place and every so often two discs of four inches in diameter are released by a sprung trap at various levels and speeds. One, say, might be flung low straight at you like Wizbangs at Wipers; that is a pair of grouse. The next might soar high into the trees; a brace of pigeons. The next, catapulted from a high Stalag Luft tower, will be pheasants.

The sport first really had sportswriters reaching for their reference books in 1968 when Bob Braithwaite, the Garstang vet, won a gold medal at the Mexico Olympics. He hit 198 out of 200 'birds'. But it is still an unconsidered pastime when it comes to publicity. Entries today include unknown 'greats' such as Eames, Poskitt, Secker, Bidwell, Hebditch. It all dates from 1880 when a Scot called McCaskey invented a target composed of river silt and pitch. In the same year an

American from Cincinnati named Ligowsky developed the first mechanised trap. The foundation of the sport had been laid a century before when pigeons were used and killed regularly in London. The participants then were nicknamed Old Hats because the fun of the thing was keeping the poor pigeon covered with their head gear before releasing them to take their luck. The nobs would perhaps go out and knock off a few on the lawn after supper for a wager.

The sport grew thereafter so that small game shooters could practise out of season. Others, of course, now participate because they enjoy shooting but dislike killing or maiming live birds. The governing body in Britain, founded in 1893 as the Inanimate Bird Shooting Association, became the CPSA in 1928. More than 250 clubs are affiliated. In the last Olympics more than 40 nations competed.

There was a colony of wild partridges in the Ruislip woods, I was told. 'Good heavens no, no one would even consider taking a pot shot at *them*.' He looked me square in the eye: 'Not at all good form that, old boy.' Every sport has its 'in' rituals which only dolts ignore. Especially in England. Like the day a new shot was invited to a certain squire's shoot in Northamptonshire. The gamekeeper had been preparing the birds all year and this was the big day. A straggly old bag of feathers flew across the horizon and the new boy was the only one to let fly with both barrels. 'What the hell are you doing?' raged the squire. 'Nobody *ever* shoots at old Jeremy here, sir.'

'Sorry,' said the young man. Five minutes later another kamikaze clatter of wings soared down from a tree towards them. Again every gun was silent. 'You see, nobody ever shoots at Rodney, either.' Then another bird flew out of the bush right in front of the youngster's barrel. He held his fire. 'Why the blazes didn't you shoot it?' fumed the squire. 'Here, sir, *everyone* shoots at Claude.'

Sheikh Zaid Ben Sultan might like that one.

# TALE OF THE FOUR CHANNEL TRIPPERS
*September 1981*

Down the Dover Road, composing little more than a dashed-off piece of waffle about the White Cliffs in the silvery dawn – you know the sort of stuff: the twinkling lights of barques on an oil-black sea, the bark of Roy Plomley gulls overhead and a quick interview with a Channel swimmer, nice one, Cyril, and might even be home for breakfast. Not a bit of it. Sometimes you feel you could write a whole book about one day. Actually, this turned into a two-day trip and as uplifting a sporting experience as I can remember in a long time. I had thought that every nut who felt so inclined could potter across the Channel these days – why, even a 12-year-old Londoner, Marcus Hooper, got across last month. Again, not so: this year only the 200th swimmer managed it and there have been over 2,100 attempts since Captain Webb waded ashore in 1875 and the Mayor of Dover predicted: 'Never in the future history of the world will any such feat be performed by anyone else.'

Some, of course, have done it many times. At the start of this year's Channel season in July, there had been a total of 298 solo crossings. The legendary Des Renford is the king of the Channel. Talk about the Calais Commuter. On Wednesday he succeeded for the 16th time and flew back home Thursday morning to Australia.

The zany zig-zag can only be attempted on the spring of neap tides when the flow encourages a good south-easterly course from Dover, a few hours of slack when you can strike out straight and so catch the returning whoosh from the south-west to plop you on to the beach at Cap Gris Nez and so collect your prize – for which, by the way, you have to pay £25 for the privilege of a copperplate vellum scroll from the Channel Swimming Association.

It is a wondrously amateur sport. With training expenses, a boarding house to hole up in while you wait on the weather and up to £600 a go to hire an experienced pilot (local moonlighting fishermen) the average Channel attempt these days costs £1,000. But still they queue to dive in. Shore-based fulcrum of the whole phenomenon is half of the dining-room table in a spick and span new bungalow just outside Folkestone. There Ray and Audrey Scott, respectively chairman and secretary of the CSA, sift and sort their forms and finances and never stop answering the telephone from all the oceans of the world.

The Scotts are the glorious personification of that backbone of all amateur sport, the honorary-officer. Mr Scott, an athletic and handsome retired schoolmaster, is the sort who is bouncing with life at four in the morning. That's when he woke me. I was kipping in his summer house. Mrs Scott, who looks like everybody's favourite auntie (well certainly like all mine) squeezed the pot and then we went down to the docks in the darkness.

There were just four little pockets of light and life. Four men had taken the chance in the early hours that tide and time was ready for them – Norman Albert, an American student interested in endurance; Paolo Pinto, a Milanese lawyer and European marathon man who has won the Greece-Italy race and Venice-Capri but twice previously had failed to cross our Channel; Trounce Guy, a powerful 30-year-old Cornish farmer making his first attempt hotfoot (to coin a phrase) from ploughing the 21 miles from Portholland to The Lizard; and Peter Winchester, a stocky, friendly 38-year-old contracts manager from Grimsby, also having a first go but whose record, they said, made him the likeliest to be raising a glass of Calvados to himself in a café near Calais that evening.

I could take my pick, said Auntie Audrey. I chose to go with the likely lad, Peter Winchester, and so we chugged off, a convoy of four fishing smacks, winking at each other in the darkness before the dawn. The sea was flat. They put us off at Shakespeare Beach. On the steep shingle Peter's 'trainer' Des, and I larded the swimmer with evil, thick handfuls of lanolin mix. Soon Peter looked like something that only a chef could do anything with. My hands were so greasy I couldn't open the second tin and felt a right fool. You have to cover every

276

intimate crevice and total panic set in when I did what I used to do as a nipper in the Stroud paddling pool and lost one end of the cord that tied up his Union Jack trunks. Somehow I fished out the lace and tied a bow. He dived in confidently.

The American and Cornishman were first away. The Italian, Paolo, was obviously all set – but he just wouldn't go in. Everyone was urging him to start. He put his toe in the water and retreated. He feared the Channel which had foiled him twice. He was finally persuaded a good 10 minutes after Peter had started his crawl. Des, Peter's trainer, had arrived in Folkestone only a few hours before we set off; he had hitchhiked from Grimsby that evening. Also in the boat was the obligatory CSA volunteer observer and three of Peter's friends. They had slept in their cars. Also Peter's son and his schoolfriend.

At 10, Peter and his dad were first inspired to think of a go at the Channel by the exploits of the Grimsby girl, Brenda Fisher, who won the *Daily Mail* race in 1951. He has swum the mouth of the Humber many times and down to Kings Lynn. He had also done very well in the Torbay Marathon. Now here he was, trained on Guinness, having his first meal in the Channel after going well for two-and-a-half hours. The sun came up and, on a pole, they passed him out some swigs of Scott's Emulsion, glucose, coffee and half a Mars Bar. The first crisis came after four hours when he wanted some rice pudding, but no one had remembered to bring the tin opener. They gouged it with a penknife.

Then the cramp in his thigh progressively got worse. He could not rub it, for some of our oil would have been transferred when he wiped his goggles. The leg trailed sadly and then even more sadly. He kept going, but all the pressure now was on his arms and shoulders. On and on, but the spirit got lower with his shoulders. He knew he was done for. He'd been in almost six hours when they hauled him out.

'The leg was giving terrible pain, but the main feeling was one of heartbreak,' Peter said. 'I felt a failure. The look on my son's face was terrible. He didn't know where to look, he was that upset.' They scraped some grease off him and covered him in blankets. 'My throat was so sore with the salt I couldn't say anything.' They turned back for home. 'I sat there and thought of having to phone my dad and wife. They were going to be so upset,' lamented Peter. He did not once mention the waste of £1,100 but later asked for a mention for his firm, his pub, The Wellington Arms, the Scout group down the road and the uncle and aunt who had all helped to raise his fare.

An hour later, in another part of the Channel, the American student decided that he had studied enough about endurance for the time being, thank you very much. The Truro farmer, Trounce Guy, threshed on mightily until well past 10 p.m. They lugged him out two-and-a-half miles from France after 18 hours. The CSA had never heard of him before, but everyone was impressed. He is self-trained, argued about his route, trod water for a total of 75 minutes to eat, as someone said, 'a few full-scale Christmas dinners' while the tide carried him backwards. On his return to Folkestone he bought two books on Channel swimming and means to have another go on one of the final neap tides of the season later this season. They all reckon he'll do it then.

Guy was still in the water when, lo and behold, the Italian lawyer Paolo Pinto was tottering on a gammy, cramped leg through the surf to kiss the sand of La Belle France. He came straight back to Folkestone and was soon fast asleep with a seraphic smile on his face in the tiny wheelhouse. When he arrived he was still so happy he could scarcely speak Italian, let alone pidgin English. 'When I landed, I wanted to be so happy, but I still had a pain in the leg. Now I am much more happy than even the pain in my leg.'

Peter slept long and then went sadly home to Grimsby. On Saturday night his old dad, bless him, threw a surprise party with 40 friends. 'A damn good try,' they all said. I read him out the four little words carved on Captain Webb's memorial plaque – 'Nothing Great Is Easy.'

He is going to spend the winter catching up on jobs about the house, laying new floorboards in his bathroom. And all the time thinking of having another go at the Channel come next July.

# A HENLEY REST-CURE

*July 1979*

From sparkling morn to balmy eventide (that's the only type
of language which is appropriate) the whole ambience at
Henley came as a refreshing relief from the demented, dusty
sweat and toil of Wimbledon. A day off! Aboard the breakfast
stopper at Paddington, a change at Twyford for Wargrave
and Shiplake – I felt as a Saturday morning miner must,
coming up from the tunnel and into the showers.

Henley, I fancy, must be what Wimbledon was like in the
days of old when Edward ruled and the Robinson's Barley
Water was actually served by Old Heathers and not a
booming senior executive from the Special Events Public
Relations Department. Mind you, I cannot resist the actual
sport, the 15-30 bit at Wimbledon, so it has to be admitted
that I accepted the order for a trip back in the time capsule
only on condition that I could follow the fortune of J.
Connors electronically on the suburban sward. I was assured
I could. Not a hope, however.

'Is that a portable wireless receiver?' asked the spotty and
boatered young boatsman manning the stewards' gate. 'No,
it's a transistor,' I replied. He examined it. 'This is a portable
wireless receiver,' he said. 'Please leave it in that tent with
those confiscated perambulators.' The pushchairs he indi-
cated were apparently not allowed either, but I did see a
number of senile gentlemen being wheeled around in
wheelchairs. Wheelchairs at Henley are not perambulators.

You may think I am already finding it easier to be cynical,
but not a bit of it. To be there yesterday on this little land's
most blissful summer's day for three years was a privilege.
John Rodda had primed me: 'In the summer that tennis and
cricket have never been offered more gross amounts of
sponsors' prizes it is worthwhile remembering that this other
legendary event in the English summer is still modelled on
the old idea of amateur sport. No Sports Council grant, no

sponsor, no brown envelopes with unsigned cheques for cash, no promoters of golden regattas waiting on the bank.'

Yesterday those were one's feelings exactly as the Pimms were haughtily ordered and, high on the river banks, the breeze tickled the chestnut and larch trees to a contented deciduous chuckle. If Olde England has gone, it certainly was not forgotten here. The girls were quite sensational in the hats they had planned for months, and the chinless slack-lipped old buffers standing at the front of the judges' launches could each have been mistaken for Robert Morley.

'C'mon Jesus for God's sake!' shouted an undergraduate. 'Pull your finger out Clare!' hollered another. 'It's deeply gratifying,' someone else remarked, 'that the Canadian crew all have English names.' All the while, with symmetrical rhythmic grace, the oarsmen streamed on, even while Americans came and went in expensively-cut Madison Avenue denim suits – 'Sorry sir, no jeans' – and old men in badged prep-school caps walked about like happy zombies straitjacketed into minuscule wetbobs blazers.

Tim Crooks, one of Britain's finest ever international oarsmen, was asked why he was not rowing. 'Because I've retired,' he answered. When was that announced? 'I've just decided to announce it,' he said. 'Come and have a drink on it.' That's Henley. 'How's Jimmy getting on?' I asked someone in the stewards' bar. 'He's okey doke, old boy,' he said, indicating his buddy. 'But I dare say you could put him in a large Plymouth Pink, what?'

---

# PIERCING EXPERIENCE
*January 1978*

There was an incongruous touch about the whole day. For a start the venue, in dusty, down-at-heel west London, was a posh-impersonal, glittery new, Hilton-type hotel. Then, after a Musak-march through the hushing foyer, a hangar of a banqueting suite was as jostlingly, laughingly, brown-ale full as a Butlin's ballroom in August.

It was the world masters darts championship: 40 players from 13 countries egged on by an uninhibited throng of 2,000 people. Andy Capp and Florrie was the first feeling, but it was quickly dispelled when we got down to the challenge. A lovely day. And though ITV, the people's choice, covered the riveting climax live, unaccountably the only activity in the press room was me with the brown ale and the frenzied scribbling of the gossip columnist from *Double Top*.

He had a lot to write home about. The winner was John Lowe, from Clay Cross in Derbyshire, a toothy hunk of a fellow who looked like an amiable extra from Coronation Street. But, by golly, he could play darts all right. And subtract from 501 like an IBM computer. Time and again he had finished a game with a quick-fire 17-6-double-3-or-whatever before the poor scorer could shout out what was needed. You have got to be good at maths to play darts. And that's not a throwaway line.

'A good player who can count can always beat a brilliant player who can't. He doesn't have to stop and lose concentration,' said last year's Welsh runner-up, Leighton Rees, on Saturday morning. All day the Welsh had fancied their chances. Rees went, then their 1975 world champion, Alan Evans, was beaten by Lowe 3-2 in the most compelling match of all. Evans, squat and scarlet-shirted like a centre three-quarter from the valleys, Cuban-heeled like a disco bouncer, had his chances but ultimately cringed in the face of Lowe's unerringly calm aim.

In the final, which Lowe won 3-0, he reduced another Welshman, Phillip Obbard, who looked like Gerald Davies and had started with an equally confident dash, to tears. Obbard, like most of the players, was decked out in multi-coloured badges like the back window of a fourth-hand Cortina. Lowe played in a badgeless fawn British Home Stores shirt with a zipper down the front. Between each clutch of darts he blew gently on the end of his fingers like Jimmy Connors. But he smiled like Tommy Steele at the end.

Lowe won £1,000. As a professional he might be able to multiply that by 10 in the 12 months, playing exhibitions, asking appearance money and endorsing the suddenly booming darts industry. He is already British Pentathlon champion, which means he's pretty handy at trick-darts as well as 501 subtraction. He admits the likelihood of even more unknown men challenging him truculently in any pub he visits. Darts is pulling itself out of the pubs and into big business. These championships were sponsored by Winmau, who make dartboards. But representatives of far bigger companies were lurking around on Saturday. It is a natural for tobacco and brewery men to start with.

Four years ago darts was still a friendly, Shanghai foursome at the Bull and Bush. In 1973, a young, side-burned Cockney businessman, Olly Croft, formed the British Darts Tournament. His verve has put a match to the touchpaper. And globally. An Australian was hot favourite on Saturday. Others from Sweden, Denmark, Holland and even Gibraltar were highly fancied. A Californian pub owner (sic) who looked like a James Bond erudite Odd Job was beaten by Lowe in the semi-finals.

Already, Croft reckons one in nine adults plays serious darts in England, which makes it the country's most popular game. The thought that toothy, gentle John Lowe might one day be Sportsman of the Year is quaint but, when you think of it, not all that unreasonable.